Narco-terrorism

NARCO-TERRORISM

—————— ▪▪▪▪▪ ——————

Rachel Ehrenfeld

BasicBooks
A Division of HarperCollins*Publishers*

Library of Congress Cataloging-in-Publication Data
Ehrenfeld, Rachel.
  Narco-terrorism / Rachel Ehrenfeld.
    p. cm.
  Includes bibliographical references and index.
  ISBN 0–465–04800–5 (cloth)
  ISBN 0–465–04801–3 (paper)
  1. Terrorism. 2. Drug traffic. I. Title.
HV6431.E395 1990
363.4′5—dc20   90–80249
                                                              CIP

To the memory of my father,
Benjamin E. Ehrenfeld, 1918–1969

Contents

———————— ▪▪▪▪▪ ————————

	Preface	ix
	Introduction	xiii
1	The Little Brothers from Bulgaria	1
2	The Cuban Connection: Castro, Cocaine, and Terror	20
3	The Lebanese Inferno: Drugs and Terror	52
4	Colombia: The Superstate of Narco-terrorism	74
5	Peru and Bolivia: The Spreading of the Empire	113
6	The Other America: From Grass to Crack	136
	Postscript	184
	Notes	187
	Index	215

Preface

———————— ▊▊▊▊▊ ————————

When I began my research on narco-terrorism in 1986, I had assumed that terror and drug trafficking could be used by any political group to advance its purposes and were not a monopoly of the left, much less the communist left. As my research advanced, it turned out that Marxist-Leninist–oriented regimes and terrorist groups have, in fact, initiated, developed, and nearly totally dominated this particularly dirty business.

My curiosity had been aroused when I first came on a visit from Israel to the United States in 1981. It was one thing to read about America's drug problem, and another to see it in New York, Los Angeles, Washington, D.C., even in Tuscaloosa, Alabama.

As a criminologist, I was invited by the United States Information Agency to explore the methods used to deal with drug addiction in America. I was closely acquainted with the drug problems of Western Europe, and was fully familiar with the literature on drug addiction in the United States, but neither prepared me for the harsh reality of this country's drug problem.

At the time I was not aware it had any political implications. It seemed, simply, a human tragedy of enormous and growing proportions, and it was one, I felt, that would soon, like other fads and fashions, be adopted in other Western societies.

While in the United States and after my return to Israel, I began to realize that drug addiction was more than a medical, social, or legal problem. There was an economic aspect to it as well. Not only was it increasingly expensive to deal with the problem, but enormous sums of money were being earned by drug traffickers. I therefore began to investigate who the traffickers were and how they conducted their business, including the laundering of their profits.

I took the startling results of my research and presented them first to Professor Warner Schilling from the Institute of War and Peace Studies, Columbia University, who trusted my instincts and facilitated the beginning of this project. He deserves not only thanks but also respect for his ability to identify the importance of this subject. Special thanks go to Professor Raphael Mechullam from the Hebrew University of Jerusalem, one of the first who encouraged me to begin and subsequently urged me to finish when the work seemed difficult and the end far away.

The research for the book would not have come to fruition but for the support provided by the Lynde and Harry Bradley Foundation, and especially Dr. Hillel Fradkin, its Program Officer; Richard Larry, President of the Sarah Scaife Foundation and his continuing support and encouragement throughout this project; and the United States Institute of Peace and its Director of Research and Studies, Dr. Kenneth Jensen, for their contribution. Finally, thanks to Freedom House and its Executive Director, Bruce McColm, for the use of their facilities and support of this book.

Because of the global nature of the issues, my research has taken me throughout the world and it would be impossible to thank all those hundreds of people in countries from Singapore to Costa Rica, from Colombia to Taiwan, who have helped. They know who they are and I thank them all for their continuing assistance. While they remain anonymous, often at their own request, they will recognize their invaluable contribution.

A few individuals whose outstanding encouragement and contributions made the struggle to deal with this very difficult and complicated subject possible are: James Ring Adams; David Asman from the *Wall Street Journal*; Roger Brooks from the

Heritage Foundation; Jose Cardinas from the Cuban-American National Foundation; Midge Decter; Audna England; Louis Freeh, Deputy U.S. Attorney, New York Southern District; Walter Haan; Ambassador Allan Keyes; Professor William Kluback; Marlo Lewis, Jr.; Lt. Col. Samuel Pope from the Department of War Studies, King's College, London; Sol Sanders; Professor Paul Seabury; James Sherr, Lincoln College, Oxford; Ambassador Lewis A. Tambs; Kenneth Thompson from the Department of State, Bureau of International Narcotics Matters; Dr. Carlton Turner, President Reagan's Director of the Office of Drug Abuse Policy; William von Raab, Commissioner of Customs in the Reagan administration; and retired Coast Guard Captain Robert Workman. Special recognition also goes to Roger Fontaine whose invaluable help was much appreciated.

To the many friends who kept my spirits up during difficult times, and reminded me how necessary it is to bring this information to the public in spite of the seeming disinterest and denial from many sources, I give my warmest thanks. Many thanks to my skillful editor, Michael Wilde, and finally, special thanks to my publisher, Martin Kessler, for having the intellectual courage to undertake this controversial project.

Introduction

———————— ▮▮▮▮▮ ————————

HONECKER AS PUSHER[1] (1990)

DRUG TRAFFICKERS IN CYPRUS WERE PLO REPRESENTATIVES[2] (1990)

COLOMBIAN POLITICAL VIOLENCE SURGES,WITH RENEWAL OF DRUG WAR AWAITED[3] (1990)

INDICTMENT LINKS CASTRO TO NORIEGA, DRUG CARTEL[4] (1988)

NARCO TERROR: LEBANON AND THE BLOODY POLITICS OF DRUGS[5] (1987)

SMUGGLERS DETAIL NICARAGUAN DRUG ROLE[6] (1985)

Since the early 1980s, readers around the world have become inured to headlines like these. Connections between drug traffickers and terrorist organizations occasionally have been described in the media. The "absolute war" declared by Colombian drug traffickers in December 1989 on the legitimate government of President Barco and the U.S. invasion of Panama to oust macho narco-terrorist, Generalissimo and "Absolute Leader" Manuel Antonio Noriega have helped to familiarize readers throughout the world with the narco-terrorism phenomenon.

Narco-terrorism has a widely disputed meaning.[7] My definition of narco-terrorism is the use of drug trafficking to advance the objectives of certain governments and terrorist organizations. As we shall see, connections between drug traffickers and terrorists are not new, but in the 1980s came to assume a new prominence. One of the first glimpses of the phenomenon came early in 1982 in the testimony of Thomas O. Enders, then assistant secretary of state for Inter-American Affairs, in hearings on the role of Cuba in international terrorism and subversion. Ambassador Enders charged that the U.S. had "detailed and reliable information linking Cuba to traffic in narcotics as well as arms. Since 1980, the Castro regime has been using Colombian narcotics rings to funnel arms as well as funds to Colombian M-19 guerrillas."[8] This became public on November 15, 1982, when a federal grand jury in Miami indicted fourteen people, including four close aides to Castro, for operating and participating in an arms-for-drugs connection between the United States and Colombia via Cuba.[9]

The major target for this deadly and illicit activity is and always has been the United States, as a natural consequence of economic and political factors. For the trafficker, the United States is the wealthiest and biggest consumer of illegal drugs in the world. The United States remains the "main enemy" for the Marxist idealogue and other anti-democratic and anti-Western forces for whom drugs serve a threefold purpose. First, they destabilize American society; second, they undermine non-Marxist democratic governments in this hemisphere and elsewhere; and best of all, the results come at no cost to these regimes and their terrorist allies, since the whole enterprise in effect is paid for by the American and other Western drug consumers.

Therefore, the focus in this book is on the threat to the United States; other Western countries remain secondary. Although there are a number of Marxist-Leninist and fundamentalist terrorist organizations around the world that deal in drugs, this book concentrates on the major players who represent the chief threat and in turn help to sponsor smaller action groups.

Why has so little attention been paid to narco-terrorism, and attention even denied, if all of these allegations are true? In part, because it is a diplomatically touchy issue. Some feel that U.S.

foreign relations would be unnecessarily strained. With regimes such as that of Syria other priorities intervene; in this case, a comprehensive Middle East settlement, and the release of the American hostages in Lebanon. It is the difficulty of recognizing a problem without having a ready solution, a quandary that policy makers are only too happy to avoid. And finally, narco-terrorism bureaucratically falls between the cracks. Mainline intelligence services like the CIA traditionally did not collect or analyze criminal intelligence; that was left to such agencies as the Drug Enforcement Administration (DEA), which is not responsible for weighing its political implications.

Most terrorist organizations operating in the world today are influenced to some degree by Marxist ideology. Modern terrorism as far back as the early 1960s was sponsored and supported initially by the Soviet Union and its surrogates. In fact, many terrorists were trained in the Soviet Union itself; even those who were trained elsewhere by Soviet allies received Marxist-Leninist indoctrination as part of their training. Thus, it is reasonable to assume that their comprehensive training included how to conduct unconventional warfare to subvert and destabilize the countries in which they operate. As part of their military doctrine, the Soviets had provisions for the subversion of potential enemies, which officially linked drugs and terrorism. The 1979 edition of the Soviet Military Encyclopedia provided a list of *measures to be used in peacetime* (emphasis mine), in order to promote Soviet foreign policy objectives. These measures, which include the use of poisons and narcotics, are contained in the definition of *spetsal'naya razvedka*; literally, "special reconnaissance," but more broadly it embraces all functions of intelligence and clandestine operations associated with that term.[10]

In an era of *glasnost* and *perestroyka,* when the Soviet Union and the United States joined in memoranda of understanding both on drugs and terrorism, such a proposition may seem fanciful, even outlandish, and most certainly provocative. Nevertheless, it remains the truth.

Many people in the West feel it imprudent to bring up past sinister Soviet activities, particularly at this time when there is no direct evidence to link Gorbachev to international drug trafficking. However, in all of his attempts to appear to be a European moderate, Mikhail Gorbachev has never renounced one iota of Marxist-Leninist doctrine. To the contrary, on November 26, 1989, in a special article published in *Pravda*, Gorbachev answered those who hope or think that Marxism has failed. In the article, he reinforced his belief that Marxism-Leninism is the correct ideology to follow, but its implementation and application had been wrong in the past and now he would see to it that it be revived and applied correctly.[11] To those who have said for years that he and other Soviet leaders actually do not believe in what they profess, the apologists have yet to produce a single shred of evidence to support that airy assumption. True, changes in Eastern Europe have occurred in the later part of 1989, but it remains to be seen how profound these changes will be, and how they will affect the Soviet Union. In spite of apparent changes in Soviet strategy at the end of 1989, in fact they have occurred only within the military rather than the political-idiological realm. The intentions in Soviet Marxist-Leninist military doctrine as voiced in the Military Encyclopedia (wherein specific concepts and principles are set out for the subversion of potential "enemy" countries during "peacetime") remain unchanged.* Political changes already have led to an apparent renunciation of Marxist ideology by former allies of the Soviet Union in Eastern Europe, yet Gorbachev is reinforcing Marxism-Leninism instead of renouncing it. An official assessment of Lenin published in Moscow three days before Gorbachev was elected by the Communist Party Central Committee to his new post as Executive President (approved by the Politburo in March

---

*In addition to the Soviet Military Encyclopedia, this was verified by consulting with experts on Soviet military strategy. Among them are Colonel Sam Pope from the Department of War Studies, King's College, London, and Dr. Leon Goure, from SAIC in McLean, Virginia, December 1989.

1990) described Lenin as a pragmatic reformer, very much like Gorbachev himself.[12] One also should remember that most of the changes in the Eastern bloc were not initiated by the people of Eastern Europe, but were sparked by Gorbachev and set in motion at his direction. Furthermore, in most East European countries the military and intelligence services remain largely intact and under Communist control. What effect this will have on their relationship with the Soviet Union and their readiness to continue to maintain terrorist and narco-terrorist affiliations also remains to be seen.

This book is not an attempt to describe the activities of individual, small-time criminals who profit from the drug trade, or the involvement of organized crime, per se. Rather, I shall concentrate on the partnership between the international drug trafficking organizations—who sometimes are state sponsored—and international terrorist groups and states, who use Marxist-Leninist tactics and strategy and whose major goal is the subversion of legitimate democratic governments. This is not to say that all international drug trafficking or every narco-terrorist operation is Marxist-Leninist in orientation; indeed, the available evidence suggests that the Soviets discovered the virtues of drugs cum terrorism relatively late. But the followers of Lenin are immensely practical in advancing their aims. If it works and the cost and risks are low, why not? If undertaking undue risk is adventurism, the fatal disorder of infantile leftism, then timidity in the face of opportunity is equally to be avoided.

Reports in Western media[13] on Erich Honecker's drug-trafficking activities to the West as part of a Soviet strategy to undermine NATO and the United States and on massive drug and terrorism money-laundering operations just started to appear in early 1990, but it is important to emphasize that although greed unites all those who participate in the drug business, Marxist-Leninist regimes and organizations have used and probably continue to use it as a political weapon in their war against the West. Although I am concerned with countries such as Mexico and the Bahamas where drug-related corruption certainly flourishes, this book does not discuss them, because as yet narco-terrorism has not taken root. Nor does this book deal with the laundering of drug profits through the international banking system, although the political implications of this activity will be discussed.

A word must be said on the question of evidence. As is always the case in these matters, the proof for narco-terrorism is found in bits and pieces scattered across the globe. Some elements are missing. Some only can be surmised. And since I am not putting anyone on trial, the body of evidence is not airtight.

Nevertheless, what I have assembled is a mosaic in which the patterns are distinct enough to form substantial conclusions. I hope that after reading about the activities presented in this book, the reader will be persuaded of the following propositions.

Narco-terrorism is a particularly sinister manifestation of the international terrorist phenomenon because its effects are insidious, persistent, and more difficult to identify than the sporadic, violent outbursts of the armed assailant.

For various reasons, the manufacture and delivery of narcotics is part of the terrorist portfolio. Most obvious is that drugs are a source of revenue to support the activities of terrorist organizations. Another reason is that the use of drugs in target countries such as the United States is part of the terrorist program to undermine the integrity of enemies. The fact that the populace of the target country is a willing participant in the escalation of the drug phenomenon does not detract from the seriousness of the problem with all its international political and economic implications. Those governments and political organizations who use profits from drugs to fund terrorist activities to undermine and destabilize legitimate governments must be identified by the victimized countries and societies and brought into the open. The failure to do so results in a losing battle. The narco-terrorist seeks to weaken the moral fiber of the target society by encouraging widespread addiction, and by nurturing the socially enervating criminal activities that flourish around the drug trade. Drug trafficking requires an environment of lawlessness and corruption to enhance the production and marketing of illicit drugs, and to enjoy the huge profits of illegal activities. Terrorists seek to promote fear and uncertainty and create a sense of chaos and disorder in order to gain political power for themselves. Terrorists always have enjoyed a special status of having their crimes deemed "political." Drug traffickers, on the other hand, always have been viewed purely as criminals. When the two combine, terrorist organizations derive benefits from the drug trade with no loss of status, and drug traffickers who have forged an alliance with terrorists become more formidable and gain in political clout.

To many, narco-terrorism may seem a fantasy; one more conspiracy theory that litters the ideological landscape. There is also a basic reluctance in human nature to believe that any government in the twentieth century would be so evil as to use narco-terrorism as a political weapon. Nevertheless, the purpose of this book is to describe, analyze, and make clear the relationship between drug trafficking perceived as a commercial endeavor, and terrorism perceived as an ideologically justified form of violence. This is in no way to suggest that Marxist-Leninists invented drug trafficking. Examples of drug abuse and the drug trade can be traced back in history to the Hashishim in Syria and the Chinese opium wars. The Marxist-Leninists over the last two decades have taken advantage of an already existing evil.

The accumulation of evidence for the Soviet Union's part in the promotion of narco-terrorism comes through its surrogates; that is, countries allied with Moscow, including Bulgaria, Cuba, Nicaragua, and Syria, all with central roles in the exporting of terrorism and trafficking of drugs to Western countries, including the United States. Most of these regimes have had unusually close ties to the Soviet Union and depended on it not only for political and economic support; they were heavily influenced by Soviet military and foreign policy advisers. The evidence, such as East Germany's involvement in drug trafficking, suggests that similar to the better-known and better-documented terrorist activities of these regimes, drug trafficking could not exist without the knowledge and approval of the Kremlin.*

This book describes how certain states and political organizations have taken advantage of democracy and the drug culture to corrode Western societies through the use of narco-terrorism as one of the most successful weapons in their arsenal of "active measures"—Soviet parlance for covert activities.

Neither the narcotics trade nor political violence—terrorism, if you will—are new to human history; nor is their lethal combination. The legendary but by no means mythical "assassins"—in reality, the Nizari branch of the Muslim Ismaili sect—of medieval Syria and Persia, who combined hashish and political murder, are an example. But ignored as contemporary narco-terrorism has been by the "scribbling set" (to use Joseph Schumpeter's caustic phrase for intellectuals) it comes as a shock that drugs and terrorism now have become interdependent to a degree unimaginable even a decade ago.

It is a deadly symbiosis that tears at the vitals of Western civilization—not just the United States. It did not simply happen, or continue to spread, without direction or purpose. Moreover, from relatively modest beginnings a few decades ago, narco-terrorism has become increasingly global in nature, to become a favorite weapon wielded against the West by its sworn enemies.

Now that the evil genie is out of the bottle, there is little likelihood that this imp will be stuffed back in—at least in our lifetime.

For comfortable, tolerant, and self-absorbed societies to acknowledge they have enemies is a major revelation and difficult to accept. That these adversaries would use both terrorism and the poison of narcotics in their war against those societies smacks of nightmare and paranoia. How could it be? Surely a handful of

---

*East Germany's involvement for twenty years in narco-terrorism on Moscow's behalf, led by its former Communist leader Erich Honecker, was revealed in the West by Alexander Schalck-Golodkowski, a former East German official who defected to the West in December 1989.[14]

criminals might do so. But those who have studied the phenomenon of narco-terrorism are arguing far more. They contend that
it is not simply a few private individuals at war with the West,
that far more than illicit profits are at stake.

Students of narco-terrorism argue that for several decades at
the very least, governments have been in the drug trade. This is
to say that by and large narco-terrorism has become a state-
sponsored phenomenon that without state protection neither
prospers nor increases, an allegation almost wholly ignored until
the 1970s. Indeed, the notion that some states actually sponsor
terrorism—narcotics aside for the moment—was a scandalous
proposition only a decade ago.

Even now it is widely discounted within a good portion of our
own political and media establishments. The most that is admitted is that state-sponsored terrorism is confined to only a few of
the world's more erratic regimes, headed by certifiably mad heads
of state—Libya's Colonel Muammar Qaddafi or the late Ayatollah
Khomeini of Iran. Wishful thinking.

Far more is involved and the evidence now is overwhelming
thanks in part to captured documents from places as distant as
southern Lebanon, the eastern Caribbean island of Grenada, and
recently, Panama.

As outrageous as Marxist-Leninist–sponsored narco-terrorism
is, we must look at what we know, what we don't know, and
what reasonably can be inferred in our examination of this contemporary, dangerous phenomenon.

One final point. The evidence for Marxist-Leninist state-
sponsored narco-terrorism is not based on esoteric or classified
information, but on accessible public sources. However, despite
the evidence and the daily impact of its deadly, depraved operations, narco-terrorism receives little public exposure. This is
particularly evident in the United States, where narco-terrorism
is given little official acknowledgment or publicity. But American
officials have not been entirely silent. Former Secretary of State
George P. Shultz in September 1984, said:

[Drug trafficking is part of a] larger pattern of international lawlessness by communist nations. The complicity of communist nations in the drug trade is cause for grave concern among the nations of the free world. . . . Money from drug smuggling supports terrorists. Terrorists provide assistance to drug traffickers. Organized crime works hand in hand with these other outlaws for their own profit. And what may be most disturbing is the mounting evidence that some governments are involved, too, for their own diverse reasons. Cuba and Nicaragua are prime examples of communist countries involved in drug trafficking to support guerrillas in Central America. . . . The link between narcotics, terrorism and communism is not confined to Latin America, but also exists in Italy, Turkey, and Burma.[15]

What Secretary Shultz said speaks for itself. What we have done about it since he spoke also speaks for itself. What we are doing now is still open to question.

This book is about the origins and the development of narcoterrorism. It is not about solutions. Placing the presently available evidence with all its ramifications before the public is what this book is about.

New York City, January 1992
A failed coup attempt late August 1991 in Moscow took the world by surprise. Since then the Soviet Union has ceased to exist and what is known as the Commonwealth is rapidly changing. The "republics" have declared independence and are moving toward some form of democracy. However, the declaration of political independence has not brought economic freedom. An agreement for economic cooperation was signed by the republics in early September 1991. Breaking the political union has not yet changed the political leadership in the republics, therefore we have yet to see what form the newly established independent republics will take and how—and for whom—the KGB and the GRU will operate in the future.

Narco-terrorism

1
The Little Brothers from Bulgaria

———————————— ▮▮▮▮▮ ————————————

Foremost among Soviet client states in this business of narco-terrorism—in length of service certainly, and very likely in volume as well—is Bulgaria.[1] Gorbachev's program for openness and restructuring of the economy had reached Sofia on October 29, 1989, when then-Communist party leader Todor Zhivkov promised reforms. Zhivkov was forced to resign on November 11, 1989, and Petar Mladenov, former foreign minister and avid supporter of Gorbachev, gained control, apparently with Gorbachev's blessing.[2] Mladenor changed the name of the Communist party to the Socialist party, and won the election on June 11, 1990. Once again, the Bulgarians proved to be Moscow's most faithful followers.

Bulgaria. The small, backward Balkan country the size of Ohio, with nine million inhabitants, is best known for its cheap red vin ordinaire and for harrassing its Turkish minority. It is more often the object of derisory amusement than alarm.

Yet, Bulgarian involvement in narco-terrorism is not a laughing matter, nor is it Lilliputian in size or scope.

Through the decades Sofia has helped poison the lives of hundreds of thousands of Americans and Europeans. It helped feed a war of savage terrorism that nearly brought down Turkey, a key NATO ally, a decade ago. It is still probably very much in the business.

But why Bulgaria? Why not some other East European satellite? The preliminary answer is twofold. First, Bulgaria's geography places it as an ideal transit point between Europe and Asia. A major trucking route from the Middle East to Western Europe slices through the Balkan People's Republic, which carries the bulk of land-transported goods between the two regions. Second, Bulgaria is (or was) the most faithful of the Soviet Union's allies.[3] No one can equal Sofia in servility to Moscow. Unlike the Poles, Czechs, Hungarians, and Rumanians, the Bulgarians seemed to like the Russians, an affection that has deep roots going back to at least the nineteenth century, long before the communists took over Bulgaria (September 9, 1949) and proclaimed it a People's Republic. This time, however, bayonets were unnecessary.

The traditional enemy for the Bulgarians has always been the Turks, not their fellow Slavs. Indeed, it was Imperial Russia that helped liberate the Bulgars from five centuries of Ottoman despotism, and it was the Tsar's forces that kept the Bulgarians from being swallowed by the equally aggressive Serbs—an animosity that was the core of the pre–World War Balkan wars, and the basis of the intra-Balkan struggles that continued during the Great War itself.*

Naturally, lacking a common border helps the Bulgarian feeling of good neighborliness. The Rumanians, who are immediately north of Bulgaria, act as a buffer. The Rumanians hate the Russians and have never forgiven Stalin for annexing Bessarabia in

---

*The Turks were never welcome in Bulgaria. Their occupation of Bulgaria from 1371 to 1393 had been cruel and bloody. The Turks had a rather clever method of occupation: they murdered and suppressed the aristocracy. They took the male children at ages 11 to 12 and turned them into professional Turkish soldiers. Upon their release from the military service, as devout Muslims of course, they were given land and resettled in Bulgaria. Bulgarians were in periodic revolt in the nineteenth century—a hostility that broke out in all-out revolution in 1876. Turkish reprisals were so harsh that they prompted Russian intervention and victory over Constantinople. With the 1878 Treaty of San Stefano, an independent Bulgarian state eventually was established, complete with a Russian prince (Alexander) as its Tsar.

1944. Not surprisingly, even ordinary Bulgarians feel close to the Russians today—ideology aside. For example, the Bulgarian language retains the Cyrillic alphabet, as does the Russian, even though other Slavic languages—Polish, Serbo-Croatian, and Czech, use the Roman alphabet.

Apparently even communism has not shaken the faith in Big Brother. Bulgarian communists have been almost abject in their willingness to follow the Soviet model, no matter how absurdly inappropriate, with few discernible objections from the bottom. If the Soviets believed in "Five Year Plans," the Bulgarians worshipped the "Five Year Plan." And even though the country was manifestly an agricultural and pastoral economy, with few natural resources that could provide the basis for industrialization, Bulgarians engaged in forced-draft industrial development, with disastrous results. Agriculture, naturally, was collectivized Soviet-style, with inevitable ill-fated consequences. Despite these follies the Bulgarians pursued their worship of things Russian to even greater heights of absurdity. During Nikita Khrushchev's visit to Bulgaria in 1962, Zhivkov declared that "we (Bulgarians) must say that our political watch-dial is exact to the second with the watch of the Soviet Union, that our watch is working to Moscow time. This is a matter of great pride for all Bulgarian people."[4] At the beginning of *glasnost* and *perestroyka,* the enthusiams in Eastern Europe—not to mention Cuba—for Gorbachev's reforms could be measured with a teaspoon. The orthodox communists in East Germany and Czechoslovakia feared any change and disapproved. The reformers in Poland and Hungary considered them hopelessly inadequate. However, at the end of 1989 political changes in accordance with *perestroyka* took place in these countries. In Bulgaria, they were embraced with sophomoric enthusiasm, where the Soviet idea of change was soon taken up with such roller-coaster abandon that chaos ensued, prompting the country's leader of thirty-five years, Todor Zhivkov, to make an abrupt and embarrassing 180-degree turn-around.* The political changes in Bulgaria that followed Mlad-enov's rise to power were initiated and implemented by him, which is the way the Bulgarian people seem to like changes— from the top. In early 1990, the Bulgarian people, following trends in other Eastern bloc countries, demonstrated in droves in the streets of Sofia, seeking change.

Fidelity to the smallest whim from the Kremlin was unique in the supposedly ideologically cohesive socialist camp that helps to explain, in part, the Bulgarian connection with narco-terrorism. But Sofia's involvement in drugs did not simply begin with an order from Moscow (although the Kremlin, as we shall see, had much to do with it); instead, Bulgarian narcotics dealing is rooted in a petty intrigue that attempted to boost the country's ragged economy during the 1950s. The Bulgarians always had taken advantage of their geographical position between Asia Minor and Europe. With the connivance of the regime the Bulgarian gov-ernment set about establishing a money-laundering service that facilitated, among others, big-time Turkish criminals who smug-gled cigarettes, watches, and other contraband into Turkey. They also provided safe haven and passports for criminals in return for cash. At first, it would earn them a trickle of hard foreign currency that seemed at the time a never-ending stream of wealth to the impoverished Bulgarians. It was all vintage Eric Ambler with steam locomotives and battered, pre-war lorries wheezing through the passes of the Balkan mountains.

It was all too easy. By the 1960s, Bulgarian officials began to consider more profitable ventures. First they turned to heroin and its morphine base, all imported from Turkey then transhipped to the rest of Europe and, finally, America. Weapons came next. Soon both narcotics and weapons would be married into the clas-sic combination that formed the narco-terrorist paradigm. And Bulgaria would play a central role. "The Bulgarian Secret Service

---

*Although virtually unknown in the West, Zhivkov, who led Bulgaria from 1954 to 1989, was the senior socialist dictator, outranking elderly Fidel Castro by five years and North Korea's aging Kim Il-Sung.

buys drugs from the Palestinians and Middle Eastern terrorists in exchange for weapons, and funnels the drugs to Europe and the United States. . . . The weapons have been used to kill thousands in Lebanon, Turkey, Iraq and Iran, while the drugs have swelled by tens of thousands the numbers of addicts around the world."[5]

Consider the Palestine Liberation Organization (PLO), which does not simply rely on handouts from frightened Arab regimes, as is commonly reported in the Western media. According to a 1984 special report published by the U.S. Department of Justice, "in 1974 and 1975 Bulgaria sold shiploads of arms to . . . terrorist groups in Lebanon."[6] Earlier, in 1983, Nathan Adams, a journalist well acquainted with this part of the world and its politics, reported, "the PLO purchases an estimated 40 percent of its light infantry weapons with either heroin, hashish or morphine base produced by PLO- and Syrian controlled laboratories in Syria or in Lebanon's Bekaa valley."[7] The Justice Department's *Special Report* confirmed this information.[8]

How did the Bulgarians fit into all of this? The answer is simple: U.S. intelligence and law-enforcement officials believe a state-owned export company, KINTEX, formed in 1968 from three smaller firms, with headquarters in Sofia, supplied up to 90 percent of the weapons to the PLO and its myriad splinter terrorist organizations that have made so many dramatic headlines over the years.*[9]

KINTEX modestly describes itself as "an importer and exporter of special equipments and materials, explosives, cables, detonators, apparatus, and other equipment used in industry and mining; shooting, fish and sports articles; multilateral set-off transactions and transit operations."[10] Not quite. The Bulgarian

---

*The profit motive is alive and well in Bulgaria's KINTEX, at 66 Anton Ivanov Boulevard. For several years the firm sold Soviet-made weapons to the CIA through a West German cutout, intended for the Nicaraguan Contras. It is certain KINTEX knew where they were going, but it is not certain if American intelligence officers knew precisely where their AK-47s were coming from.

connection may have grown a bit like Topsy, but it was never simply a matter of gradually falling into the guns-for-drugs business. Nor was it merely a question of profits, although hunger for hard currency in bootless Bulgaria never should be discounted. In fact, thanks to a Bulgarian defector, the genesis of Bulgaria's involvement in narco-terrorism now can be traced and understood for what it is today. When Stefan Svirdlev, a former colonel in the Komitet za Durzhavna Signurnost (KDS), Bulgaria's equivalent to the KGB,* defected to Greece in 1971, he described a Moscow meeting of Warsaw Pact intelligence services in 1967. This was the year, incidentally, that Yuri Andropov became head of the KGB and forged an agreement to exploit the corruption in Western societies to the advantage of the Socialist camp. Svirdlev brought along a rather interesting directive from Bulgaria's State Security, dated July 1970. The directive dealt with "the destabilization of Western society through, among other tools, the narcotic trade." The vehicle for the execution of this strategy was KINTEX.[11]† Svirdlev added, "The movement of narcotics from the Middle East through Bulgaria to West Europe and North America was well known to us. It was, of course, illegal, and drugs were seized when found. Now, it would be a weapon."[13]‡ Nevertheless, the KDS needed the proper vehicle. It was not hard to find. In thrifty Bulgarian fashion, their intelligence did not have to create a slate of brand-new agencies; it would make do with what it already had.

---

*The KDS and the Razvedochni Otdel (RO, the Bulgarian military security agency's equivalent of the GRU [Soviet military security agency]), copied Big Brother's (Soviet) intelligence services.

†The directive smuggled out by Colonel Stefan Svirdlev was dated 16 July 1970 and carried identification no. (DS) M–120/00–0050. Svirdlev defected in 1971 with his wife and child. He worked for Greek intelligence for eight years, but was forced to flee again, this time to West Germany after the Greek government began an *ostpolitik* of its own. The more than 500 documents he snatched from KDS files were left in Athens.[12]

‡Jack Anderson's column in April 1972 (quoted in the Justice Department's *Special Report*) disclosed that a classified CIA document called Bulgaria "the new center for directing narcotics and arms trafficking between Western Europe and the Near East."[14]

KINTEX fit the bill very well. Located on a narrow cobblestone side street behind the TSOUM department store in the center of Sofia, its four-story headquarters is off-limits to diplomats and foreign journalists. Obviously, the Bulgarians were sensitive about protecting the identity of their "business partners."[15]

Like its Soviet counterpart AMTORG or Czechoslovakia's OM-NIPOL, KINTEX already was laced with senior KDS officials who used the export-import business as a convenient cover to make repeated trips to the West for the purpose of espionage, which made the transformation of KINTEX into an all-out illegal enterprise relatively simple. Its previous experience in gun running for Soviet clients in the Middle East and Africa and smuggling also proved valuable. In short, the Bulgarian trading agency didn't miss a beat in picking up its new assignment.[16*]

How did it all work?

KINTEX has about 500 employees, at least a full quarter of whom are intelligence officials from KDS (now renamed more simply the Durzhavna Signurnost, or DS), all of them in leading positions. KINTEX reports directly to the DS's First Directorate which, like its model the KGB, has a monoploy on all foreign operations. The First, like other similar Eastern European directorates, is stuffed with KGB advisers who in effect are liaison officers, linking it with the Soviet bloc's senior intelligence service.

The thrifty Bulgarians did not attempt to manage everything in the illegal arms and drugs business; rather, they piggyback on existing organizations such as Lebanese narcotics smugglers, the Sicilian Mafia, and corrupt Swiss bankers, to name just a few. KINTEX acts as a facilitator, an honest broker if you will, providing others with the cover and protection of a sovereign

---

*KINTEX did not waste much time. In December 1969, West German police in Frankfurt seized 200 kilos of morphine base that German chemists identified as coming from Sofia. How did they come to that conclusion? The presence of chemicals found in the base were those only used in Bulgaria. Later, the Turks who were arrested in the drug raid said the source of morphine was a Turkish national living in Sofia.[17]

state—an invaluable, indispensable support infrastructure for drug criminals and terrorists alike. A typical drug deal, according to Adams, runs as follows:

traffickers applying to ship heroin or morphine base through Bulgaria or to buy it from KINTEX must agree to reinvest a portion of their profits—sometimes up to 50 percent—in the purchase of other KINTEX supplied contraband. Nearly always the deals are consummated in hard currency—American dollars, West German marks, and Swiss francs being the preferred mediums of exchange, almost, but not always. KINTEX, in fact, pioneered a once unique barter arrangement where guns and drugs were swapped directly. No fancy or cumbersome arrangements for KINTEX or its patron the Bulgarian DS; a direct deal was fine with them.[18]

Once the drugs were delivered from Syria or Lebanon, the weapons were smuggled to the terrorist groups. It was—and is—simplicity itself.

The U.S. Drug Enforcement Administration (DEA), based on scores of informants, eventually put together a typical scenario of a KINTEX operation first published in the Justice Department's *Special Report* on Bulgarian involvement in drugs and terror:

A European arms dealer, a sanctioned customer of KINTEX, purchases weapons from Western or Eastern European countries through licit or illicit channels. The arms dealer sells these weapons to KINTEX through a representative in Sofia. These weapons, in turn, are resold to a Middle Eastern trafficking group, which then supplies an insurgency group. Payment to KINTEX from the Middle Eastern group may take the form of heroin in selected cases. The heroin is then sold through KINTEX to selected Western European trafficking groups.[19]

Over the years, Sofia became the locus of scores of narcotics traffickers, many of them Turks. They were given living, office, and storage space—usually first-class accommodations in Sofia, and the Black Sea port towns of Varna and Burgas—along with all the usual protections and exemptions that only a government can provide.

As far back as the early 1970s, the American authorities already had obtained some leads of their own concerning Bulgaria's involvement in the drug business.[20] Many were supplied by Henri Arsan, a Syrian with a long record in dope smuggling. His mistake was trying to sell 200 kilos of morphine base in the spring of 1973 to a U.S. undercover agent. While implicating other narcotics traffickers, Arsan neglected to mention his own special relationship with KINTEX which, in fact, he resumed and continued right through the early 1980s until his arrest by Italian police.[21]*

By the late 1970s, business was booming and Bulgaria, no doubt, was taking in billions of dollars in illegal profits that showed up on no one's books except those kept at KINTEX. By 1980, however, U.S. officials had figured out the KINTEX connection in some detail. In a briefing to State Department officials, intelligence analysts told them, "There no longer can be any doubt that Bulgaria is profiting both politically and financially from the traffic in narcotics and arms which is supported by drug profits. KINTEX is the primary vehicle, and KINTEX is simply an arm of the Bulgarian State Security."[22] That kind of money, in addition to the fact that Bulgaria was helping to refine and tranship via Sicily growing quantities of America's heroin supply, eventually got the attention of U.S. officials. In the fall of 1981, the U.S. government responded by suspending "normal working contacts between U.S. and Bulgarian law enforcement agencies . . . . The accumulation of reliable reports citing that, at a minimum, the Bulgarian authorities tolerated the activities of known arms and narcotics traffickers who operated from Bulgarian territory, led to this decision."[23]

What they found after receiving leads from Italian investigators

*Arsan later would be arrested again by Italian police, only to die in jail.

was a complex arrangement whereby unrefined drugs from the Middle East were being sent through Bulgaria to refining labs in Italy, where the heroin was sent on to European and American customers. The cash generated from the sales of the narcotics then would be laundered by Swiss banks with the help of hundreds of dummy corporate accounts. The freshly washed money would be used to purchase weapons for terrorist groups around the world, but especially those concentrated in the violent and volatile Middle East.[24] At the center of this evil empire was Bulgaria's KINTEX.

But it would take nearly an entire decade before Washington lodged an offical complaint, in January 1983, against the Bulgarian government for its involvement in narcotics and terror.[25] In March 1983, the State Department, together with DEA and Customs, read the following statement into the congressional record:

The United States government has in fact been aware for some time that, at a minimum, the Bulgarian authorities tolerate the activities of known arms and narcotics traffickers who operate from Bulgarian territory. The accumulation of reliable reports regarding this activity led the U.S. in the fall of 1981 to suspend normal working contacts between U.S. and Bulgarian law enforcement agencies and to halt negotiations on a customs agreement which were then underway with the government of Bulgaria. Since then we have made our concerns known to the Bulgarian govenment in a number of high-level discussions both in Sofia and Washington. The Bulgarian response to the questions we have raised has been disappointing, though we continue to have hopes of convincing the Bulgarian government to bring a halt to arms and narcotics trafficking based on Bulgarian territory. We do not intend to resume regular bilateral contacts with Bulgaria in this field unless it becomes clear they will lead to concrete results.[26]

Four years later, U.S. officials were willing to go public on Sofia's contribution to narco-terrorism, largely because the Bulgarians had completely ignored U.S. inquiries. John C. Lawn, then acting director of the DEA, speaking to the House Foreign Affairs Committee in May 1984, explained his frustration:

[W]hen the DEA passed information to the Bulgarians for follow-up action over this 10-year period, the results were not responsive. On at least 5 separate occasions, information was provided on scores of Turkish, Syrian and Jordanian traffickers based in Sofia. The Bulgarian side promised a full and prompt investigation. In these cases the Bulgarians either did not respond or only provided the DEA with a list of recent narcotics seizures made by their Customs Service.[27]*

The test of Bulgarian sincerity took place from 1971 to 1981, when Washington finally suspended cooperation with Sofia—over ten years, in case anyone is concerned that the U.S. government was unduly hasty in suspecting Bulgarian complicity. Then in 1983, a curious incident occurred that finally led the DEA to conclude that Sofia was not playing the game honestly. It involved the question of gun running. In June 1983, a DEA agent stationed in Vienna met with a top-ranking Bulgarian customs official in Sofia. When the DEA representative queried the man on Bulgarian arms smuggling, the official insisted huffily that the U.S. was *also* a major supplier of weapons. The DEA concluded by inference that this constituted an admission of Bulgarian guilt.[29]†

In 1984, a number of officials, including William von Raab, U.S. Customs Commissioner; Francis Mullen, former DEA director; Clyde Taylor, then chief of the State Department's

*As part of their deception Bulgarian officials would ostentatiously seize "tremendous amounts of contraband, primarily hashish" from "amateur traffickers," that is, drug runners who were not working for or with KINTEX.[28]
†The DEA office in Vienna is responsible for following Bulgarian narcotics activities. Bulgarian officials as early as 1973 denied KINTEX's guilt. In response to a series on heroin published by *Newsday,* Sofia rejected the story and warned that its publication might damage the U.S.-Bulgarian narcotics agreement.[30]

narcotics bureau; and Robert Sayre, who then headed the department's office for combating terrorism, appeared before U.S. Senator Paula Hawkins. In addition to confirming what others had learned before, these U.S. officials also charged that KINTEX's intelligence officers would "task" the Turkish nationals (often of Kurdish origin), Syrian, Iranian, Jordanian, Lebanese, and European nationals, their partners in crime, with intelligence-collection missions carried out in both the Middle East and Western Europe.[31]

American intelligence now knew how close the Bulgarians were to their friends in the drug business. Paul Henze, a former NSC staffer under Jimmy Carter and an expert on the Bulgarian-Turkish connection, in the same hearings reported that "The smugglers were given more and more favors. When the Turkish government cancelled their passports and put them on international wanted lists, the Bulgarian regime gave them fake passports and let them take over villas in Sofia and Burgas. It even provided naval escorts for their ships."[32]

American intelligence also had learned that KINTEX was only part of the Bulgarian picture. Arms and drug deals mean nothing if the goods can't get to the buyer in time. With experience, the Bulgarians had it down to a science.

But let the Drug Enforcement Administration tell the story:

A preferred method of smuggling narcotics aboard [Transport International Routier, TIR] trucks is within "traps" built into the vehicle itself; "traps" built into the gas tanks are the most reported method. To a lesser extent, narcotics from Southwest Asian source countries are concealed within legitimate cargo, undergoing only cursory examination at the source with the knowledge and complicity of a customs official. Because of their exemption from customs examination and the volume of traffic, TIR trucks are rarely searched en route to their destination unless specific intelligence information is transmitted to appropriate customs officials.[33]

It should be added that the TIR system is an international agreement whose signers, including the United States, agree to facilitate the international transport of goods by eliminating as much red tape as possible. This means that once vehicles have been cleared at the beginning of a trip they are not inspected again until the end of the journey. That's good news for cargo trucks that recieved their seal of approval originally from Bulgaria. It also should be noted that in mid-1980s some 50,000 trucks per year crossed Bulgaria on their way to the Middle East or Western Europe. Half that number were TIR trucks.[34]

Did this spurt of publicity about Bulgaria slow down Sofia in its pursuit of the almighty American dollar? The answer is some, but not much. While cross-Bulgarian drug trafficking may have slowed a bit since the mid-1980s, Sofia continues to branch out in other, quite profitable directions. Thus, the Bulgarians have expanded their money-laundering services—up to $2 billion a year—for which they earn $10 million a year, by one estimate. That figure is almost certain to go up, perhaps exponentially, as Western countries tighten their banking laws. As a result, Bulgaria takes drug-earned cash, flies special couriers to Switzerland where the money is converted to untraceable gold, and then returned, for a fee, to its anxious clients—many of whom are in the jewelry business in Turkey.[35]

Of course, things do change, and as a result of KINTEX's sordid reputation, the Bulgarians created a new covering company dealing with the nasty business of arms and narcotics—its name is Globus.[36] Globus seems to specialize in the cash-for-gold laundry business first started under KINTEX. According to *Forbes*,

When it arrives at Globus, the gold is unpacked and weighed. For this service, the Bulgarians charge $60 for every kilo of gold that they move. This fee plus the $1 to $3 per $1,000 charged on the smuggled bank notes earns Bulgaria most of the $10 million or so in yearly laundering fees.[37]

Even better, the Bulgarians do their job with all due modesty: "Hand this to the Bulgarians. Their fees are modest and their service impeccable. 'In all my dealings with the Bulgarians, not a single gram of gold or a single deutsche mark ever disappeared,' says [a] Zurich money dealer."[38]

Clearly, a good case could be made that Bulgarian participation in narco-terrorism can be chalked up to greed. Some observers believe that short of running directly against Soviet-bloc interests, Sofia would have sold weapons to anyone. Consider the following:

Item. KINTEX sold weapons to the Nigerian government during its civil war with the Ibo-dominated Biafra in the 1960s.

Item. KINTEX sold several boatloads of weapons to right-wing Christian militias shortly before the Lebanese civil war broke out in 1975. The weapons flow ceased only after protests from the local communist party reached Moscow.

Item. The Bulgarians also have sold arms surreptitiously to the South African government.[39]

But simple greed can hardly explain Bulgaria's participation in at least three episodes of state-sponsored terrorism, two of which struck at the heart of Western interests. The first involves Sofia's role in the destabilization of Turkey in the late 1970s. The terrorist war that nearly destroyed a key NATO ally and did provoke a military takeover has received little attention in the United States. For their part, West European governments took little notice until the army restored order; characteristically, they blamed the Turkish armed forces for the problem. Yet, most assuredly that was not the case. As for Bulgaria, at the behest of the Soviet Union its role was to supply money, arms, and training for both right-wing and left-wing terrorists.[40] Those terrorists trained by the Bulgarians operated both in Turkey and around the world where "Armenian" murder squads assassinated Turkish diplomats.

The billion dollars that was poured into the Turkish effort did not come from Bulgarian pockets, to be sure. Although Bulgaria's leaders had little historic love for the Turks—witness their brutal persecution of the country's Turkish minority—destabilizing Turkey essentially was a Soviet project. As former NSC staffer Paul Henze explained to a Senate subcommittee, "Turkey guards the straits that lead from the Black Sea into the Mediterranean and its solid land mass blocks Soviet access to the Middle East. Since the Middle Ages Russian Tsars had coveted Constantinople (Istanbul). So did Stalin and his successors [who] have not given up this ambition."[41]

The same could be said of Bulgaria's role in subverting Italy, another key NATO ally, at about the same time as the Turkish venture.* Proof? Captured Italian Red Brigade members testified that Bulgaria had offered them arms and money during the December 17, 1981 kidnapping of American Brigadier General James Lee Dozier to encourage them to further "destabilize Italy."[44] But Sofia's attempt at promoting more terrorism in Italy via the Red Brigade is a mere Bulgarian bagatelle compared with its supreme contribution to the Soviet effort to undermine the West, referring, of course, to Bulgaria's almost certain participation and sponsorship in the attempted killing of Pope John Paul II.

The issue is hideously complex, but Bulgarian participation is now beyond a doubt. To begin with, Italian investigators who labored for years putting the pieces together are certain that Sofia did not do it solely for the money. So is much of the Italian press, including the left-wing *La Republica,* which joined with uncustomary relish in the investigation of Soviet and Bulgarian links to Turkish gunman Mehmet Ali Agca, who actually pulled the trigger in St. Peter's square on May 13, 1981.

Here are only the highlights:

*Vladimir Sakaharov, a KGB officer who defected in 1967, provided information about Soviet recruitment and training of Turkish agents in subversion and terrorism beginning in the early 1960s.[42] As for Soviet and Bulgarian subversive activities in Italy, "They've been operating in Italy so long without being bothered—why should they worry in this case [the attempt to assassinate the pope]?"[43]

- An Italian police report dated May 27, 1981, implicates a Bulgarian identified as Mustaeof as a possible suspect in the attempted assassination.
- Agca confesses he received the gun from an unidentified Syrian and a false passport from a Turkish national in Sofia. At the time, Agca was staying at the plush Hotel Vitosha, a favorite working place for the Bulgarian DS.
- In the Bulgarian capital, Agca in a later confession detailed contacts with Bulgarian officials who were stationed in Rome and who planned the details of the attempt on the life of the pope.
- One of those officials, airline official Sergei Ivanov Antonov, was arrested in Rome for complicity in the assassination attempt on November 25, 1982.* Other Bulgarian government officials would be charged, but would leave Italy before being arrested.[45]

Bulgaria became involved because its Soviet Big Brother, KGB boss Yuri Andropov, feared that the Polish pope John Paul II was undermining Moscow's control of Poland. It was not an irrational fear, considering that eight months after the attempted assassination Polish communist officials proclaimed martial law, arresting numerous Solidarity leaders in the meantime.

One might think that exposure would have dampened Bulgarian enthusiasm for narco-terrorism, especially since the answer to cui bono is nearly always the Kremlin; contrary to appearances, however, that is not the case. The State Department decided to ignore the evidence. On June 8, 1987, the Senate Caucus on International Narcotics Control heard a startling testimony by Louis Freeh, then head of the Organized Crime Unit of the U.S. Attorney's Southern District of New York office, that

---

*Antonov was released and returned to Bulgaria after the Italian court could not find enough evidence to convict him—a direct result of Bulgarian and Soviet political pressure.

Bulgaria was the key link in the heroin-trafficking chain between the Middle East and the U.S.:

What we found was that the Bulgarian government would warehouse the material [morphine base] and in some cases refined heroin. . . . They would sell it [morphine base] from time to time directly to the Sicilian [Mafia's] lab refineries . . . they would arrange to be paid . . . [in] dollars, which were collected here in the U.S., which made [their] way through Switzerland to Bulgaria.[46]

Freeh continued to report that the U.S. Attorney's office "documented in this case (the 'pizza connection'),* $60 million between 1980 and 1984 which were collected as heroin proceeds and sent to Switzerland, Sicily and back to Bulgaria."[47]

The State Department's Bureau of International Narcotics Matters released its 1989 *International Narcotics Control Strategy Report* in March of that year. In its section on Bulgaria it admitted that that country had long been a transit point for drug smugglers, but insisted that Sofia had "cracked down on them" in the mid-1980s, partially as a consequence of U.S. pressure:

There is some evidence that some traffickers still operate on a temporary basis from hotels in Sofia. There is no evidence of any current involvement of government agencies in drug trafficking. There has been no evidence that would indicate any Bulgarian law enforcement official has been engaged in narcotics-related corruption since 1986. There was one isolated case of corruption in that year.[48]

But others in the American government did not look at Bulgaria with such rose-colored glasses. This is especially true of the DEA and Customs, which had spent years dogging Bulgarian efforts at promoting narco-terrorism. In fact, a DEA and Customs in-

*The infamous Pizza Connection, the Sicilian Mafia's involvement in drug trafficking to the U.S. and money laundering, was one of the biggest organized crime cases, broken and tried by U.S. authorities in 1986.

vestigation report was leaked to the *New York City Tribune.*
Dated January 3, 1989, it went into considerable detail about
ongoing Bulgarian drug and arms activities, paying particular
attention to Globus, which has largely replaced KINTEX as the
agency of choice for Sofia's illicit operations.[49] According to the
report,

Shakarchi Trading Company receives cash that is smuggled from
Turkey to Switzerland via Sofia, Bulgaria. The smuggling of the
money out of Turkey and into Bulgaria for transportation to Switzerland is processed by a Bulgarian import/export firm called "Globus," which in reality is an agency of the Bulgarian government
operated by the Bulgarian Secret Police. The Bulgarian government
takes a percentage of the value of the goods, whether it be illegal
cash, drugs, or weapons, and guarantees safe passage of the material
through Bulgaria.[50]

This report was sent together with a letter dated January 6,
1989, from Customs Commissioner William von Raab to William
Webster, Director of Central Intelligence, in which von Raab
expressed his concern "with . . . the involvement of Bulgarian
officials in narcotics smuggling and money laundering . . . and
the serious impact of such Bulgarian activities on the United
States."[51] He asked for Webster's assistance in dealing with the
problem.

Just why the State Department has chosen to back away from
rather than to condemn Bulgaria in the face of overwhelming
evidence is unclear. The old standby that the diplomats are always
looking for ways to improve bilateral relations may once again be
correct, especially if one considers the Soviets' reaction when
Bulgaria's involvement in drug-money laundering became public.
After all, Bulgaria was one of the most loyal surrogate states in
the Eastern bloc. Just how sensitive the Soviets were to the Bulgarian connection can be gauged from Moscow's vigorous denials
of Sofia's involvement in narco-terrorism. On April 12, 1989,

Kremlin spokesman Geradny Gerasimov labeled charges against Bulgaria and a Soviet request to the U.S. for help against Bulgarian trafficking into the USSR "a total invention."[52]

In July 1991 the Bulgarian Parliament adopted a noncommunist constitution, which is concerned with human rights and will introduce a market-oriented economy. Not everybody blesses President Zhelyu Zhelev's democratization of Bulgaria. The main opposition comes from the Union of Democratic Forces (UDF), which claims that the Parliament has a communist majority and that Bulgaria's infrastructure is still in place. Interpol is concerned with growing drug-trafficking activities throughout the Eastern bloc, including Bulgaria. But due to the political changes, it is very hard to obtain concrete data.

2

The Cuban Connection: Castro, Cocaine, and Terror

───────── ▖▖▖▖▖ ─────────

If the Bulgarians have been little brothers to their Russian allies, the same cannot be said for the Cubans. True, Havana has more or less faithfully followed the Soviet line on most major questions—especially in foreign policy—since the end of 1967, but not out of great love or admiration for the Soviet Union. Yet the Soviets have been subsidizing Cuba to the tune of $5 billion a year for the past thirty years.

Cuba's alliance with the Soviet Union, based on a perceived universal U.S. threat to the revolution, is rooted in a profound hatred of America and Americans—Castro's apologists notwithstanding. The Cuban leader who has completed three full decades of undisputed power has an almost pathological hatred for the United States that is irrational, irreversible, and unrelenting, the origin of which is not at all clear. Castro himself has never made it clear, but in contrast to his defenders, his anti-Americanism did not begin with the 1961 Bay of Pigs or with the alleged (but fabricated) incidents in 1959 that supposedly had been directed at the young revolution by Washington.

In fact, Castro privately held feelings of animosity toward the U.S. even before his seizure of power. In a letter to his friend Celia Sanchez, written from the Sierra Maestra in June 1958, Castro made clear his views: "When this war is over, a much longer and more important war will begin for me: I shall have to wage against the Americans. I feel that is my destiny."[1] In reality, all that matters to Castro is unending enmity directed at the main and nearby enemy, the United States of America—but it is a personal animosity. That is both the strength and weakness of Cuba's anti-Americanism as well as of its pro-Sovietism. Indeed, as an ample number of observers over the years have quickly discovered, most Cubans have little love for the Russians.

Unlike the Bulgarians, Cubans had little experience with Russians before 1960, when Anastas Mikoyan visited the Caribbean nation, the first high-ranking Soviet official to do so. Cubans knew firsthand of the United States and to a lesser extent Spain, the former metropole. Cuba's only experience with Bolshevism was their Partido Socialista Popular (PSP), the small and orthodox pro-Soviet party loathed by nearly all politically active Cubans in the 1940s and 1950s including, quite probably, the young Fidel Castro himself, who at the time belonged to the left-wing but strongly anti-communist *Ortodoxos*.*

The PSP made the mistake of joining Fulgencio Batista's cabinet in the early 1940s, and then refusing to join the guerrilla war against him when Batista returned to power through a coup in March 1952. Yet once in power Castro would either jail or force into exile old comrades who refused to join forces with the despised communists, such as Blas Roca and Carlos Rafael Rodriguez. The power of Castro's fear and loathing of the United States swept away all objections, and so the alliance with the Soviets was forged.

Fidel Castro's record over the last thirty years is ample testimony of his willingness to promote terrorism—but what about drugs? Unlike Bulgaria, Cuba did not have a rich history of smuggling or involvement in narcotics. The island, is, however, strategically situated in the Caribbean. Stretching nearly 700 miles

*But not Fidel's younger brother Raul, who is the longest-running minister of defense in the world and is the elder Castro's slated successor. Raul is certain to have been a communist since his youth—an attendee of the Soviet-sponsored 1950 World Youth Festival held in Vienna. He has remained an admirer of all things Soviet, a fact that reassures Moscow, assuming, of course, that the younger will succeed the older.

from tip to tip, it commands the central Caribbean lying between the Gulf of Mexico and the Caribbean proper. It is a natural connecting point linking South America with its northern border.

Fidel Castro once contended that before he took power in January 1959, Cuba had been a poor country. Cuba "had not developed economically or technically for dozens of years," Fidel stated in an interview in 1964.[2] As with much of the Maximum Leader's rhetoric, this description is not only self-serving but untrue. In fact, before the 1959 revolution Cuba was one of the most developed countries in Latin America, ranking second and third in most of the economic and social indicators.[3] Blessed with fertile soil, a year-round growing season, a relatively large entrepreneurial class, and proximity to the United States market, a majority of Cubans enjoyed a standard of living that was the envy of much of the hemisphere. This is not to say that there were no poor and even hungry in Cuba, but compared to nearby Haiti or distant Bolivia, there could be no comparison.[4] Cuba did have deep and serious societal problems—problems that gave Castro an opportunity to seize power after a relatively short and bloodless insurrection, compared to the decade-long, communist-led guerrilla war in El Salvador, which may have cost as many as 70,000 lives and with no end in sight.

Cuban history is one of frustrated aspirations. By the third decade of the nineteenth century almost all of Spain's New World empire had vanished and a score of new republics replaced the old vice-royalties and captaincy-generals. Only in the Caribbean was Spain able to hold on to Puerto Rico and its prize jewel, Cuba—which is not to say that most Cubans were happy with their status; they were not. Spanish-born officials ran the government and kept the best jobs for themselves. Spanish governors-general came and went, but not without having made their fortunes in Cuba through graft and other forms of corruption. Favors seldom were granted to native-born Cubans.

Cuban attempts to achieve independence were steadily frustrated throughout the eighteenth and much of the nineteenth century. The so-called Ten Years War that began in 1867 was brutally suppressed by Spanish troops. When another revolt broke out in 1895, it was not the Cuban patriots who got the credit for finally driving out the Spaniards but the Americans, who declared war on Spain in 1898. Cuban nationalists of every political persuasion always have insisted that the American involvement in the war was not necessary. They argue, too, that Cuban rebel troops under generals such as Calixto Garcia eventually would have defeated the Spanish after 1895. Perhaps. In any case, the U.S. war with Spain created another layer of frustration for most politically active Cubans. The United States's special relationship wth Cuba embodied in the Platt amendment enacted by Congress in 1901 (and not rejected by the Cubans until 1934),[5] giving the right to American intervention, only deepened it. But complete political independence did not solve Cuba's problems, either. Corruption flourished under both dictatorships and elected governments. By the time of Fulgencio Batista's second period of power after his March 1952 coup, Cuba was well on its way to social and political disintegration. Politics and university life, for example, revolved around "gangsterismo," in which armed political gangs struggled with each other for control of Havana University and patronage from various government ministries. Cuba's reputation for vice—gambling, prostitution, and drugs—has become gaudier in the retelling, especially from the current regime's propagandists. Nevertheless, there is more than a kernel of truth in it.

The dark side of Cuban life resembled that of Mexican border towns like Tijuana and Juárez. Havana, too, became an escape for Americans seeking illicit pleasures, including drink, beginning in the prohibition era. Unlike Canada, where thirsty Americans also repaired, Cuba and Mexico did not have our northern neighbor's tradition of law with order. Instead, another morality was at play: anything could be had for a price, including narcotics. What Cuban gangsters did not know about the business, they soon learned from their American counterparts.

Shortly after Castro's rebel army had marched into Havana, several thousand Cuban narcotics dealers set up shop in the United States—mostly, but not entirely, in Miami. They dealt in cocaine, supplying Miami's growing Hispanic population, and heroin for the voracious New York market.[6]

Fidel Castro and his apologists have made the claim that one of the revolution's virtues was the elimination of vice in Cuba, including drugs, This is a half-truth, at best. It is true that drugs became difficult to obtain for the local population, but this did not apply to the American market. Unlike the Batista government, which does not seem to have been directly involved in narcotics trafficking, there is ample evidence that even in its early years the Castro regime was directly involved in drug trafficking, principally cocaine. Castro's pursuit of drug trafficking as a vehicle and weapon to spread revolution was documented by Captain Robert Workman, U.S. Coast Guard (retired), a 1984 Senior Fellow at the National Defense University. In 1958, Fidel Castro stated publicly that he was going to export his revolution beyond Cuba using "his" methods. His methods included a twofold purpose for involvement with the narcotics trade: to damage U.S. society by aiding drug traffickers and to finance Marxist terrorists and guerrilla activity in Latin America, including training and arms shipments for insurgency.[7]

According to a declassified DEA intelligence report, Cuban government involvement in drug trafficking goes back at least to 1961. During that summer top Cuban officials met with then senator from Chile, Salvador Allende (according to a confidential informant) to discuss setting up a cocaine-distribution network in order to help finance the revolution in Chile and the already economically strapped Cuban regime.[8]* Ten years later, accord-

*Attending the meeting were Ernesto Guevara, Ramiro Valdes, Captain Moises Crespo of the Cuban secret police, and then senator from Chile, Salvador Allende. The meeting began with a discussion of Chilean politics, but soon Comandante Valdes turned the talk to setting up a cocaine-trafficking network in order to raise

ing to the same DEA report, Cuban embassies in Canada and Mexico regularly facilitated heroin trafficking to the United States. The report continued: "A heroin dealer operating in Mexico obtained heroin directly from Havana in exchange for auto and farm parts, medical supplies, etc."[9] And according to Sal Vizzini, a Federal Bureau of Narcotics special agent in the early 1960s, two Cuban agents were arrested in Miami with large amounts of cocaine in their possession. That agent would later write that the investigation that followed their arrest clearly and definitely indicated that they were Fidel Castro's agents selling cocaine for money or trading it for guns for Castro.[10] Castro took a most pragmatic attitude about making revolution: Whatever worked.[11] It was some time, though, before supporting the narcotics traffic to the United States became a fixed part of Cuban foreign policy.

But while Castro's use of drugs to promote revolution is a relatively new tactic, his foreign policy objectives have remained fixed since 1959, the year of his triumph over Fulgencio Batista and, he thought, the first victory over American imperialism since Pearl Harbor. His overall objectives are threefold: (1) the survival of the Cuban socialist revolution, stamped in his image; (2) the advancement of international proletarianism, as once defined by the Soviet Union; and (3) the quest for Cuban leadership in Latin America and, preferably, the entire Third World.

Driving these somewhat abstract goals (the first being an exception) is a rabid anti-Americanism, as we have seen. For Fidel, everything done must be at the expense of the United States. Why? Because, according to him, the United States is the fountainhead of all of the world's major evils. Colonialism, neocolonialism, poverty, racism, the arms race, the debt burden, and

money to help finance Allende. At the time Santiago, Chile, was the leading cocaine-processing center in the Western Hemisphere. Valdes, who ran the secret police, suggested that Roberto Alvarez, chief of Cuban espionage, head the new organization.

pollution are only a sample of the trouble the United States of America makes for the world, especially for the Socialist camp and its friends in the Third World.

To accomplish these grandiose objectives Castro has fashioned an equally ambitious set of interlocking strategies. He has sought: (1) Cuban leadership of Third World as a weapon to be used against the United States; (2) the extension of Cuban diplomatic and military presence in Latin America and Africa; and (3) the promotion of radical left and Marxist-Leninist regimes in Latin America and Africa.

Castro's vision of a world without *yanquis* could be chalked up to small-power megalomania were it not for Cuba's alliance with the Soviet Union, an alliance Castro sought before the Soviets even dreamed that such a thing was possible. Indeed, the ever-cautious Soviets spurned Castro's initial advances as reckless adventurism, and to this day have not included Cuba in the Warsaw Pact. Castro sought membership because an attack from the United States meant automatic Soviet defense of his regime, something Moscow is not ready to pledge in black and white. Nevertheless, while the relationship has not been entirely harmonious, it has settled down into a durable and mutually profitable marriage of convenience.* Unlike Bulgaria, Cuba to this day retains a measure of independence and with it, self-respect. In short, Cuba may be a Soviet proxy, but it is not a pawn, a mere vassal in Soviet state calculations, and it is in this light that we must consider Havana's role in the spread of narco-terrorism within the Western Hemisphere.

What is curious is not that Castro adopted narco-terrorism as a policy as did the Bulgarians but that it took Fidel so long to proceed with it. As mentioned earlier, there is some evidence of

---

*Wracks in the Soviet-Cuban marriage appeared to take a more serious turn by the spring of 1990, when this book was written. It seemed that Castro's strong objection to *perestroyka* was about to drive a permanent wedge in the relation, and predictions about the end of the Castro brothers' regime became a daily event.

Cuban involvement in trafficking in drugs to the United States, but not enough to indicate drug running as a systematic Cuban policy before the mid-1970s. It has taken Fidel some time to implement the decision to use drugs as a potential weapon. This decision was part of a larger pact designed to destabilize the United States. In the Tri-Continental Conference of world revolutionary groups that was held in Havana in January 1966,* one of the decisions called for the planned destabilization of the United States and explicitly detailed such activities as the exploitation and undermining of American society through the trafficking of drugs and the promotion of other corrupting criminal activities.[12]

Based on all the evidence, it appears that Castro indeed accepted this decision and began systematically to exploit any perceived weakness in the United States. At this time the flow of drugs became a salient part of Cuban strategy. Not only has the spread of drugs expanded, but Castro has been able to capitalize on the growing "support network" surrounding the drug business. In particular, he has exploited the tentacles of narco-terrorism and strengthened Cuba's influence in strategic areas of this hemisphere. While in the early years narco-terrorism was used opportunistically as a source of profits and as a convenient means of creating self-sustaining insurgencies, later it became a major channel through which the Cuban-Soviet strategy was implemented to exert political influence on the state level in Latin America.[13]

The Angolan adventure toward the end of 1975 was a low point for Cuban revolutionary adventurism. The Cuban economy in the late 1960s was battered after Cuba's commander-in-chief insisted on producing a record 10 million tons of sugar, an act of economic monumentalism that defied the laws of supply and demand, with predictably disastrous results. At the time of Che

*Officially the conference was called "The First Conference of Solidarity of the Peoples of Africa, Asia, and Latin America" (OSPAAAL).

Guevara's ignominious death in the Bolivian *yunga* in 1967, it had become apparent even to Fidel Castro that his foreign policy of promoting revolution indiscriminately with a handful of fanatical guerrillas equally was a bust. So he decided to change his modus operandi.

Castro's lodestar remained the same—the destruction of the United States—but his tactics changed. If his minions in Latin America could not win power outright, they would simply terrorize. And so in the late 1960s and early 1970s, carefully trained urban terrorists unleashed a wave of violence throughout the southern cone of South America in Argentina, Brazil, Chile, and Uruguay. None of these Cuban-sponsored groups won power, of course, but they did poison the well of politics in each of these countries for years, possibly decades.

Although the use of the rural guerrilla war strategy has never been entirely abandoned in either theory or practice, Cuba's sponsoring of urban-based terrorism became more and more a substitute although it has never been formally acknowledged by Havana. Nevertheless, terrorism—primarily urban-based terrorism—came to be, through earlier failure, the principal weapon in Cuba's arsenal as it continued to promote anti-American insurgencies around the world.[14]

Yet the years of rage in South America also brought frustration. Despite Fidel's destiny, he personally had not done much actual damage to the Yankee colossus in years. By 1975, he could rejoice in the victory of the "Vietnamese people," but his own successful contributions to the anti-imperialist struggle had been limited to propaganda and those yellowing notices on Playa Giron.*

---

*Fidel's craving for the limelight in those lost years is vividly illustrated by his courting of then Secretary of State Henry Kissinger. Castro praised Kissinger repeatedly as a "realist"—a man who could be talked to. In fact, Fidel promised to see him any time the Secretary wanted. Kissinger merely ignored the overtures.

It is hardly surprising that besides discovering opportunities to expand the revolution in Africa beginning (but hardly ending) with Angola, Fidel Castro also discovered the advantages of narco-terrorism. Castro did not have to look far—drugs from South America were going right under his nose. Illicit narcotics by the shipload were plying the Caribbean waters from Colombia to south Florida via the Windward Passage, a narrow strait of water that separates the eastern tip of Cuba from Haiti. The smallest error of navigation by the *narco-buques* could place the drug vessel within Cuban waters, where an alert coast guard could seize and search with characteristic police-state thoroughness. This is precisely what began to happen. The cargoes were confiscated and the crews imprisoned. The losses to the Colombian traffickers became serious; far more so than the small finds made by U.S. officials at the time.

As a result, in late 1975 some of Colombia's best-known and biggest cocaine kingpins met secretly in Bogotá, Colombia's mountain capital, with the Cuban ambassador Fernando Ravelo-Renedo in order to negotiate the release of their property—boats, cargo, and crews.[15]

It was all quite extraordinary. But out of that meeting came an alliance that has proved enduring and mutually beneficial to each side. Even more extraordinary was the arrangement itself; the Cubans made the initial offer. Ravelo, in fact an agent of Cuba's elite intelligence service, the Departamento de América (DA), conveyed it from his chief, Manuel Pineiro Losada. Havana not only was prepared to ignore drug-laden mother ships operating in its waters but also to provide fueling and repair services in its ports—shelter privileges that would come in handy in the treacherous waters of the Florida Straits. Havana also offered to escort the narcotics boats upon leaving Cuban ports, as well as provide Cuban flags to disguise their origin all the way to feeder vessels stationed off the Florida Keys. In return for this package of protection and provision the Colombians would pay $800,000 per vessel—a bargain to the cash-laden Colombian *narco-traficantes*.[16]*

But the drug traffickers could count on more than the sanctuary of Cuban waters. Havana's airspace was also for sale. According to DEA chief Francis Mullen, "DEA frequently receives information alleging that traffickers fly aircraft over Cuba during their drug smuggling operations. No previous arrangements are necessary. The aircraft enter a commercial flight corridor over Cuba without being challenged by Cuban authorities."[18] This is no minor service being provided by the Castro regime. Cuba sits astride the central Caribbean stretching from Cabo San Antonio in the west to Punta Maisi in the east, a distance of over 700 miles. It is a corridor as wide as the distance from Washington, D.C., to St. Louis, Missouri.†

The precise motivation for Castro's decision to directly involve himself in the drug trade remains unclear. But Cuba, then as now, was hungry for hard currency. That drugs would help undermine an already rotting bourgeois American society merely added to the pleasure of the game. Moreover, not much in the way of original thinking was needed in terms of the services— the Bulgarians had already provided a ready model. Cuba's active support and participation in drug trafficking to the United States

---

*The DA was created in 1974 as a counterbalance to the much larger and senior intelligence service, the *Direccion General de Inteligencia,* which was "colonized" by the Soviet KGB in 1961. The DA is found within the General Department of Foreign Relations of the Cuban Communist Party, and its chief, Pineiro, nicknamed Red Beard, reports directly and exclusively to Fidel Castro.[17]

†But no one and no scheme is perfect. In the same testimony, DEA administrator Francis Mullen details a flight that went awry. In September 1983, a plane crashed in the Florida Keys, killing the pilot. The flight had originated in Jamaica carrying a load of marijuana. One of the fascinating items on board was a "let down chart" for Varadero, Cuba. Such a chart is an approach plan that details instrument flight-rule information for pilots unfamiliar with airports. Moreover, the fuel found at the wreckage was not of a type used in either Jamaica or the U.S. According to Mullen: "There is a strong possibility that the fuel was procured in Cuba." Also, the pilot was seen a few hours before the crash. The time elapsed between his observation and the actual crash was not enough for the pilot to have flown around Cuban airspace. But there was time to cross Cuba, land at Varadero, and make his rendezvous with death in the Florida Keys.[19]

has been publicly documented by American intelligence since the early 1960s.[20] Nevertheless, the initial reports were greeted with skepticism inside and outside of the intelligence community. Castro couldn't be that bad, the skeptics argued. Besides, his revolutionary days seemed to be over. The only time that Fidel mentioned drug trafficking or money deriving from drug business was in an interview with the Cuban newspaper *La Habana*, in which he admitted that Cuba earned $70 million from confiscated drugs seized with the airplanes and boats carrying them.[21] In 1979, after negotiating with the Carter administration Castro agreed to take action against drug traffickers, at the same time continuing Cuba's profitable involvement in drugs and arms running. During the next couple of years, subsequent to Fidel's empty promise, there were many incidents reported by U.S. intelligence and others on continuing Cuban involvement in the drug business.[22]

By the fall of 1981, proof of Cuba's involvement in drug trafficking was undeniable.[23] The America Department under Pineiro Losada had become the coordinating agency linking the Cuban government, South American drug dealers, and Latin American insurgents. The relationship became close and symbiotic. Here is how it works: The DA coordinates with other Cuban officials (principally in the navy and air force) to provide major drug smugglers access to Cuban ports and territorial waters. For this service, the cocaine merchants pay millions of dollars. The DA then uses the smuggling routes of the drug traffickers: a pipeline through which tons of weapons and war supplies are funneled back to Marxist insurgents in Latin America. This involvement finally was acknowledged publicly on September 29, 1982. During an interview with Brian Ross on NBC's Nightly News, then Vice President George Bush, who headed the Federal Drug Task Force in Florida, stated that " . . . there is an involvement of Cuba in . . . the overall drug problem."[24]

On November 15, 1982, a federal grand jury indicted four top Cuban officials—all members of the Cuban Communist Party

Central Committee—including Ravelo-Renedo; his minister-counsel in Bogotá, Gonzalo Bassola-Suarez; Santa Maria-Cuadrado, a vice admiral in the Cuban navy; and Rene Rodriguez-Cruz, a senior official in the DGI. They were not alone. Also indicted was Jaime Guillot-Lara, "a good friend of Cuba," whose drug-running activities were known to the DEA as far back as 1976. Guillot-Lara was in charge of major Cuban-Colombian drugs-for-arms operations in which a Colombian narcotics ring was used to funnel arms as well as funds to Colombian M-19 guerrillas.[25] According to the indictment, the drug running was no penny-ante operation. Guillot-Lara's flotilla of boats carried 2.5 million pounds of marijuana, 25 million methaqualone tablets, and at minimum a thousand pounds of cocaine *per year*.[26]

The evidence submitted to the grand jury came primarily from three key witnesses: Juan (Johnny) Crump, David Lorenzo Pérez, and Mário Estévez Gonzáles. Johnny Crump was a Colombian lawyer and drug dealer who was a close friend of Ambassador Ravelo-Renedo. David Pérez, a Cuban-American also in the business, was in charge of the Florida end of the operation as distributor. Finally, Estévez Gonzáles was a Cuban intelligence agent who was slipped into the United States via the Mariel boatlift. His mission: to assist the drug-smuggling effort and, most critical, arrange for the return of the drug profits back to Cuba. For a while the Cuban-Colombian arrangement worked like a charm. When Guillot-Lara's boats left Colombia they carried the Cuban flag in order to let Havana know that they were friend-lies. The Cuban navy then would escort the drug boats onto a Cuban key, in the area of Paredon Grande, where Cuban intelligence officers oversaw the transfer of the drugs to smaller vessels that in turn would be escorted into American territorial waters, flying different flags of course.

The whole operation was going too well; something had to go wrong. Things began to unravel when the Colombian army seized a cache of weapons from the Cuban-supported M-19 guerrilla movement. The arrested terrorists implicated the Cuban embassy and Departamento de América personnel in recruiting new members and providing training in Cuban-based camps. As a consequence, Colombia broke off diplomatic relations with Havana and expelled the DA's resident Ambassador Ravelo-Renedo and his staff.

What went wrong? Pulling off covert activities is never easy, but the Cubans and the Colombians were becoming careless and they had to depend on those who essentially were amateurs. Here is how it went awry. Acting on instructions from the M-19, Guillot-Lara travelled from Colombia to Panama, where he met with the guerrilla group's chief, Jaime Batemen, and the Cuban first secretary of the embassy in Panama, González Bassols Suárez, formerly stationed in Bogotá as its minister-counsellor. At that meeting Bateman underlined the importance of getting arms through to the M-19 and arranged for Guillot-Lara himself to receive a shipment delivered to Colombia's remote Guajira peninsula.

On October 10, 1981, after a further meeting with the Cubans, Guillot-Lara went to the Colombian port of Dibulla where his boat, the *Zar de Honduras*, arrived loaded with seven tons of arms. The weapons then were transported to a nearby farm that conveniently had an airstrip. In exchange for the guns, the M-19 loaded 8,000 pounds of marijuana onto the vessel to be transported to the United States via Cuba. Ten days later, the M-19 insurgents moved the cached arms, consisting of FAL rifles and 90,000 rounds of ammunition, onto a hijacked C-47 that the guerrillas had stolen in Medellin. The cargo was flown south to Caquetá province. It didn't make it. The rickety pre-war plane was forced to ditch in the Orteguaza River, where thirty-six hours later authorities found it still intact, floating down the river. The weapons in the meantime had been off-loaded into the hands of the local M-19.

One little setback, however, was followed by a bigger one. On November 14, the Colombian navy sank the good ship *El Karina*—also belonging to Guillot-Lara—while it was attempting to make an arms delivery on the Colombian Pacific coast. Meanwhile, Colombian officials impounded his *Zar de Honduras* in the Caribbean port of Barranquilla. He had had enough; Guillot-Lara soon fled to Cuba and then to Mexico. A week later, Guillot-Lara met a Bolivian military officer in Mexico City. His Cuban contact had told him the Bolivian had 500 pounds of cocaine for sale. Guillot-Lara's instructions were to fly to La Paz to confirm the information. But before he could comply, despite warnings from Cuban and Nicaraguan intelligence officers, the Colombian was arrested by Mexican police and charged with possession of false documents.

Through their many friends in the Mexican government the Cuban embassy knew almost immediately that Guillot-Lara had been arrested. Its officers made extraordinary efforts to get him released, to no avail. Meanwhile, the Colombian had told the Mexicans more than they probably wanted to know, information that was reported promptly to U.S. intelligence by Washington's friends in Mexico City. The United States suddenly knew far more about Cuba's role in narcotics trafficking than it ever had suspected—and the information from Mexico would constitute a large portion of the evidence used in the Miami indictments. It was not a total loss to the Cubans, however. The Mexican authorities eventually released Guillot-Lara despite American protests, after which he promptly fled to Spain; he currently resides in Cuba.

Of course the publicity over Guillot-Lara prompted heated denials from Havana. Precisely as in the Bulgarian alibi, Cuban officials pointed to Havana's arrest and conviction of numerous petty drug smugglers. In DEA chief Mullen's words:

The Cubans apparently deal only with those drug smugglers they trust or those who can provide some benefit or service to Cuba such as smuggling weapons, illustrated in the Guillot investigation. Cuba continues to seize vessels and aircraft carrying drug cargoes into its territory that do not have necessary official contacts in Cuba.[27]

All this and more was made public by special congressional hearings in Miami, Florida, in April 1983 (better known as the Paula Hawkins hearings).[28]* Castro continues to deny any Cuban involvement whenever he is asked about Cuba's drug trafficking by the American press.

According to a 1986 U.S. government confidential report, the Guillot-Lara case was "only the tip of the iceberg of Cuba's ultrasecret involvement in the drug trade." The report went on to say that since 1982 the U.S. government had recorded at least fifty cases of direct Cuban involvement in trafficking in drugs to the States. The report continued, "Castro's officials not only provided equipment and chemicals to refine the cocaine, but the operation was set up on an armed military base, offering maximum security."[29] Additional information about Cuba's arrangements with and profits from the drug business was provided by David Lorenzo Pérez and Mário Estévez Gonzáles, co-defendants in the Guillot-Lara case. On February 9, 1983, Pérez testified before the Miami federal court that Cuba's profits from the sale of $10 methaqualone tablets in the U.S. was $800,000, in addition to the 30 percent profit from the 23,000 pounds of marijuana sold by him in the U.S. Mário Estévez Gonzáles, a former Cuban agent, testified that his major task in the U.S. was to distribute cocaine, marijuana, and methaqualone tablets in New York, northern New Jersey, and Florida, and that during a fifteen-month period he delivered the two to three million dollar profit of his operation to his Cuban bosses.[30]

On April 30, 1983, former U.S. Ambassador to Colombia Tom Boyatt, in testimony before Joint Senate Committee hearings said " . . . the Guillot-Lara case proves that the drug trafficking structure, the same people, the same plans, the same means of transportation, were used to carry marijuana northward to hurt the U.S. and to bring guns south to Colombia to supply those guns

*Paula Hawkins, the former senator (R) from Florida and chairman of the Senate Drug Enforcement Caucus, was a leading force in the early 1980s in the investigations about Cuba's role in trafficking in drugs to the U.S.

to the M-19 for the purpose of overthrowing the freely elected government of Colombia, and that it is a matter of evidence and record." To the question of whether he had any doubts about Fidel's knowledge and approval of these activities, his answer was "NO."[31] At the same hearings, James H. Michel revealed that the State Department had a report that the Cuban Communist Party Presidium, and specifically Fidel Castro, decided in early 1979 to deal with drug traffickers using Cuba as a bridge and support for the network to the United States. Their reasoning, according to Michel, was that these activities would aid Cuba's economy as well as contribute to the deterioration of American society.

In the U.S. government confidential report, a few more lesser-known cases were listed. Among them was a February 1984 DEA report on an unnamed drug trafficker and money launderer who flew from Havana to Panama. There he was met by one Richard Bilotnick, a known drug and arms dealer with close ties to Cuban officials, including the Cuban ambassador to Panama. At the time, Mr. Bilotnick was the manager of INAIR, a Panamian air company that was charted to the Cuban Corporation for Import and Export (CIMEX). INAIR was shut down later that summer after one of its planes was seized in the U.S., carrying 1,070 kilograms of cocaine from Panama. "Havana Haven," read a headline in the *Wall Street Journal*, April 30, 1984:

While maintaining an outwardly tough posture toward drug smugglers, the Cuban government has secretly singled out a few for special favors . . . these selected traffickers have been permitted the use of Cuban waters as a haven from the U.S. Coast Guard while transshipping narcotics to the U.S. from Colombia . . . in return Cuba gets scarce hard currency—as much as $500,000 per shipment . . . it uses some of this money to buy arms that are secretly ferried by the drug smugglers to gurerrillas in Latin America.[32]

The following items documenting Cuban involvement in international drug trafficking are listed chronologically:

May 1984. According to a DEA source, the Colombian government pressure on drug trafficking forced *narco-traficante* Carlos Lehder to move his entire operation to Cuba. In the summer of 1982, Lehder was working with fugitive Robert Vesco in the Bahamas before the Colombian was forced to take refuge in Cuba in December 1982. Lehder reportedly planned to transport coca base from Panama to Cuba on Panamanian-registered ships. Cuban military personnel off-loaded and transported the unrefined coca to a Cuban military base near Havana. The same source reports that the Cubans provided the equipment and chemicals to process the coca into cocaine. The refined drug then would be shipped from Cuba's north coast to Andros Island in the Bahamas, where it would be picked up by smugglers for transport to the United States.[33]

June 1984. The U.S. Coast Guard discovers several charts on the U.S.-registered vessel *Vera*, seized during an attempt to transport marijuana to the United States. On one chart, generalized lines led from the Colombian coast to the port of Cárdenas, Cuba, which was circled. On another chart, the port of Manzanillo, Cuba also was circled.[34]

March 1985. A Joint State Department and Department of Defense report on Soviet-Cuban influence in Central America and the Caribbean warned that one of the outcomes of this cooperation is an "emerging alliance between drug smugglers in support of terrorists and guerrillas."[35]

April 20, 1985. The *New York Times* reported that James A. Herring, Jr., in testimony before a U.S. Subcommittee on Narcotics said that he "worked with Cuban government officials and with the American fugitive Robert Vesco to help the Nicaraguan government build a cocaine processing laboratory near Managua. Our purpose was to earn foreign exchange for Nicaragua's troubled economy."[36]

July 11, 1985. The *Miami Herald* reported that Jose Antonio Fernandez, an admitted drug trafficker who smuggled more than $200 million worth of marijuana to the United States, told U.S.

officials of a secret meeting with special Cuban agents who worked closely with Castro in arranging "safe passage of marijuana ships through Cuban waters."[37]

March 23, 1988. Major Florentino Azpillaga Lombard, former Cuban chief intelligence officer in Czechoslovakia who defected in Vienna in June 1987, told a *Washington Times* reporter that Cuba's Cayo Largo, a small resort island south of the mainland, is being used for drug-trafficking purposes. Azpillaga was told by the Cuban chief of the DGI that a "powerful drug syndicate" has been using Cuba for transhipment of illegal drugs to the U.S. at least since 1978. A fleet of thirteen ships and twenty-one aircraft were operating in Cuban territory under the protection of the Cuban "Special Troops," an elite unit within the Ministry of the Interior and under the direct command of Fidel Castro himself.[38]

July 28, 1988. The *Washington Post* quoted U.S. Attorney Dexter Lehtinen as saying: "The evidence in the trial demonstrated that Cuban territory was used with the knowledge, approval and cooperation of the Cuban government." Fifty to sixty videotapes were presented to the Miami federal court detailing explicitly the links between Cuban government officials and a massive smuggling ring. Assistant U.S. Attorney Thomas Mulvihill asserted in court that the tapes showed drug smugglers explaining how the Cuban coast guard used radar to warn them about the whereabouts of U.S. drug law-enforcement vessels, and how they advised them about safe passages to cross the channel between Cuba and Miami. Both father and son Reinaldo and Rueben Ruiz were the leaders of this drug ring. In addition to five other criminals, both were convicted for smuggling cocaine worth at least $10 million to the U.S. via Cuba. Rueben Ruiz spoke out specifically implicating Raul Castro in this drug-trafficking operation.[39]

As in the case of Bulgaria, the evidence for Cuban involvement in narco-terrorism, in which profits generated from drug sales in the U.S. are used to finance revolutionary activity in Latin America, is abundant. And apparently these activities have not lessened one bit. Indeed, very little had changed on that score until June 1989, when in a series of articles, editorials, and speeches the Castro brothers astonished the world by announcing the arrest of Cuba's top military combat officer, General Arnaldo Ochoa Sanchez. Even more astonishing was the charge that Ochoa not only was guilty of corruption but of narcotics trafficking as well. As State Department spokesperson Margaret Tutwiler observed, it was "the first time the Cuban government has admitted involvement in drug smuggling operations."[40] The real reasons for such an admission are known only to Castro. From the limited information available from Cuban-censored publications and videotapes from the trial, it seems that Fidel feared that his security forces and his Ministry of Interior (MININT) in charge of the drug smuggling operations were penetrated by the U.S., and that undeniable evidence about his and his brother Raul's personal involvement in the drug business was about to surface. It was all too close for comfort.

In addition, Castro needed a reason to get rid of General Ochoa. General Arnaldo Ochoa Sanchez, who was "hero of the republic," member of the Cuban Communist Party Central Committee, Raul's close friend, and who fought with Fidel in the revolution and commanded Cuban "internationalist" forces in Ethiopia, Nicaragua, and Angola, was arrested on June 12, 1989. He was very popular in Cuba at the time of his arrest, especially among the veterans who returned from Angola and had to face the harsh reality of empty promises of the good life that should have been theirs after fulfilling their military duties. Returning visitors from Cuba reported that hundreds of veterans lined up daily outside Ochoa's home in Havana waiting to bring their grievances before him, and according to these sources Ochoa not only was sympathetic to their complaints but also used his connections in order to provide assistance. In addition, as was revealed in Fidel's speech to the State Council on July 9, before Ochoa's execution, Ochoa opposed Fidel's anti-*perestroyka* pose and other military decisions.[41] It should be noted that Ochoa was schooled and trained in the Soviet Union and supported *perestroyka* openly. Judging from his popularity and considering the effects of Gorbachev's visit to Cuba only six weeks earlier, Ochoa quickly was becoming a serious threat to Castro.*

Fidel's response was to suddenly "spring clean" Havana. Consequently, on June 12, 1989, Ochoa was arrested and charged (according to *Granma*, the Cuban Communist Party newspaper) with "serious acts of corruption and dishonest management of economic resources." The editorial stated, "The true revolution cannot leave unpunished those who violate its principles."[42] Only later, on June 19, were drug-trafficking charges added. In yet another editorial *Granma*, informed the world that "much worse and without precedent in the history of the Revolution is that Ochoa and some MININT officials in connection with him made contact with international drug dealers. They made agreements, attempted [sic], and possibly cooperated, with some drug trafficking operations close to our country."[43] As it turned out, in the Stalinist-style trial that sentenced Ochoa to death, many levels of the Cuban government also were involved in this conspiracy. Ochoa was executed at dawn on July 13, 1989, together with three other co-defendants, also formerly close aides to Castro. Ten more received heavy prison sentences ranging from ten to thirty years.[44]

Apparently Fidel feared for the weakening of his position, as well as for his heir, brother Raul. His admission after thirty years of denial that Cubans indeed were involved in the drug business was for domestic political purposes. Immediately following Ochoa's execution Castro distanced himself from the issue. In his traditional speech to mark the anniversary of the revolution on July 26, 1989, he spoke about the "complete disintegration"

*Due to strict censorship in Cuba, the analysis by foreign scholars and observers of what goes on there usually is based on interpretations and general understanding of political developments in Cuba, as well as reports from defectors from and visitors to Cuba. The analysis of Ochoa's case was no different.

of the Soviet Union, about an upcoming American invasion of Cuba, but never once mentioned Ochoa or the trial.[45]

All available evidence suggests that while numerous agencies of the Cuban government, including the intelligence agencies, the interior ministry, the Cuban navy and coast guard, and the air force, all have contributed to drug trafficking to the United States, the Cuban army seems to be a major exception. How General Ochoa could have been involved in narco-terrorism when he spent most of the last ten years of his life outside Cuba—and the Western Hemisphere—is difficult to explain.[46] Nor have Cuban authorities attempted to do so. Clearly Ochoa had run afoul of both Raul and Fidel for opposing the prolongation of their venture in Angola, and if the history of the regime is any guide, it would seem that the higher the figure to be purged the more outlandish and serious the charges.

Castro's belated admission fell on a few willing ears in the U.S. Tad Szulc, on the op-ed page of the *New York Times* stated, "The Bush administration would be well advised to at once take Mr. Castro at his word instead of responding with worn out legalism and ideological foot-dragging."[47] And Senate Foreign Relations Committee Chairman Claiborne Pell immediately commented that the arrests in Cuba "could open the way to naturally beneficial cooperation between the U.S. and Cuba in narcotics trafficking that is taking place in the sea and air space that we share."[48] Such talk must please Fidel, for there is, to be sure, more to this dark affair than is presently known. But it is simply preposterous that the Castro regime can off-load decades of promoting narco-terrorism on the back of one cashiered army officer.

Nor did Fidel ever seriously consider giving up the profitable drug business, especially now that he faced Soviet demands to improve Cuba's dwindling economy. Castro's public stance was one of disgust and dismay with those involved in drug activities, yet even as the Ochoa case was unfolding, business went on as usual. On June 28, 1989, the *Washington Post* reported that

"Drug smuggling flights over Cuba have continued at a steady pace." The article quoted U.S. Customs Chief of Enforcement Patrick O'Brien as saying "the pattern is continuing." He also identified the drug flights over Cuba as "the major threat" to U.S. drug interdiction efforts in South Florida.[49] The Associated Press later reported that "Sixteen hundred pounds of cocaine were recovered by federal agents, from a speedboat observed earlier in Cuban waters catching bales dropped from a suspected drug running plane."[50]

Meanwhile, the war being waged with the United States continues, according to Castro. What is presented here is only a sampling of massive evidence that links Cuba with the international drug trade and international terrorist organizations. The evidence thus is compelling that drugs, more than "simply" a plague spawned by forces festering in modern "post-industrial society seeking instant gratifications," have been shaped into a powerful strategic-weapons system—one that wreaks its "direct damage" in lethal and disabling addiction, and its "collateral damage" in the corruption and criminal activity that flourishes around the drug trade, as well as in the overall undermining of the target society.[51]

In a strange, significant respect and contrary to general opinion, it seems that the strategic link between Moscow and Havana has been strengthened by Gorbachev's "new thinking" in foreign policy that was codified at the 27th Soviet Communist Party's Congress in February 1986.[52] In keeping with the priority domestic objective of restructuring and bolstering the Soviet economy, the "new thinking" essentially calls for sustaining the "march of socialism" at a lower cost—of avoiding the creation of client regimes (particularly in the Third World) that would impose crippling burdens on Soviet treasury and resources. Cuba, which has been such a burden over the years, forever sensitive to a further dwindling of Soviet assistance to Havana, can well sympathize with this imperative. The joint agenda of Soviet-Cuban strategy in the Western Hemisphere thus reads: preservation and expansion of Marxist-Leninist regimes with minimum economic support and the further estrangement of the United States from Latin America, in large part by moving the Organization of American States (minus the United States) toward the ranks of the global "nonaligned movement."

The flow of narcotics, arms, and terrorism fits ideally into a strategy that has the added advantage, especially from Moscow's viewpoint, of being economically self-sustaining. This strategy forms the background for the spectacle unfolding in Panama. Jose Blandon Castillo, former intelligence aide to General Noriega, has described how Castro acted as mediator among Noriega, the Medellin cartel, and the M-19 movement to keep the flow of drugs and money-laundering activities in place and how he, Blandon, was sent by Noriega to Havana to arrange for Castro's intervention in the latter's behalf. He found Castro eager to cooperate: "Fidel feared that Noriega would be replaced in Panama. . . . His [Castro's] interests were political, they were economic and they were interests linked to the war which was being waged with the United States. . . . Fidel Castro made Panama a window of opportunity for business, in order to import Western technology and export some of his goods from Cuba."[53] As later events in Panama evolved it became clear that Castro had even bigger plans for Panama. The huge quantity of arms and ammunitions discovered by the Americans during the invasion of Panama and the overthrow of Noriega in December 1989, bore Cuban markings. It appears that Fidel intended to help Noriega in his efforts to avoid honoring the Panama Canal treaty stipulations.

Blandon's testimony not only provided evidence that enabled United States prosecutors in Miami to indict Noriega for his involvement in drug-trafficking activities to the U.S., but also paints a very clear picture of how drugs can be used to corrupt and subvert a government. His descriptions lead to an understanding of how narco-terrorism contributes to the undermining of democracy by a mere handful of thugs. He also gave evidence that describes Cuba's role in the drug flow to the United States. Blandon testified that Castro had implemented an overall system for the management of drug and arms traffic in Central America and the Andean countries, and the United States. The effect was to deepen Cuban inroads in these areas. According to Blandon, "Fidel Castro's theory went back to this. . . . If you want to have an influence on Colombia's political world, you have to have an influence on the drug-trafficking world, too." He went on to describe Castro's rationalization of the central thrust of the effort: "The war in Central America waged by the United States made it easier, or at least gave him the moral justification, to do anything against the United States, anything that was necessary."[54]

Blandon described the joint ventures of General Noriega, Fidel Castro, the Colombian insurgent movement M-19, and the Medellin cartel in overseeing and protecting drug shipments from Colombia to the United States via Cuba, the laundering of the money in Panama, and the provision of arms to Marxist-Leninist rebels in Central America. Blandon revealed that in 1984 such operations were carried out simultaneously in Panama, Nicaragua, and Colombia, and that Nicaraguan leaders were paid in cash for their part in the transactions. He testified:

Fernando Ravelo-Renedo, the Cuban Ambassador to Colombia, was the contact person between the guerrilla movement, the M-19, and the drug movement. . . . In the case of Colombia, there is a link between drug-trafficking and the guerrilla movement, and part of their coordination is done by the Latin American Department of the Communist Party of Cuba, led by Manuel Pineiro, who is also the head of all subversive movements in Latin America. . . . Ravelo traveled to Panama and dealt with Noriega as an officer who was in charge of those operations. . . . The Republic of Panama was converted into a huge empire in order to commit certain crimes, and it was part of a general project in the hands of Colombia's drug-traffickers. This project aimed to penetrate other countries like Nicaragua and other armed forces, such as in Honduras. . . . Only two or three months ago, there was a large shipment which was hidden in lumber exported from Honduras to the United States [and seized in Miami]. This international network has been able to penetrate the Central American armed forces and, because of this, security problems . . . affecting the democracies in Latin America, especially in Central America, are jeopardized.[55]

Meddling in the affairs of autonomous governments and undermining legitimate institutions were not the only specialties of the Cuban government. The opportunity to spread their gospel presented itself with the rise of the Sandinista regime in Nicaragua.

———————— ▦▦▦▦▦ ————————

Nicaragua and the Cuban Connection

Cuba lost little time after the consolidation of the Sandinista regime in Nicaragua in harnessing its Nicaraguan allies to the narcotics operations. No one familiar with the Sandinista regime that seized power in Nicaragua on July 19, 1979* will be surprised at its involvement in narco-terrorism as well. In every aspect, it faithfully echoed the anti-American themes that its Havana sponsors have propounded over the years.

Like the Cuban communists, the Nicaraguan Sandinistas are admitted Marxist-Leninists and supporters of the Kremlin.† For their loyalty they have been supplied with at least $3 billion in arms and military construction—for a population less than three million—and with economic aid that runs about $500 million a year.[56] In return for the money the Nicaraguan government faithfully supported Soviet foreign policy in every form available. It

---

*In national elections held in Nicaragua on February 25, 1990, the Sandinista regime lost to the opposition coalition led by Violetta Barrios de Chamorro. Many observers compared this turnover to the changes in Eastern Europe, where communism seems to be replaced by more democratic regimes.
†In early 1990, the former Nicaraguan president Daniel Ortega made many public statements in favor of Gorbachev's *perestroyka,* and objecting to "socialism to death" that Castro was still supporting.

also helped promote insurgencies in the rest of Central America, especially in El Salvador. Managua and Havana were the only governments in Latin America that publicly supported the odious General Manuel Antonio Noriega of Panama until he was deposed. As for Sandinista complicity in drug trafficking the evidence has begun to mount, owing to the defection of key Nicaraguan officials and alert, clandestine intelligence courtesy of the CIA.

The CIA has provided that for which it is best known: revealing and compromising photographs. These show that in April 1984, a planeload of cocaine—750 kilos—flown from Colombia to an airfield northwest of Managua was met by a senior official of the interior ministry, Frederico Vaughn. Vaughn, who was close to top Sandinista *comandante* Tomas Borge Martinez, had been called to the airport because the pilot Adler Barriman (better known as Barry Seal), who was working for American intelligence, had (purposely) damaged his plane on landing. That required Vaughn's help to transfer the drugs to another plane, providing splendid black and whites for the edification of the world's attentive public. Vaughn, incidentally, was paid $1.5 million for his government's help in transhipping narcotics to the United States, a sum that most likely went into the depleted coffers of Nicaragua's hard-currency strongbox.[57]

That was not the end of pilot Seal and his Nicaraguan connection. Let the report of the president's bipartisan commission on organized crime chaired by Judge Irving R. Kaufman, a distinguished U.S. federal judge, tell the story:

In July 1984 Seal made another trip to Nicaragua from the United States to bring supplies for a new cocaine processing center under construction there. In a subsequent taped conversation with Seal, Frederico Vaughn stated that the processing center was ready for use. Eleven persons including Vaughn were indicted by a federal grand jury on charges stemming from this trafficking arrangement.[58]*

*Vaughn remains a fugitive from American justice. Pilot Barry Seal was killed

That is hardly the end of the Sandinistas' *known* involvement in the drug trade. In April 1985, Frederico Vaughn and his boss, Interior Minister Tomas Borge, were implicated by James Herring in a drug-smuggling ring to the U.S. Mr. Herring, a Tallahassee businessman, turned government agent while working for Robert Vesco. His testimony regarding the Cuban-Nicaraguan partnership in the drug business directly helped to arrest and convict Jitze Kooistra, a drug kingpin from Holland who worked with Vesco in Managua and Havana, smuggling cocaine to the U.S. and Europe. Kooistra was sentenced to ten years, which he now serves in a Florida federal penitentiary. Herring's testimony led to eight more convictions, which makes his information even more credible.[59] In testimony before the Senate Labor and Human Resources Subcommittee he provided the following:

1. In 1983 the Sandinista regime "made a deal" with Vesco to process cocaine and ship it to the U.S.
2. Tomas Borge and Frederico Vaughn were in charge of this business.
3. Official Nicaraguan planes and diplomatic couriers smuggled cocaine worth millions of dollars to processing laboratories in Managua from Colombia and Bolivia.
4. The Managua regime supplied airfields and armed troops, secured the processing laboratories, and provided transportation of the refined cocaine to the U.S. and Europe. Herring himself worked in one of these laboratories in Managua. In 1983, while walking one day with Vaughn in the lobby of the Intercontinental Hotel in Managua, he was introduced to Tomas Borge, who thanked him for his help. The U.S. Department of Justice, as well as the U.S. Customs service, considered Herring "a most reliable eyewitness."[60]

---

in early March 1986, outside of New Orleans. His work as an undercover DEA agent made him a marked man in the underworld of Soviet-bloc "wet affairs."

Thanks to another defector, Nicaraguan diplomat Antonio Farach, we know that the Sandinista then defense minister Humberto Ortega (brother of former president Daniel Ortega) met
with his Cuban counterpart, Raul Castro, to discuss "a new business venture" which called for Nicaragua to help an assortment
of international *narco-traficantes*, each of whom had contacts
with Cuba. According to Farach, one purpose of the younger
Castro's visit had been to establish a narcotics infrastructure "for
the Nicaraguan revolution"—with Havana's help, of course.
When Farach questioned this, he was told by his superiors two
moral and political justifications for drug trafficking in Managua:

In the first place, drugs did not remain in Nicaragua; the drugs were
destined for the United States. Our youth would not be harmed, but
rather the youth of our enemies. Therefore, the drugs were used as
a political weapon against the United States, the drug trafficking
produced a very good economic benefit which we needed for our
revolution. We wanted to provide food to our people with the suffering
and death of the youth of the United States.[61]

And finally, Alvaro Baldizon, another defector who worked for
Borge's interior ministry, testified that his boss was fully involved
in smuggling Colombian cocaine into the United States via Nicaragua.[62]

The Sandinistas continued to use the drugs and arms business
not only to obtain badly needed foreign exchange, but also to cut
inroads into neighboring Central American countries, principally
by providing cocaine at discount rates as payment for support
and services rendered to Managua. Neighboring Costa Rica has
been a major proving ground for this method. When drug trafficking began on a large scale from Nicaragua, the rural police
in Costa Rica initially were bribed with payments in U.S. dollars.
Very quickly, drugs were substituted for dollar payments at a
liberal rate, with the incentive that recipients could earn much
larger sums by selling the narcotics. Thus, in December 1986,

one gram of 75 to 80 percent pure cocaine was sold in the streets of San José for six dollars—one tenth of what it cost even in Bogotá (never mind New York). What happened was that given the easy availability of the drugs, the payees themselves became users. Corruption thus was compounded by addiction, setting a pattern of destabilization evident not only in Costa Rica but in other regional nations as well.[63]

Baldizon, in testimony before the Senate Subcommittee on Security and Terrorism, reported on the explanation given to him by Tomas Borge's assistant that Nicaragua was involved in the cocaine trade because it earned dollars "needed to finance espionage activities for the Fifth Directorate and some operational expenses of the Interior Ministry's Superior Directorate." Baldizon continued:

I was also informed that the activity involved giving protection, lodging, refueling and access to the landing strip in Montelimar to Colombian traffickers traveling to the United States. They added that this protection was extremely profitable for the Government of Nicaragua. The explanation concluded with a statement that the connection with the (Colombian) Mafia had been established by Captain Paul Atta, head of H-and-M (Heroes and Martyrs) investments company, and that this information was known to some of Captain Atta's officials. They pointed out to me that some Aero Commander and Navajo aircraft, seized from people related to Somoza's government, had been given to the (Colombian) Mafia.[64]

Nicaragua's Heroes and Martyrs had a counterpart in Cuba. According to Baldizon, they are investment holding agencies created to invest in other countries on behalf of their governments "in a way that is covert—in other words, that would not show these governments as the investors. . . . This was not limited to drug trafficking but also investments in hotels, real estate and restaurants, and also they are making a lot of money with the pirating of videotapes."[65] In short, one more broke "socialist" state was looking desperately for a capitalist dollar.

Baldizon then described a meeting attended by a Cuban adviser from the Fifth Ministerial region in August 1984:

Cocaine traffic was discussed over lunch, touching on different aspects: They expressed the Sandinista view that Yankee imperialism was armed to the teeth, believing that the Soviet Union was going to attack the U.S. as part of a nuclear war. But the Yankees did not realize that Yankee imperialism was going to perish, eaten from within by covert ideological subversion, the drug traffic and the economic competition with Japan and the European Economic Community.

In terms of the drug traffic, Borge's assistant explained that cocaine: "(1) destroys and corrupts American youth so as to weaken and harm future generations; (2) it provides a mechanism whereby American youth finances liberation movements; and (3) the network used for cocaine distribution is used for the traffic of weapons bought on the black market."[66]

For Fidel, as for the Sandinistas, anti-Americanism is the sugarcoating for Marxism-Leninism. The Sandinistas had lost their popular support already, and if recent events in Eastern bloc countries, including the Soviet Union are any indication of future change for Marxist-Leninist regimes in Latin America, it may be reasonable to assume that we are coming to the close of Cuban narco-terrorism—not because Fidel Castro has lost interest in pursuing the issue, but because he may be losing his importance as a key player in Latin America. His domestic standing seems to be weakening and the Ochoa case is indicative of problems he faces with the military. His conservative Marxist-Leninist views and objection to *perestroyka* isolate him from the rest of the Soviet bloc. It therefore was probable that Cuba would sustain cuts in Soviet economic subsidies and reductions in arms supplies. But apparently Cuba is more important in the eyes of the Soviets than many American analysts seem to realize; in April 1990, when it was expected that the Soviet Union would finally cut the umbilical cord, a new one-year trade pact valued at $14.7

billion was signed between the Soviet Union and Cuba, an 8.7 percent hike from previous trade agreements.[67] Although it seemed that Castro had little to offer ideologically and economically, apparently he does have something to offer. The narco-terrorists in Latin America have more than enough funds to purchase arms anywhere in the world, but this should in no way undermine or diminish Castro's architectural skills in designing, building, and maintaining the infrastructure of narco-terrorism in Latin America.

As of July 1991 Cuba's economic condition has worsened, although the Soviet Union has not cut off financial aid. Cuba is trying to fill the gap in its economy by expanding drug trafficking. Reports on such activity by air and by sea have increased to the extent that even the Soviet newspaper *Moscow News* has reported it. In spite of *perestroyka,* Cuba's role as the foothold in the backyard of the United States is still strategically important to the Soviets. Despite promises at the negotiating table of the INF treaty, the SS-20 Soviet ballistic missiles remain on Cuban soil.[68]

3

The Lebanese Inferno:
Drugs and Terror

———————— ▪▪▪▪▪ ————————

Long before the South American republic of Colombia became synonymous with cocaine and corruption there was Lebanon.* This small Middle Eastern country was carved out of greater Syria by the French in 1920. They dubbed it the Greater Lebanon in order to protect the Levant's largest Christian enclave. It is also narco-terrorism's link to Asia and Europe and by extension, to North and South America.[1]

In fact, modern narco-terrorism began in Lebanon. It started in a small way, but eventually evolved and expanded until it came to embrace all the fighting factions in Lebanon, the pocket armies of the night that puzzle, horrify, and terrorize Lebanon and the civilized world.† Synonymous with endemic, irrational, and apparently endless violence, the orgy of destruction in Lebanon has reduced the region's only democracy (aside from Israel) and its dynamic economy to rubble and dust. A conservative estimate puts the death toll at well over 150,000. Beirut, once a Riviera-style capital of 1.3 million people, the financial and communications center of the Middle East, is ruined. It is a post-nuclear

---

*Lebanon occupies 4,000 square miles on the eastern shore of the Mediterranean, between Syria and Israel.

†It has been estimated that Lebanon has some 80,000 men under arms, not counting the regular army and the 43,000 occupying Syrians. And this in a country with a population of 2,800,000 people, less than that of the city of Philadelphia. One question never asked is this: with a ruined economy, who pays for all those gunmen, who, after all, represent a large percentage of the labor force?[2]

wreck where less than 200,000 people live in fear and perpetual anger, on borrowed time.

As of early 1990, Lebanon has a new Syrian-supported government and a new President, Elias Hrawi. After Amin Gemayel finished his term of office in September 1988, Lebanon had no head of state or government until November 5, 1989, when René Moawad was elected President. Alas, his reign was short, for on November 22, 1989, a roadside bomb planted apparently by The Party of God (Hisballah)* ended his life.[3] President Hrawi was elected to replace Moawad on November 24, 1989.[4] In fact, Lebanon has another, Christian government, headed by General Michel Aoun. But in spite of their power and army neither government exercises control and authority over much of anything. The Syrians do, however. In order to emphasize their presence and their support of Hrawi, the Syrians moved at least 10,000 soldiers with armored vehicles to reinforce the 33,000 Syrian troops already in Lebanon since 1976.[5] As a consequence, Lebanon flourishes not only as a producer, but also as a refiner and distributor of hashish, heroin, and cocaine.[6] Much of the fighting that occurs in Lebanon concerns who gets what in the narcotics business. As the country descends further into chaos, the flow of narcotics continues. So does the violence.

Supplementing the two "official" governments of Lebanon are a variety of ethnic, communal, and religious factions, each with its own militia fighting to hold on to their various bits of turf in a country no larger than Massachusetts. The sheer complexity of the groupings and their gunmen baffle most outsiders. A recent capsule description by the London *Economist* has the virtue of being both brief and for the most part accurate, if incomplete:

[The militias] include the Lebanese Forces (which are Christian), Amal and Hisballah among the Shia Muslims, and a rather efficient

*The Party of God (better known as Hisballah), a pro-Khomeini organization of Shiite fundamentalists comprising three separate factions, operates from South Lebanon, Beirut, and Baalbek.

little Druze force. In all, these boast some 80,000 armed fighters, according to Western intelligence sources. The occupying armies are the Syrians in the east and north, and the Israelis (with a client local militia, called the South Lebanon army) in their "security zone" in a strip of the south. This armed chaos is an ideal environment for terrorists and hostage dwellers.[7]*

Lebanese terrorists who hold hostages, particularly U.S. citizens, have become the country's signature, and to most Americans even more familiar than the senseless slaughter carried out by Lebanese against Lebanese, who are aided in their grisly task by outside forces. The gruesome murder of U.S. Marine Lieutenant Colonel William Higgins in 1989† in a Beirut basement by Iranian-supported Hisballah gunmen provided the Bush administration with its first, television-driven crisis. That crisis simply underscored what most Americans already feared: that Lebanon is a lawless society run by terrorism unique in the world. This is the picture of Lebanon as a Hobbesian state of nature, where each man's hand is raised against the other in perpetuity, that comes to mind. According to Hobbes:

To this war of every man, against every man, this also is a consequent; that nothing can be unjust. The notions of right and wrong, justice and injustice have there no place. Where there is no common power, there is no law; where no law, no injustice. Force, and fraud, are in war the two cardinal virtues. It is consequent also to the same condition, that there be no property, no dominion, no *mine* and *thine*

---

*Of course, this brief account does not include other armed groups including the remaining units from the Palestine Liberation Organization (PLO), many of whose fighters were expelled after Israel's 1982 Operation Peace in Galilee— shattered remnants of the once powerful Sunni Muslim militia. Nor does it make clear that the Christian community, divided among Maronites, Greek Orthodox, and Roman Catholics, is not one as a military force. Various clans within the Maronite community, for example, have been at war with each other in a desperate bid for supremacy.

†Investigations by U.S. authorities could not determine whether Higgins was murdered soon after his kidnapping in 1988, or in 1989, when the Hisballah released the picture of his body hanging from a rope.

distinct; but only that to be every man's, that he can get; and for so long, as he can keep it. And thus much for the ill condition, which man by mere nature is actually placed in; though with a possibility to come out of it, consisting partly in the passions, partly in his reason.[8]

But Hobbes was wrong about one thing in his observation that in a lawless state there is no distinction between property, dominion, justice, and injustice. There is one form of cooperation in the general state of every man to himself that continues to flourish in Lebanon with the total abandon of law and order: the relationship between drug traffickers and terrorists.

Indeed, the flood of drugs that goes to Western Europe, the United States, and now increasingly to Israel,* is the very fuel that stokes the Lebanese inferno. But more than Lebanese lives are involved. Narcotics provide the funds for terrorist groups operating in Lebanon, including the PLO, which help them continue their war against both Israel and the West. This aspect of life in Lebanon rarely is touched on by observers. Even though the various fighting factions have been described in clinical detail, its psychology seldom is discussed.† But this omission not only leaves out a critical part of contemporary narco-terrorism, it also greatly distorts and downplays the danger that present-day Lebanon presents to the West. Any counter-terrorist and antidrug policy that does not take this central reality into account has no chance of being successful. How did Lebanon become a drug haven in the first place? Who benefits and who assists the trade—and how does it work today?

*In an off-the-record interview with a high-ranking Israeli police officer during the summer of 1989, the author was told of this growing activity by most terrorist groups in Lebanon, especially PLO members and supporters, and by the Syrian military.
†Barbara Newman in her book *The Covenant* cursorily mentions the problem of the drug traffic in Lebanon, but asserts that the Gemayels, and Bashir in particular, were not involved in the trade. Newman's bias in this case may be explained by the fact that she and the younger Gemayel were lovers.[9]

━━━━━━━━━━━━ ▖▖▖▖▖ ━━━━━━━━━━━━

In the Beginning and What Happened Next

The Lebanese are no strangers to the drug trade. Centuries before there was a Lebanon, a particularly potent cannabis plant known locally as "hashish" was grown by dirt-poor peasants living in Lebanon's fertile Bekaa valley. By present-day standards, production in the past was small and markets limited. Mostly they were confined to the Arab Near East, primarily Egypt, and its capital, Cairo. Caravans of drug dealers would leave the Bekaa for Egypt, crossing through Palestine. Later, the camels were replaced by boats crossing the Mediterranean Sea. The drug merchants seldom were arrested until the late 1960s, when the Israelis stepped up the patrol of their borders because of the PLO terrorist threat. Some of the hashish that was carried to Cairo remained there for local consumption. The rest continued to other hashish-hungry markets in North Africa and Western Europe. Lebanon also was a crossroads and a transit point for Asian opium and heroin on its way to European markets. But the quantity was small, and no large numbers of Lebanese were involved in the trade.

This all changed after the Second World War when the French withdrew and left Lebanon technically independent. The part of the Levant that became Lebanon simply was detached from greater Syria (a reality that contemporary Syrian leaders do not yet recognize or accept) in order to provide greater security for France's protégés, the local Christian community. Its most important members are the Maronite Christians, who since the arrival of Islam in the seventh century have found refuge largely in the Lebanese mountains, and later in French arms. Without the French, or even the Ottoman Turks, Lebanon's Christians were embarking on a precarious voyage into the unknown. The political arrangement the French helped to install, based on the somewhat suspect 1943 census that showed the Christian and

Muslim populations as roughly equal, offered some hope for Christian survival, if not dominance, in this corner of the eastern Mediterranean. Political offices were divided in half with a slight edge given to the Christians, especially the Maronites. The president always was to be a Christian; the prime minister a Muslim. The cabinet was balanced. The parliament would have six Christian deputies for every five Muslim and Druze, leaving that body's total membership as a multiple of eleven. The army and other security forces would be Christian dominated since the latter community supplied nearly all of their officers. While the system worked, more or less, in spite of a number of built-in inequities, what was granted to the Muslim community in reality was given only to the Sunni population, while Lebanon's large and rapidly growing Shiite population virtually were ignored by Christian and Sunni alike. The 1943 census was never updated, for obvious reasons: the French political formula on which it was based became more and more remote as the Christian percentage shrank due to a lower birth rate and a high level of emigration to the United States, South America, West Africa, and Australia.

The first signs of real trouble came in 1958, when Egypt's Gamal Abdel Nasser, after forming a union with Syria, attempted to change the rules by siding with the country's poor Shiite community. Only the appearance of American marines that summer kept the country from coming apart. But enforced tranquility proved temporary. By the early 1970s, the tensions among the various communities had grown so great that full-scale civil war began in 1975. The added strains of Syrian intervention and the rise of the PLO in Lebanon after its forced departure from Jordan in 1970 proved too much for the intricate Lebanese system of checks and balances. Even before the outbreak of hostilities, the Lebanese were arming to the teeth. The first to do so were the Christians, especially the Maronites, who saw their position in Lebanon threatened both from within and without.

Sunni- and Alawite-run Syria, with close ties to the Soviet Union, made Lebanon's Christian community extremely nervous. So did the PLO, who came in droves to Lebanon after "Black September" 1970, in Jordan.* Egyptians already had demonstrated they could not be trusted, even after Nasser's death in 1970. The entire Muslim community, Sunni as well as Shiite, was increasingly restive. The Maronites had never forgotten the slaughter of thousands in 1860 at the hands of the small but extremely warlike Druze community. Beginning in the 1960s, the fear, if not the panic, of the Maronite Christian community led its leading families—the Chamouns, the Franjiyehs, and the Gemayels—to become deeply involved in what had been the traditional drug trade in Lebanon: hashish from the Bekaa and opium and heroin from Asia. Shipped from Christian-run ports, Christian militias protected the product. In this way the Christians earned the huge sums of money needed to buy arms on the world market.

Until the late 1970s, the three principal Christian clans divided the trade among themselves much as they had parceled out the real power in Lebanon for a generation; power, drugs, and politics became one. Anyone not in the guild was left out and would have remained out except for a small matter of demographics: the Muslims were having more babies. Time was running out for the Christians.

At first the Christian trade was mostly in hashish. The Lebanese variety called Lebanese Gold or Cherry Flakes was prized especially by marijuana connoisseurs for its potency. The plants are grown in the Bekaa Valley, which runs for nearly seventy-five miles northeast to southwest between the country's two great mountain ranges, the Lebanon and the Anti-Lebanon. The northern end of the Bekaa is especially fertile. Its alluvial soil is replenished constantly from the erosion of the two mountain chains. A mild Mediterranean climate with abundant sunshine

*September 1970, was named Black September after King Hussein's forces killed thousands of fedayeen, and drove the rest of them out of Jordan. A subgroup of Al-Fatah subsequently adopted "Black September" as its nom de guerre.

and just the right amount of morning moisture makes for almost perfect growing conditions.

With the increase in inter- and intra-communal tensions, hash-ish production exploded. In 1986, more than four million pounds of hashish were harvested in the Bekaa, representing some 75 percent of world consumption.

Travelling by car through the narrow roads of the Bekaa, it is as though a multicolored carpet extends majestically over the country-side. Thousands of acres of shoulder-high marijuana plants grow in clearly delineated plots. Before the outbreak of the 1975 Lebanese civil war, only ten percent of the valley was used to cultivate hashish. Since the breakdown of law and order [fourteen] years ago, however, the acreage taken up by hashish in the Bekaa has expanded steadily. Today, over 90 percent of the valley is covered with marijuana plants.[10]*

How much is this worth to the Lebanese economy? Drugs now have become its mainstay, its single most important export, worth several billions of dollars. There are no other known sources of income to generate enough money to support the ongoing war. An indication of the economic power that derives from drugs in

---

*The authors continue: according to eyewitnesses who traveled through the area,

The third week of October signals the beginning of harvest season and close to 80,000 peasants swarm into the valley for this purpose. Under the hot sun, women in bright dresses and head scarves chop plants with hand sickles, tossing the tops into bundles on the ground. Tractors and huge trucks piled high with towering heaps of hashish rumble along the roads. The pungent fragrance of the drug hangs over much of the region.[11]

Colorful pictures of Lebanese harvesting opium while armed Syrian soldiers stand by have been taken on at least two separate occasions. The first, a film, was photo-graphed and produced in 1988 by Christopher Wenner, a London-based documentary photographer. The second, a videotape from 1989, was given to the author by a U.S. reporter who wishes to remain anonymous. In addition to information similiar to that in the film, the tape shows interesting footage of Pablo Escobar, the Colombian cocaine kingpin, meeting Syrian officials in Larnaca, Cyprus. They were not dis-cussing the weather.

Lebanon may be observed from the annual financial reports by *An-Nahar*, a Beirut daily newspaper. Comparable to the stock quotations listed daily in the *New York Times*, the reports carry both local and international prices of drugs produced in Lebanon. *An-Nahar* prices are based on reports from Lebanese drug-trading groups. [12]*

If the Christian minority in Lebanon at first monopolized the drug trade, they lost that monopoly soon after Syria overtook the Bekaa Valley in 1975 when the civil war began, starting the arms race inside Lebanon. The Sunni, Shiite, and Druze communities strove hard to catch up, which meant grabbing their share of the drug trade. The drugs-for-guns upward spiral continued, driven by factional fears and actual fighting.

Anyone who has been in battle knows that war is an enormous consumer of lives and matériel; the losses constantly need to be replaced and replenished, which to the Lebanese meant that more hashish must be offered for sale, especially to the drug-hungry Western world. It was not long before the hashish industry could no longer supply the dollars needed to keep war among the Lebanese going. In 1982, poppy growers from Turkey were brought into the Bekaa Valley, and their guidance made possible the production of opium, morphine base, and heroin. This was inevitable. Opiates per weight are at least ten times more profitable than hashish. As a result, poppies and marijuana plants now compete for scarce land, with the poppy now occupying more than 15 percent of Bekaa acreage. Last available figures in 1990† show that at least five tons of pure heroin were processed from poppy plants. [13]‡ The poppies are cultivated and

*Hashish prices for 1984 and opium and heroin prices for 1984–85 per kilogram in Lebanese pounds.
†The latest figure for spring 1990, as estimated by INM.
‡The poppy harvest occurs in August in the Bekaa. The opium that is taken from the bright red flowers is then turned into a morphine base from which heroin is the ultimate product. As in Colombia, small, highly mobile laboratories do the work. There are estimated to be at least a hundred of them in the valley. According

then processed into opium, morphine base, and heroin. This is not done by the Lebanese peasantry. Chemists from Italy, France, and the United States provide the technical skill that now produces some of the highest-grade heroin in the world. At least a quarter of that heroin has gone to the United States, making Bekaa's contribution to the American heroin habit approximately 20 percent by 1986,* and the Lebanese connection continues to grow, according to U.S. drug officials. Meanwhile Western Europe, which has been experiencing a drug epidemic in the last few years, receives the lion's share of Lebanon's narcotics production.[15]

Even more recently, the Syrian and various Lebanese factions have become involved in the highly profitable cocaine trade. Coca leaf is not grown in the Bekaa, but the Lebanese merchant communities that thrive in South America are sending large quantities of coca paste from Colombia, Peru, and Bolivia to Lebanon for refinement in the Bekaa labs, which help supply the increasingly voracious European craving for cocaine and with it the relatively cheap and highly addictive crack. Indeed, the overseas Lebanese are vital for the drug trade:

Whether in North America, South America, Europe, or other centers of the Lebanese diaspora, these communities lend the rare element of trust to this worldwide drug traffic. These worldwide ethnic and family links aid tremendously in the export and marketing of drugs. In the U.S., for example, the largest Lebanese community lives in Detroit. It is no coincidence that of all the Lebanese heroin entering the U.S., more than half enters through Detroit.[16]

---

to State Department reports, the larger, more sophisticated refineries are across the border in Syria.[14]

*As with all drug-related statistics, this figure also may be in dispute. The general statistics for heroin production worldwide are: 18 to 20 percent in Southwest Asia; 50 to 52 percent in Southeast Asia; and 30 percent in Mexico (INM figures for 1990).

The production, refinement, and transportation of Lebanon's various illicit drugs are fought over jealously by the country's warring factions. Transportation especially is a delicate question of turf. Hashish and opium traditionally are moved over land or sea, since they are bulky products. This means that the various groups involved in the trade must have secure roads and ports to move their merchandise. Opium's by-products—heroin and morphine base—and the latest product on the Lebanese market, cocaine, are usually transported by air, often from Damascus.[17] As in Colombia, Lebanon has seen a vast increase in primitive landing strips, where single-engine planes make pickups and are soon on their way to European destinations.

Exactly how does it work? In truth, most of Lebanon is involved—including the government, the military, the fighting factions—Muslim, Christian, Druze, rich and poor alike. Everybody gets a piece of the "drug pie."

All Lebanese governmental bodies derive most of their revenues from the drug industry. The government collects drug-based revenues in two ways: taxes collected through local officials in regions where hashish and poppies are grown; and fees levied at checkpoints and roadblocks, as well as from "customs officials" at many ports, especially Jūniyah, Aliminia, and Sidon, three cities that flourished after turning into drug-handling ports. In recent years, the first method of collection has been virtually impossible to enforce due to the state of lawlessness that exists in the Bekaa. The second method is easier and more reliable, as soldiers accompany collectors to ensure payment.[18]

With the near-total dissolution of governmental control in Lebanon has come an even keener competition among Lebanon's armed factions, and the factions within factions, for control of their own ports or even a single pier. Holding a secure area on the Lebanese coast can mean hundreds of millions of dollars per year, while the lack of one can mean military extinction.

In the far north is the ancient seaport of Tripoli, largely under

Syrian control, from which a good portion of the Bekaa's hashish and heroin is exported to Europe via Cyprus. But the Syrians have not worked alone in Tripoli; the Christian Maronite Franjiyeh clan also uses the city for drug trafficking. With its fishing fleets serving as transports, hashish, opium, and heroin are also sent to Western Europe, protected, naturally, by the Franjiyeh-controlled "Tiger Militia."[19]

Approximately 100 miles south of Tripoli is the small Christian-held port of Jūniyah that once was held exclusively by the late Bashir Gemayel, who was elected president of Lebanon in 1982 and killed by a car bomb a few months later—a killing that caused some consternation in Washington at the time. But the younger and more aggressive son of Pierre Gemayel had been no saint. Thanks to profits earned from drug exports through Jūniyah, Bashir had built his father's fairly insignificant Phalange militia into a formidable fighting force during the 1970s, when the Christian Maronites began to feel besieged from all sides. Before the killing of Bashir Gemayel, the port of Beirut also had been part of the Gemayel drug-exporting empire. In exchange for drugs came Belgian arms that equipped the Christian militias in East Beirut. But since the decline of the Lebanese Christian community and the Gemayel family, Beirut port, when it functions, has become a free port in every sense. All the factions in the battered capital are fighting for a piece of the action, even if it comes down to a single pier or warehouse.

Further south, the ancient city-state of Tyre is yet another outlet available for drug smugglers. Until 1982, the year the Israelis entered Lebanon, the town had been controlled by the Palestinians, specifically by George Habash, a Christian, and his PLO offshoot, the Popular Front for the Liberation of Palestine (PFLP). In fact, the PFLP was no breakaway faction of the PLO, as it conventionally has been depicted, it was and still is part and parcel of that organization. In her book *The Soviet Union and Terrorism*, Roberta Goren wrote:

The PFLP came into existence in late 1967 and was made up of three principle groups: one set up by George Habash in the aftermath of the Six-Day War (The Vengeance Youth), one made up of PLO Anti-Shuquairy members (The Heroes of the Return) and one formed in the early 1960's by Ahmad Jibril and Ali Bushnaq, Palestinian ex-officers of the Syrian army. . . . The need for the adoption of a strict Marxist-Leninist revolutionary ideology was emphasized in their own publications.[20]*

Indeed, Habash's drug profits were made possible by a PLO-owned shipping company called SUMUD, the Arabic word for steadfastness. SUMUD exports hashish, opium, opium base, heroin, and, lately, cocaine, to Europe and in return obtains weapons needed to pursue the PLO war against Israel and any other targets they choose.

No one is neglected in these operations. The Sunnis have Sidon for drug-running purposes; the Shiites have Ouzae, which is part of greater Beirut; and the Druze control the port of Khalde, also in Beirut.[21] But the division of the drug trade among Lebanon's factions suggests more agreement than actually exists. In fact, the struggle continues among them for a larger share of the drug trade as the cost of the war escalates. The reason is simple: the more one can control, the greater the resources that will be available to pursue the war against the rest.

Lebanon is not simply a matter of feuding religious communities; assuredly, it is nothing as simple as the bad Muslim McCoys battling virtuous Christian Hatfields. In fact, the war for the drug trade began within the Christian "family": "In 1978, a small detachment of soldiers under the direction of Bashir Jemayal assassinated Tony Franjiyeh, son of the former Lebanese president. This bloody murder heralded the beginning of violent inter-Christian [sic] feuding. Disagreements between the Chris-

*The group headed by George Habash apparently is the most active and had carried out the most violent attacks against both Western and Arab targets. The usual modus operandi is plastic explosives, often Cimtex, made in Czechoslovakia.

tian factions over equitable divisions of drug revenues soon followed."[22]* If Christians kill Christians with abandon, why should Christians and Muslims and Druze have any higher regard for each other—especially when it involves money, self-enrichment for the few, and survival for the many? The answer, of course, is that they don't.

It must be remembered that the war among the communities and the clans is not a static one; since Lebanon's independence, the tide has turned steadily against the Christians. As we have seen already, they hardly are victims of a growing brutal majority. Much of the destruction has been caused by Christian leaders, including a good deal of murder and mayhem among themselves. They do not suffer only from self-inflicted wounds. Their feud with the Syrians, who have controlled the Bekaa for the last fifteen years, has also deprived them of access to the valley's narcotics mother lode, which, in turn has further helped fuel the increasingly bitter clash between the Christians and the Syrians—who once were allies against the Palestinians and the Sunni militias.

The Lebanese Christian and Syrian armed rivalry that broke the Beiruti bubble in the summer of 1989 was not the only problem faced by the Christians. At that time, the 1982 Israeli invasion of Lebanon had been widely viewed as a Save-the-Maronites expedition. But the law of unintended consequences, particularly when it comes to military interventions, rapidly came into effect. The long-neglected, numerically powerful, indigent Shiite community in Lebanon for the first time became conscious of its numbers and its kinship with the Iranian revolution. It was the Shiites who took the brunt of the Israeli northward thrust, where the bulk of that community's population is clustered in Lebanon's neglected, poverty-stricken south. Now the two highly volatile

---

*The murder did not slow them down. Franjiyeh's family continued its involvement in the drug trade. According to the *Sydney Morning Herald*, a link existed between a heroin importing racket and the Zgharta militia, headed by Soloiman Franjiyeh, who was Lebanon's president from 1970 to 1976. This link was identified when 1.4 kilos of heroin were discovered by the NSW police.[23]

elements of old grievances and newly discovered power exploded, first against the Israelis and then, more lethally, against the Lebanese establishment—against the comfortable Christians and the nearly equally comfortable Sunni Muslims, who even in 1982 had thought that Lebanon was forever theirs. The Shiites soon put them both on notice. They wanted more, including a bigger slice of the drug revenue pie, and they were prepared to back their demands with military force, the formidable Amal militia.

After 1982, Lebanon would never be the same again. In the end, the Israeli architects of Peace in the Galilee knew their neighbor no better than anyone else, least of all the Americans, who blundered in and blundered out again at the cost of hundreds of dead American marines, with no clear plan or purpose.

———————— ▮▮▮▮▮ ————————

Lebanon Is Not Just for the Lebanese

The lucrative nature of the drug business and the lawless state in which the country has lived during the last decade provided a perfect entry for others to become involved in both drugs and terror, which is precisely what happened. Chief among those who have stepped in are the Syrians and the Palestine Liberation Organization, but Bulgaria, Cuba, and the Soviet Union also are involved. The Syria of President Hafez al-Assad has been a major player, if not *the* major player, in the Lebanese drug trade since at least 1975, when Syrian forces seized complete control of the Bekaa Valley. By March 1, 1987, under Section 481(h) of the Foreign Assistance Act, President Reagan denied certification to Syria.[24]

The Syrians remained in the Bekaa Valley despite the movement of the Israeli Defense Force into the area seven years later. Besides the northern port of Tripoli, Syrian control of the Bekaa means that Damascus has stategic control of Lebanon. Nothing can move in or out of the valley without crossing a Syrian army checkpoint. At these control stations, the Syrians simply "extract" hard currency from the drug merchants who wander through the Bekaa. This is the situation everywhere in Lebanon. If an armed faction has command of a road and a checkpoint it will collect a tariff from the vendor of narcotics. That is how business is conducted in Lebanon today. It is primitive, some might say medieval; but Hobbes would have understood.

In the case of the Syrians, control also means that Damascus, with its 43,000 heavily armed soldiers stationed in Lebanon,[25] can just about name its share of the drug profits. Not surprisingly, that share has gone up over the years, to the consternation of Lebanon's fighting factions, including the Christians, who worry more about this matter than any other group.[26]* But Syrian involvement in drug running goes beyond the Bekaa Valley, indeed, beyond Lebanon.[27] One recent example demonstrates how Damascus has forged ties with, among others, the Sicilian Mafia. On March 13, 1986, Italian authorities seized the *Fidelio*, a 400-ton Honduran-registered boat off the southern coast of Sicily, after a three-day chase involving six Italian patrol boats, several helicopters, and navy corvettes. As the police had suspected, drugs were found aboard: three tons of hashish and several kilos of heroin and morphine base. Even more interesting was the drug-running team itself, comprised of a dozen Syrian soldiers in uniform and Sicilian mafiosi. The captain of the boat was a member of the Sicilian Cuntrera crime family, which has its Italian branches in Rome and Milan as well as in Canada, Mexico, Venezuela, and the United States.

The *Fidelio* is not an isolated incident. Italian law-enforcement officials believe that some Syrian drug-running operations are administered worldwide by Francesco Di Carlo, a member of the Cuntrera crime family. As to Syrian involvement in drugs, Italian officials have identified such Damascus high officials as Rifaat al-Assad, vice-president and minister of the interior, who happens to be the younger brother of President al-Assad. Others, such as

*There are 30,000 Syrian soldiers in the Bekaa alone.

Defense Minister Mustafa Tlass and Syrian Army Chief of Staff Hikmat al-Shihaby, are mentioned as receiving drug commissions of at least $100,000 a year, usually in the form of gold bars. Despite the mass of evidence against them, the Syrians deny (as Cuban authorites once did) any involvement in drugs or terrorism.[28] On June 29, 1989, a bill calling for an embargo on trade with Syria was presented to the House by Congressman Robert Dornan. Among the findings listed in the proposed bill are not only many Syrian terrorist activities, but also "Syrian involvement in the cultivation, production and distribution of illegal narcotics including heroin and hashish. This has been so notorious that the US. government has decertified Syria."[29]

Before the Lebanese civil war and the Syrian occupation, the ancient city of Baalbek was a poor and neglected spot of Lebanon, with only 30,000 impoverished inhabitants. Now the town is 120,000 strong and growing. Mercedeses and BMWs race down the smooth motorways leading to Baalbek, which now could be renamed "The City of Terror." Drug prosperity makes Syrian control over Baalbek, located only twenty-five miles from Damascus, all the easier. Damascus and its friends and allies, a true terrorist international, have operated in Baalbek for years with total impunity.[30] Baalbek, for example, is the headquarters of the Hisballah, the pro-Iranian terrorist group that holds the bulk of American hostages in Lebanon. Iran and Syria share not only a common enemy, Iraq, but a common working relationship in both drugs and terror, not to mention the Hisballah, their love child.

Another group that has benefited from being located in Baalbek is the Palestine Liberation Organization. The PLO has a long, sordid, and continuing involvement in narco-terrorism. For years Lebanon has provided the organization with shelter, sanctuary, and an important source of income—revenue earned from the narcotics trade. Indeed, its super-sophisticated network of worldwide contacts has made the PLO, even more than the Syrians, the most successful purveyor of drugs originating from the Middle East. Its shipping line, SUMUD, had business arrangements with all of the PLO offices throughout Western Europe. The criminal, political, and terrorist apparatus merged into one powerful whole, while legally constituted governments and their intelligence services looked the other way.

All of this comes as a shock even to veteran observers of the region. Generally it has been thought that the PLO gets its money from other Arab governments, as well as from its own legitimate businesses (farms, construction companies, airlines) and the "taxes" it collects (extorts) from Palestinians living around the world. This is true, but only partly so. In fact, before the PLO largely was expelled from Lebanon by the Israelis in 1982, it is estimated that the organization earned $300 million from the narcotics trade yearly, approximately three times what it earned from supportive Arab regimes. Other money was earned from patently criminal activities such as bank robbery and smuggling. With this money it is estimated that the PLO is able to purchase at a minimum 40 percent of its basic weapons of terror, light infantry weapons, thereby completing the circle of narco-terrorism.[31]

The Israeli invasion, however, created a crisis within the PLO:

Six months after its expulsion from Beirut, faced with a growing financial crisis stemming from the Lebanon war, the PLO convened its Finance Committee in a secret emergency session in Algiers on February 20, 1983. Under the chairmanship of Yasir Arafat, the committee decided to broaden the PLO's activities in international drug trafficking in order to raise badly needed funds. As stated by Sallah Dabbagh, then PLO treasury chief, who spoke at the Algiers meeting: ". . . the entire future of the PLO operation for liberation may hinge on our exporting more drugs throughout the world."[32]

This is exactly what they did. The following are two examples of PLO involvement in the international drug trade:

Early in 1984 PLO agents sold 4.3 metric tons of Lebanese hashish worth more than $12 million to British drug traffickers. The U.K.'s

Customs Service intercepted the drugs onboard a yacht and arrested the traffickers and their PLO collaborators. At the trial conducted in July 1985, they were sentenced to a total of 36 years in jail. The second recent and more complicated example of PLO trafficking took place in Australia where in August of 1985 the federal police rounded up 35 persons—some of whom were Austrialians of Lebanese origin and charged them with trafficking hashish worth $40 million which were to purchase assault rifles and plastic explosives.[33]

Despite its temporary setback in Lebanon, there is every indication that the PLO continued to promote international narco-terrorism. Early in 1990, the PLO not only regained its military forces in Lebanon, but actually increased its power from 8,000 terrorists, who were forced out by Israel in 1982, to 11,000.[34] At the same time, drugs for arms on behalf of the PLO increased as well. In early March 1990, U.S. Customs arrested fifteen Palestinians in Maimi for their $1 million-a-month cash transfer to PLO-identified accounts generated from drug trafficking and other criminal activities,[35] made possible with the support and patronage of the Soviet Union, Cuba, Nicaragua and other states and movements that were or still are part of the Marxist-Leninist Soviet nexus.[36]

The Soviet-PLO relationship is long and tangled—and typical of Kremlin caution, their courtship long and sometimes tortured. In the end, in the early 1960s, Moscow became convinced that the armed wing of the Palestinians would be a valuable asset. One should not forget that the Soviet Union had been the first to sponsor, support, and train terrorist organizations from around the world in an attempt to undermine Western society. The Soviets and Soviet-allied countries trained terrorist organizations based on strategy described in the 1979 Soviet Military Encyclopedia.[37] Both this and the more recent 1986 edition provided for a list of *measures to be used in peacetime* (emphasis mine), in order to promote Soviet foreign policy objectives. Among those operations, the Soviets instruct the following:

Reconnaissance [is] carried out with the aim of subversion of the political, economic, military and moral potential of actual or possible enemies; basic tasks are:

- Acquisition of reconnaissance data on important economic and military targets, destruction or taking out of such targets;
- Organization of sabotage and diversionary terrorist acts;
- Conduct of hostile propaganda;
- Accomplishment of punitive operations against patriot forces;
- The putting together and preparation of rebel detachments, etc.

Special reconnaissance is:

- Organized by means of Military Organs and Special Services; and
- Conducted with forces of Agent Reconnaissance and Troops of special Designation.

For this purpose are used:

- Special types of weapons, personal equipment, technical resources, i.e., silenced firearms;
- Mines and explosive resources;
- Radio and other special apparatus; and also
- *Biological weapons, narcotics, poisons,* et cetera [italics added].[38]*

The PLO was seen not only as a weapon to be used against Israel (thus polarizing the Arab world even more against it and the United States); it could be employed directly against the United States. Typically, the first trainers and suppliers of the PLO came not from Moscow but from its most faithful client in Europe at the time, the German Democratic Republic. By the late 1960s, East Germany, followed by Hungary, Czechoslovakia, Bulgaria, and Yugoslavia, were assisting the PLO in the fine arts of terrorism.[39]†

---

*The author verified this by consulting with experts on Soviet military strategy. Among them are Colonel Sam Pope from England and Dr. Leon Goure from Science Application Inc. (SAIC) in McLean, Virginia.

†And later Cuba, of course. Since the early 1970s Castro formed close ties with both Yasir Arafat of the PLO and Hafez al-Assad of Syria. Cuban armored units fought with Syrian troops during the Yom Kippur war, and Cuban trainers have worked in the Baalbek terrorist training camps.[40]

But it was only when the Lebanese civil war began in June 1976, that the Soviets fully aligned themselves with the PLO. They stepped up official support for the PLO by supplying it with an unprecedented amount of arms. The PLO, with its drug connections and access to the Kremlin armory, for the first time became a major actor in Lebanon.[41] The full extent of Soviet support for the PLO in Lebanon became known to the West after Israeli troopers captured a variety of documents in its several forays into that country. Translation and analysis of the documents by Professor Raphael Israeli revealed that:

There is almost no communist country that is not represented in one way or another in the PLO network of political and military ties. First and foremost is the Soviet Union, which seems to provide the ideological, diplomatic and military backbone of the Palestinian movement.

Other East Bloc countries, such as Hungary and east Germany, act as surrogates for the Soviet Union and extend very substantial military training to PLO personnel. Even China* and Yugoslavia play their part, as do North Korea and Vietnam. Other Third World Communists, notably Cuba's Castro and the Sandinistas of Nicaragua,

---

*The nature and depth of the continuing relationship between the PLO and China is best described by a letter received in Beijing on June 27, 1989. The letter was sent from Yasir Arafat, chairman of the PLO Executive Committee, to the Chinese Communist Party General Secretary Jiang Zemin, congratulating him on his appointment to General Secretary:

On behalf of the Arab Palestinian people, their leadership, and myself, I express the warmest, most sincere congratulations to you—dear comrade—on your appointment to General Secretary of the Communist Party of China, and *take this opportunity to express extreme gratification that you were able to restore normal order after the recent incidents in People's China.* I wish you—close friends—more progress in your endeavor to achieve the hopes, goals, aspirations, stability, and security of our friends, the Chinese people.

I humbly express our deepest gratitude to the government of People's China, the great Chinese people, and the Communist Party of China for the Chinese people's friendship, and the Chinese people's and leadership's aid and support for my country's just struggle, and your unwavering and principled stand toward our country's revolution and our revolutionaries.

Dear comrade, I wholeheartedly wish you success in your new mission, and hope that People's China will continuously progress and develop.[42]

have either extended aid or served as models for PLO ideologues and military planners. . . . The camaraderie between the Soviets and the PLO is apparent as they discuss and coordinate worldwide moves aimed at strengthening the communist camp and weakening "Western Imperialism."[43]

And as scholar Roberta Goren reports:

In the Litani operation of 1978 the first massive quantities of Soviet and Soviet-bloc materiel were first discovered. The arms included a wide variety of anti-tank and anti-aircraft missiles—SAM-7s such as those found in the possession of Daniele Piffani and two Palestinians in November 1979 in a Rome apartment—and Soviet-made artillery guns, mortars and Katyusha rockets together with a wide array of small arms. In addition, the PLO is the only terrorist group to have received ultra-modern, sophisticated weapons, which have often not been available even to stable clients of the USSR and these in turn have been available to other groups.[44]

Even after the war in Lebanon quieted down, narco-terrorism continued to flourish. In October 1990 Syria finalized its plan to incorporate Lebanon into Greater Syria. It did so while the world was watching silently. Syria obtained control of Lebanon without giving up anything—not even one Western hostage. When Syria joined the coalition in the Gulf War against Iraq, it tacitly agreed to control terrorist attacks against the West. The West, however, did not use this opportunity to demand that Syria's involvement in drug production and drug trafficking cease. Syria was too important politically to the State Department to make drugs an issue, and the highly publicized war on drugs in the United States was ignored.

4

Colombia: The Superstate
of Narco-terrorism

–––––––––––––––––––– ▌▐▌▐▌ ––––––––––––––––––––

In Colombia, soon to have the second largest population in South America, the origin of illegal-drug trafficking to the U.S. "has been traced to the 1959 Castro takeover of Cuba,"[1] and since then this booming industry has been promoted and protected by Cuba and other Soviet-bloc allies, wreaking political, economic, and social havoc. Illegal drugs may be a "scourge" (to use President Bush's term in his first inaugural address) but they are a catastrophe for Latin America. The signs of narcotics-induced disintegration are apparent everywhere in the hemisphere, in some nations at a very advanced state. Colombia, Peru, and Bolivia head the list and receive the bulk of attention, but narco-terrorism has a habit of moving almost at will into other countries, in very short order. Brazil, Paraguay, and to a lesser degree Venezuela and Ecuador, also are under attack. Only Chile, which under General Augusto Pinochet kicked out the cocaine traffickers in 1973, is relatively free from their influence. With the passing of the old dictator, however, its future is uncertain.

In January 1988, Colombia's attorney general, Carlos Mauro Hoyos, said: "We are confronting a superstate." That brave man knew what he was talking about. Two months later he was assassinated, gunned down by the M-19 (Movimiento 19 de Abril),*

---

*The April 19 Movement (better known as M-19), at the beginning, was an outgrowth of a vaguely populist, nationalist, and authoritarian movement led by

a communist terrorist group hired for the occasion by the Medellin cartel.

Note that Mauro Hoyos did not call the drug traffickers a cartel or a corporation, but a superstate. He was not exaggerating. As Freedom House's Douglas Payne acutely and accurately observes, " 'the super-state,' centered in Colombia, radiates throughout Latin America and the Caribbean. Its foreign policy instruments, like those of any other state, include force, economic leverage and, most recently, propaganda and diplomacy. The goal of its foreign diplomacy is to achieve legitimacy among the sovereign states of the hemisphere."[4]* As we shall see, that goal largely has been reached, at least in Colombia, which once had comparatively strong legal institutions and a respect, if not reverence, for law.† In fact, the marriage of narco-traffickers and Cuban-trained guerrillas already has destroyed Colombia's legal system. Many doubt that it can ever be reconstructed. By comparison, the Cuban-sponsored revolutionaries of the 1960s were mere nuisances, amateur troublemakers who were outgunned, outnumbered, and outsmarted by security forces everywhere in Latin America. For Colombia twenty years later, exactly the reverse is true. As yet there is no light at the end of the tunnel—unless, of course, it is emanating from an oncoming train.

The sense of defeat and hopelessness in a war most of us did not know was going on is difficult to accept. Until recently, Amer-

---

the deposed dictator, General Gustavo Rojas Pinilla.[2] With Jaime Bateman's leadership it later moved toward Moscow and Cuba.[3]

*An early and vivid demonstration of the legitimization of the narco-traffickers was their brazen negotiations in Panama with an ex-president of Colombia acting for the government as an intermediary. The drug merchants offered to pay off Colombia's foreign debt in exchange for immunity.[5]

†It is no accident that one of Colombia's founders, Francisco de Paula Santander, was called "the man of laws." Legality, constitutionalism, orderly political procedures, or at least the appearance of same, have been respected in Colombia more than in any other Latin American country—until recently. The moral: If it can happen in Colombia, it will happen or has happened elsewhere in the region, and more rapidly.

icans have been only dimly aware of the problem, if at all. Ignorance, of course, does not change the facts; neither does rhetoric about a war on drugs. How could it happen so quickly? How could it happen at all? These are the general questions. More specifically, one should ask when and how the alliances were forged that made narco-terrorism the threat it now is to all governments in the Western Hemisphere, including our own; which regimes have been targeted and in what order; how narco-terrorism takes advantage—brilliantly, I might add—in a way that the late Che Guevara never anticipated, of the corruption and other failings already existing in Latin America; what does this say of our chances to defeat the threat? One must be clear on one point. The threat is growing, not receding. The failure of Marxism-Leninism around the world does not change the prognosis. The spread of the narco-terrorist empire continues at breakneck speed, and we have summoned neither the energy nor the resources and will to combat it. We have yet to even recognize the enemy.

By now, most have heard of the Colombian cocaine cartel, though the term itself is misleading. It is not an actual cartel, but rather a loose collection of individuals and families who work together not to set prices, but to assure a high rate of delivery to cocaine markets around the world. These drug lords, who virtually run large cities such as Medellín and Cali, dominate the drug trade in marijuana and cocaine and earn billions of dollars per year bringing corruption and violence to not only Colombia, but to U.S. cities as well; as we shall see, an identical pattern of corruption is also emerging in the United States.[6]

But why did Colombia become the narco-terrorist superstate? Despite its legal traditions, Colombia, paradoxically, is a country that rarely has been at peace. It has the most violent history in the region—no mean accomplishment—and yet has never had a full-blown successful military coup. Colombians specialize in civil wars, having had scores of them. The War of the Thousand Days in the late nineteenth century took over 100,000 lives. The most recent full-scale conflict, which occurred in the decade following World War II, known simply as *La Violencia*,[7] cost 200,000 dead. At its height in the late 1940s, Colombia's warring factions were murdering each other, and innocent bystanders, at the rate of 2,000 a month.[8]

The turmoil never ended; it merely has been transformed. To be sure, the traditional political parties, the Conservatives (now the Social Conservative party) and the Liberals, did make peace of sorts in 1957, and established a National Front where each shared power equally and alternately. The killing continued, albeit at a slower rate. That period of relative tranquility ended after Fidel Castro came to power in Cuba. New guerrilla armies sprang up in the 1960s, almost always with Havana's help.[9]

Castro himself as a university student had his first taste of Colombian violence in 1948, when he attended a youth conference in Bogotá sponsored by Argentina's Juan Perón. When the bloody *bogotazo** ripped through the capital like an earthquake after the murder of a left-wing politician, the future Cuban ruler joined the fighting in the streets in hopes of mounting an insurrection then and there in the Colombian capital. Castro's protégés continue the struggle today in the cities and the countryside. After a decline in the 1970s, most of Colombia's numerous guerrilla and terrorist groups now are larger in size, better equipped, and more politically sophisticated than ever. They, too, like their narco-trafficker comrades, have acquired a patina of legitimacy by endlessly negotiating cease-fire and peace accords with a harried and increasingly haggard central government.[10]

Still, the cocaine kingpins of Medellin and Cali are probably more dangerous than the terrorist and guerrilla groups. The drug families are relatively new compared to the guerrillas, but their violence has been far more effective in undermining the Colombian state. Moreover, the traffickers' lawlessness has inspired

---

*The uprising, which took place in Bogotá in April 1948, that touched off the Colombian civil war.

others in Colombia to use illegal force as well, including members of the security forces. The climate of insecurity also has led to the rise of self-defense groups, usually peasants, who battle alone against guerrillas, drug traffickers, and common criminals; not surprisingly, these vigilantes commit their share of atrocities as well. The spiraling violence works to the advantage of the narco-terrorists, since the government cannot guarantee either law or order and is thus even further discredited.

But no matter how deadly, the narco-traffickers cannot do it alone. This marriage of guerrilla and drug lord has made possible the swift and devastating institutional debacle of Colombia, now the model for other groups around the hemisphere.

Who are the guerrilla armies of Colombia, and how did they come to form this alliance with the men from Medellin? Colombia's insurgents are nothing if not persistent. They have waged war against the government for at least a quarter century and have survived longer than any other such group in Latin America. But they are more than merely surviving; since the mid-1960s, there have been two rural guerrilla armies in the field: the National Liberation Army (ELN), which was pro-Cuban from its beginning, and the Colombian Revolutionary Armed Forces (FARC), itself a merger of several guerrilla groups. The FARC has been the armed wing of the ultra pro-Soviet Colombian Communist Party, the PCC. For nearly a decade, both the ELN and the FARC have roamed at will through a half-dozen Colombian departments acting independently from one other and receiving only small amounts of aid from Havana, consisting mostly of propaganda support and training for top cadre. Both remain active today.

In their first decade, the ELN and FARC followed the Che Guevara school of rural guerrilla warfare. Thus the ELN *comandante-en-jefe* Fabio Vasquez, a devoted follower of Castro, propounded the un-Leninist notion that the Colombian proletariat was utterly unable to fight a war in the cities. Only in the very last stage of the revolution could it even have a role. What that eventual role would be can be only imagined, but it would not have gone down well in the Kremlin. In any case, despite his enthusiasm, by the mid-1970s Vasquez and his fellow guerrillas in the FARC were pretty much on the run as the battle-hardened Colombian army put more pressure on their strongholds. In desperation, both the ELN and the FARC were forced to accept a division of labor: the FARC would continue operations in the *campo,* but the Castroite ELN would conduct terrorist warfare in the cities among the undernourished proletariat. The guerrilla compact did not work. Urban action came to nothing more than a handful of university student strikes, to which few paid any attention. By 1976, a majority of FARC and ELN leaders were dead and their followers scattered.[11]

That respite proved temporary, like others in Colombia's long and tortured history. The next round of violence, which continues today, is far more serious. For one thing, the Cubans have played a much larger role in the campaign to overthrow the current regime than they had in the past. In addition, guerrilla strategy has become far more sophisticated than it was in the yahoo days of the Che Guevaraism: it combines military and political elements; it strikes targets in the provinces as the well as the major cities; and new life has been breathed into both by a new group, the April 19 Movement—better known as M-19.[12] Moreover, the struggle has gone international, with M-19 in the forefront linking itself with the growing network of mutually supportive terrorist groups that cover the world. In bringing it into contact with others, the Nicaraguan Sandinistas and, of course, the Cubans, have played an especially helpful role, which brings us to a major point about the revival of Colombia's insurgent groups: the revival would not have been possible without the 1979 Sandinista victory in Nicaragua over its strongman, Anastasio Somoza. Furthermore, this renaissance of violence has been sparked by the M-19, which was itself an outgrowth of a vaguely populist, ultra-nationalist, authoritarian movement led by the deposed Colombian military dictator Gustavo Rojas Pinilla, a man who had more in common with Argentina's Perón than with Cuba's Castro. The catalyst was the bitterly fought 1970 presidential election. Rojas officially lost that one by the narrowest of margins to the establishment candidate. Rojas's followers, who were for the most part lower class, thought otherwise, and for weeks Bogotá teetered on the verge of another *bogotazo*.

The Rojas phenomenon eventually sputtered out as a mass movement, but a frustrated and radicalized splinter of its youth movement went underground only to emerge in 1973 as the M-19. Early on, the M-19 imitated Uruguay's *Tupamaros* by adopting Robin Hood-style tactics. For example, its agents stole Simón Bolívar's sword and spurs. Later, they became more bloody minded when they kidnapped and killed a popular trade union leader in 1976. After that murder, M-19 dropped any pretense of being romantic urban guerrillas and unleashed a campaign of kidnappings, bank robberies, and assassinations that terrified Colombia's urban middle class.

The M-19's reign of terror received little notice outside of Colombia—much to the annoyance of its leaders, who were already thinking in grander terms. All that changed when the group committed its first international spectacular. At the same time, Castro had been using a Colombian drug ring led by Jaime Guillot-Lara, in which the sale of drugs financed arms for the M-19.[13] Their success came with the daylight invasion of the Dominican Republic's embassy in Bogotá—a raid which netted a number of diplomatic hostages, including American ambassador Diego Asencio. In exchange for the diplomats the M-19 commandos demanded the release of their jailed comrades-in-arms. The negotiations, that served also to legitimize the M-19 as a belligerent, lasted two months and ended peacefully with the M-19ers being flown at their request to Cuba into obscurity, or so the Colombian authorities hoped.[14]

The Colombian authorities were wrong, of course. Within weeks of the terrorists' *despedida* (farewell) Cuban intelligence

agents had arranged a meeting between the M-19 and their protégés in the ELN and FARC. According to U.S. intelligence
sources, the representatives discussed joining forces and coordinating strategy and tactics, the sine qua non of serious Cuban
support.[15] That gathering was preceded by an M-19 contact with
Nicaragua's Sandinistas, then in power only for a few months.
Neither set of initial talks succeeded completely, despite Cuban
encouragement. Nevertheless, beginning in 1980 a rough kind
of cooperation began among the long-divided Colombian revolutionaries.

Havana's most daring intervention in Colombian affairs came
at the end of that year. Clearly not satisfied with M-19's reliance
on urban terrorism* as a tactic, the Cubans trained, equipped,
and shipped back to Colombia a band of would-be M-19 guerrillas.
It was a clear and blatant effort by Castro to revive a rural-based
insurgency along the lines already well under way in El Salvador,
Havana's other priority of the early 1980s, after the fall of Somoza.
The State Department's December 1981 white paper† on Cuban
support for subversion in the hemisphere, based on highly sensitive classified sources and, incidentally, never challenged by
the Soviet bloc nor any of its agents, provides some interesting
details. It shows, for example, that in November 1980, the M-19
sent guerrillas to Cuba via Panama to begin training for the operation. They were given three months of military instruction by
Cuban army instructors on the use of explosives, automatic weapons, hand-to-hand combat, military tactics, and communications.
A course in politics and ideology was taught as well.[17]

Subsequently, in February 1981, two hundred M-19 guerrillas
landed on Colombia's Pacific coast after crossing Panama with
the help of Colonel Manuel Antonio Noriega, who was then leader
of the country's intelligence agency, the G-2. But the plan to

---

*Urban terrorism differs from rural guerrilla warfare not only strategically but
ideologically too.[16]
†A "white paper" is a formal government research paper.

establish a rural base for the M-19 went haywire. An alerted Colombian army battalion (alerted by whom—Noriega?*) pursued the freshly minted would-be M-19ers until they either were killed or captured. Among the survivors was Rosenberg Pabon, the leader of the Dominican embassy takeover. This failure did not mean that the M-19 would simply vanish from the scene. On the contrary, five years later once more it was in the picture carrying out acts of urban terrorism. In May of 1986, for example, it engineered in broad daylight the kidnapping of Alvaro Gomez, who had been the Conservative party's presidential candidate and a fierce opponent of Colombia's guerrillas and terrorists. He was also publisher of the country's leading newspaper, *El Siglo,* which campaigned against Colombia's narco-traffickers. The M-19 threatened to kill Gomez unless the government agreed to negotiations—the familiar tactic. President Virgilio Barco, a Liberal, called the terrorist bluff by refusing to do so, but he did allow the Roman Catholic church to initiate a national "dialogue for peace" that included a meeting of the M-19 in Panama with Colombian churchmen, labor union leaders, and representatives of human rights groups who were in fact leftist sympathizers.

The dialogue was a charade. The M-19 used it to get more recognition, and thus legitimacy, but the real negotiations for Gomez were carried out elsewhere, in Havana. Members of the Social Conservative party (including Gomez's brother) went to Fidel Castro and asked him to act as middle man between the government and the M-19; pleased to be asked, he did just that, and Gomez was released.

Meanwhile, the other three major Colombian guerrilla groups—the FARC, the ELN, and the once-Maoist Popular Lib-

---

*Noriega's criminal activities are yet to be revealed in his upcoming trial, but one should note that Noriega was not the first (and probably not the last) to exploit Panama's special location and unique economic situation. For many years Panama has been known as the Switzerland of Latin America. The canal connecting the Atlantic to the Pacific, the Free Trade Zone, and Colón have been used for contraband trading and smuggling of everything. At the same time, the banking system provided complete anonymity for every imaginable scheme.

eration Army, the EPL—while less powerful than the M-19 still can bite, and bite hard. All are now Marxist and Leninist, vociferously anti-American, and would, if they could, turn Colombia into another Soviet-style police state, sans *glasnost*. That objective has not changed, even though some of the groups signed ceasefire accords with various Colombian governments, beginning with President Belisario Betancur, in the early part of this decade.

During "peace talks" the FARC and its political representatives follow the same negotiating tactics as the Salvadoran communist guerrillas belonging to the Faribundo Marti National Liberation Front, to the letter. Among the demands are a "purification" of the armed forces; the lifting of the state of siege which has been in effect for the last forty years (except between 1982 and 1984); and the end of the army's alleged support for the death squads. None of these conditions have been met, nor are they seriously expected to be by the FARC, but this is hardly the point. By pressing its demands, the armed wing of the Colombian Communist party assumes a state-to-state status as it negotiates with its peers in Bogotá. Diplomatic success and prestige depend on military power. What are the Colombian FARC's chances for further military victories? According to U.S. intelligence analysts, its strength will probably increase over the next few years. It is likely to become a major threat to the regime by the mid-1990s.[18] The pattern is similar to that of the FMLN in El Salvador.

Despite the M-19's superior publicity machine, it is the FARC which has grown the fastest and which is expected to pose the biggest threat, according to American intelligence estimates. Less than five years ago, the FARC had no more than 2,500 armed combatants. This number now has tripled. FARC weaponry also has improved. Hijacked light aircraft are used to move weapons from region to region at will, giving these guerrillas a flexible logistical apparatus. With the FARC becoming more powerful the other guerrilla armies are rethinking their previous casual and loose relationship.[19] The ELN, the EPL, and the M-19 reformed their alliance. This coalition, originally called the National Guerrilla Coordinator (CNG), was later renamed the more politically attractive Simón Bolívar Coordinating Committee (CCSB) in September 1987. After a faulty start, the numbers within the CCSB have grown from 1,500 to 2,500 in less than two years. Though hardly a perfect coalition of forces, the CCSB has been successful in coordinating attacks. Once more, this is a pattern that closely resembles the early years of the Salvadoran guerrilla groups that formed the FMLN.[20]

The rising star within the CCSB is the National Liberation Army. Once confined to a small area of operations near the Venezuelan border, the ELN has resumed terrorist activities in its old hunting grounds, Antioquia department, whose capital is Medellin. In the last year it has bombed businesses, attacked police posts, and kidnapped mayors throughout the department. In Medellin itself, the ELN in 1988 set off a dozen bombs, one of which hit a Jewish synagogue on April 10. A review of the available evidence thus suggests the following pattern of guerrilla activity:

The FARC and the members of the CCSB are *expanding their areas of operation* and have broken out of their traditional strongholds. As a consequence, the Colombian insurgency is rapidly reaching a different and more dangerous stage.

The FARC in particular has taken advantage of the four-year-old ceasefire *by recruiting and rearming* while also building its political arm, the Patriotic Union (UP), something it and the other groups had lacked. The UP participated in the 1986 elections and achieved some success. It obtained 4.5 percent of the vote in the presidential election—more than any other minor party— and won five House and three Senate seats. The UP also has been quite successful in penetrating Colombia's trade unions in the last few years. And the UP has been busy in the countryside organizing those areas that are dominated by FARC forces, where government agents dare not go.[21]

The guerrillas are using force with increasing strategic effect.

The ELN, for example, now poses a major economic threat to the key Cano-Limon-Covenas oil pipeline located near the Venezuelan border; ELN bombings have shut down the pipeline for at least a year. Colombian authorities would like to reroute the pipeline through Venezuela, but Caracas, understandably, has little interest in attracting Colombian terrorists to Venezuelan territory.

The Colombian armed left has shown great resilience and the ability to grow and learn from past mistakes. It should be no surprise then that it is receiving continued foreign support. Cuba and Nicaragua furnish arms and training to all the groups, with the possible exception of the small and inexpert EPL. The latter had its cadre trained in China and North Korea in the late 1960s, while Libya became a major contributor to the M-19 in the early 1980s.[22]

Outside support of Colombia's violent left is not news. The success of its efforts, in turn, won respect and increased support from Moscow and Havana. But the guerrillas and terrorists belonging to separate groups are only part of the threat posed to Colombia and the hemisphere; the second and more serious threat is posed by the narco-traffickers. In contrast to the guerrillas, the drug lords are a relatively new phenomenon. Even though illicit drugs and smuggling have long been part of Colombian society, the creation of this vast criminal empire devoted to narcotics—above all, cocaine—is fairly recent. Indeed, a handbook on Colombia prepared for the U.S. Army in 1970 never once mentioned illegal drugs in what was otherwise an encyclopedia of information on that country.[23]

According to the DEA, the Colombian narco-dealers have supplied at least 80 percent of the cocaine[24] and 35 percent of the marijuana[25] exported to the United States since 1982. The U.S. General Accounting Office estimates that in 1988 the gross revenue derived from the sale of these commodities is at least $7 billion per year.[26] No doubt the profits have soared since. One study done by Switzerland's St. Gallen University, quoted in the

Economist, suggested that the figure may have been as high as
$9 billion when cocaine consumption by America's yuppies was
at a peak in the early 1980s, but is now "only" $4 billion, owing
to abundant supplies of the white crystals and relatively inelastic
demand.[27] Only the Colombian drug lords know for sure—and
possibly even they do not.

These numbers, whichever one chooses, are impressive if not
mind boggling. Yet the Colombian drug trade was a relatively
small-time affair less than twenty years ago. It only began to
expand after the fall of the Marxist Allende regime in Chile. Until
1973, cocaine processing in South America had been headquartered in Santiago. But General Pinochet's regime took a dim view
of narcotics, and the bulk of Chilean chemists and other technicians either were jailed or soon emigrated to Colombia.[28] After
that, business grew quickly during the 1970s almost without
official notice either in Colombia or the United States, until it
was too late.

According to Rensselaer Lee, "Colombia is the linchpin of the
Latin American drug trade. The country is not only a source of
coca leaf, but is also the region's largest supplier of marijuana to
the U.S. market."[29]* He goes on to explain that Colombian traffickers organize and finance narcotics production in other South
American countries. The problem seems to be spreading to Ecuador, Panama, Peru, and Venezuela. In Bolivia, the Brazilian
Amazon, Peru, and Venezuela cocaine is refined on a minor scale,
and marijuana is being produced in Colombia, Ecuador, Guate-
mala and, to a lesser degree, in Belize.[30] These comments first
appeared in 1984. Since then, the problem has grown enormously. What has been its impact on Colombia?

Let me try to indicate the extent of the devastation. In the last
eight years, the Colombian drug cartels have killed over 1,000
public officials, 12 Supreme Court judges, more than 50 judges,

*Dr. Lee has written extensively on the Latin American drug problem and is an
associate scholar of the Foreign Policy Research Institute.

over 170 other judicial employees, dozens of journalists, a narcotics police chief, an attorney general, a major newspaper publisher, and 3 presidential candidates—including the Supreme
Court justices gunned down by the M-19 (which was hired by
narco-traffickers for the occasion) in 1985. For years, Colombian
judges dealing with drug cases automatically would be the target
of multiple death threats.[31] Typically, these judges, poorly paid
and totally unprotected, are given a choice by their enemies:
either they accept a bribe or expect to be murdered along with
their families, including children. Few resist. Some flee the country. The results? "In Colombia today [June 4, 1990] there is no
way to convict someone of drug trafficking, or of illegal enrich-
ment," stated Carlos Ossa Escobar, general manager of the Institute of Agrarian Reform in Bogotá, Colombia.[32]

Moreover, the infrastucture surrounding the legal system also
has been sapped. Politicians, journalists, and police officials who
resisted the drug barons have been eliminated.* Attorney General
Carlos Mauro Hoyos already has been mentioned; he was murdered soon after he told the *New York Times* that he was pre-
paring tough new measures to combat the narco-traffickers.[34] In
addition, some 3,000 policemen and soldiers have been killed and
wounded in this one-sided war by narco-traffickers, whose targets
range from the ordinary private and patrolman to the very top of
the legal system, as we have seen.

Others who are neither frightened away nor murdered are
found to be involved with the drug empire in some fashion. The
resignation of the acting attorney general, Alfredo Gutierrez Marquez in March 1988 is a good example. Gutierrez, who replaced
his murdered predecessor, had earlier created a sensation by
favoring the legalization of the drug trade and dialogue with the
traffickers. He had neglected to disclose that his brother owned
a farm with an airstrip that had been used by drug traffickers.

---

*At least 220 judges and court employees have been murdered in Colombia since
1981.[33]

The brother's next-door neighbor was drug lord Pablo Escobar.

The effectiveness of the drug lords in intimidating or bribing the nation's judiciary is not limited to these fairly crude methods. They also have been successful in infiltrating virtually every antidrug agency in the country. Indeed, the problem has become so serious that the American DEA, for one, has long hesitated to share intelligence with the Colombians for fear of compromising vital sources and methods. In the meantime, the narcotics chieftains are not content to play the part of outlaws. Why should they? In line with their growing ambition and sense of legitimacy—the superstate mentality once again—the narcos, particularly in Medellin, have acquired an image of social responsibility and political respectability. As Lee points out: "By sponsoring an array of public works projects—such as clinics, schools, sewage projects, housing developments, and sports stadiums—they have acquired a popular following."[35] These acts of pseudo-charity have had an effect. In 1982, one leading narcotics kingpin, Pablo Escobar, whom *Forbes* believes to be one of the world's most wealthy men along with Jorge Luis Ochoa, was elected to the Colombia congress largely as a result of his housing project, called "Medellin without Slums." That project has provided 2,000 of Medellin's poorest with brick housing that includes electricity, running water, and telephones.

But not all is entirely well with the *narco-traficantes*. In 1987, the same Pablo Escobar was forced to flee his home in his pajamas after the Fourth Brigade of the Colombian army, based in Medellin began raiding his homes and businesses.[36] Rumors placed Escobar in Panama after the assassination of Liberal party presidential candidate Luis Carlos Galán on August 17, 1989.[37]

Following Galán's assassination, President Barco cut the Gordian knot of extradition by announcing a new executive decree which would eliminate the judiciary in the process of extradition. This meant that the "extraditables," the drug kingpins of Cali and Medellin, could be sent to the United States for trial. The first one, Eduardo Martinez Romero, thirty-five, was a Medellin-based money launderer. According to the seventy-five-page indictment, Martinez was responsible for washing $1.2 billion in two years.[38] After Barco declared an all-out war on drugs following Galán's assassination, 1,279 drug traffickers were arrested, 9 suspects were extradited to the U.S., and at least $250 million in property, weapons, and drugs were confiscated by the Colombian government.[39]

But the key cartel figures who went into hiding in turn declared all-out war on the Colombian government from their hideouts. "We declare absolute and total war on the government . . . and all those who have prosecuted and attacked us," read the cartel's communiqué. Barco responded saying, "We will not be cowed. We shall prevail over the forces that would destroy our democracy and enslave our nation."[40] The government then rounded up 11,000 suspects (who were shortly released), seized massive amounts of narco-trafficker property, including more than four tons of cocaine, and promised unrelenting war against the cartels.[41]

The United States, which had given virtually no material support to the Colombian government in the past, rushed $65 million in helicopters, small arms, radios, trucks, jeeps, assault boats, ambulances, field gear, and antitank weapons in record time. In addition, another $261 million in assistance were promised to Colombia by the Bush administration.[42]

But in Colombia nothing is ever simple, especially in this struggle.

The murder of Galán, for example, remains a mystery, although the rumors in Colombia are that his assassination had been contracted for by the drug traffickers. In contrast to the American media's portrait of him, the Liberal party leader was not an ardent enemy of the cartels. Like many other Colombian politicians, Galán opposed extradition of Colombian drug traffickers to America on nationalistic grounds. Nor was he outside the mainstream of political opinion on the question of drugs, which is to say not much more than a platonic opposition to them. There is not a shred of evidence that anyone other than narco-traffickers did the killing, although proof has yet to be established that they did. In fact, if the cartel leaders ordered the murder, their motive remains a mystery. The murder of Bernardo Jaramillo Ossa, another presidential candidate (for the leftist Patriotic Union) on March 22 in Bogotá, created yet again more violence and protest on the right and the left. The aftermath of Ossa's murder revealed that the Colombian government, including President Barco, had been negotiating with the cartel. Barco of course denied this, but the "extraditables" issued a communiqué confirming the talks and negotiations with the government, denying any involvement with Ossa's killing: "Why attack someone who was firmly opposed to Colombia surrendering to the United States?"[43] In April 1990, reports from Bogotá confirmed that the drug traffickers had been pursuing negotiations with the government and therefore reducing their terrorist activities, while at the same time the terrorist groups on the left increased their terrorist acts.[44] Although Colombia's Supreme Court upheld Barco's decree to extradite drug traffickers wanted in the U.S., Barco allegedly promised Escobar that he would be tried in Colombia and would not be extradited to the U.S. When this was revealed and Barco denied any kind of negotiations with the cartel, Escobar, in a communiqué, pointed out that the talks between the cartel and Barco led to the release of hostages kidnapped by the cartel, and kept the extradition to the U.S. on hold for three months.[45]

One reason the military moved against Escobar in 1987 was his smear campaign against the Colombian army. Escobar's scheme called for the hiring of lawyers indirectly through a third party to launch a publicity campaign against alleged abuses of human rights committed during the first stage of the army's drive against the cartel, which included attacks on urban safe houses and rural cocaine-processing labs. But the army campaign ended and life continues as before, at least in Medellin. The proof? Well-known narco-leaders remain in the public eye. They continue to display their wealth and power, fearing little in the way of orthodox legal methods—until Galán's assassination, when the narco-terrorist war in Colombia took an apparent turn; since mid-August 1989, the drug lords have been on the run, fearing extradition to the U.S. But for many years the drug lords continued to expand their economic empires. In the last decade alone, the traffickers have bought a drug-store chain, supermarkets, office buildings, radio and television stations, popular soccer teams and, of course, the ultimate legitimizer in Colombia, land. And by land I don't mean a condo in Miami or a few acres in the suburbs— the leading narcos own vast haciendas chock-full of grazing cattle; one has an elaborate private zoo reminiscent of Xanadu in Welles's *Citizen Kane;* many have banana plantations. According to a widely accepted estimate in Colombia, cartel members have purchased 2.5 million acres within the last ten years. If true, this figure represents one twelfth of Colombia's total of arable land.* The buying frenzy was interrupted only briefly in the last year, when the army raids conducted in Medellin forced Escobar and others temporarily into hiding. The Fourth Brigade let up on the pressure after the discovery that the unit's intelligence officer was working for the narcos. The lifestyles and the property buying went on as usual.

Another reason for the narco boldness is the quality of the legal services they buy. Like their criminal counterparts in the U.S., the traffickers can afford the very best, which includes two former Colombian Supreme Court justices hired to work out the formulas that prevent bribed and frightened judges from properly adjudicating their cases. So although the narcos almost never come from Colombia's insulated upper class, they are more than happy to use the services of its members.

As part of their scheme to legitimize themselves, cartel members also exploit the Colombian media, openly and unapologetically, when campaigning against government attempts to put

*The estimates for property owned by the drug lords in Colombia derive from U.S. DEA intelligence sources.

them out of business. As a result, narco spokesmen in print have protested marijuana- and coca-leaf eradication as well as legal extradition. Their first argument, cast in populist terms, deeply deplores such eradication as subservient to the United States. One example is Carlos Lehder, a trafficker recently convicted for his crimes in Florida, who wrote a column in Medellin's newspaper *El Colombiano* in May 1982: "From any point of view, the extradition of nationals has no reason for existing and even less reason exists for making a pact with a country which does not even have borders with us and whose customs have not one iota of affinity with ours."[46] The traffickers and the Colombian left have had great success in turning the drug dealer debate into an "Us versus Them" argument that senior Colombia government officials have had enormous difficulty in countering—when they tried.

Polls conducted in the fall of 1989 indicate that two thirds of Colombians are opposed to extradition.[47] It is not surprising then that former President Belisario Betancur's attorney general, Carlos Jimenez Gomez, said recently that "Colombia should neither practice nor allow the surrender of its nationals to foreign justice."[48] A few years earlier, in 1985, Gomez, along with former president Alfonso Lopez Michelsen, met secretly with top narcotraffickers in Panama, where the latter offered to pay two billion dollars to help retire the foreign debt in exchange for amnesty. The offer was not accepted, but it hardly ended the narcos' diplomatic version of "Let's Make a Deal." A year after the rendezvous in Panama, the indefatigable narco-lords made another bold offer, this time to the United States government. In exchange for the dropping of all drug charges, the Medellin cartel would provide Washington with intelligence on Colombia's guerrillas, including information on Cuban and Libyan activities. In contrast to the offer on the debt, the second Colombia proposal was ludicrous. Needless to say, it was rejected out of hand.[49]

Nevertheless, at home they have been successful in neutralizing public opinion. Proof of this can be found in a 1985 public opinion poll published in another Bogotá daily, *El Tiempo,* which listed drug trafficking well below unemployment, street crime, and inflation as national problems. There is no evidence that in the ensuing years narcotics dealers will be seen as any larger a threat than before.

It is not surprising that only rarely will anyone speak out publicly against drug trafficking in Colombia. One exception, however, is the editor of Colombia's second leading daily, *El Espectador,* Juan Guillermo Cano, who responded to *El Tiempo's* broadside against extradition. Cano said, in part:

Mr. Plinio Apuleyo Mendoza has written in favor of the human rights of the assassins of Colombia's attorney general and the kidnappers of Bogotá's mayoral candidate Andres Pastrana Arango. . . . Congratulations, Mr. Mendoza. Your fine character has guaranteed your life, just as other esteemed national personalities, including prominent conservative party leaders, have guaranteed their lives too.

That is courage, indeed, that is really setting an example for the youth of Colombia and in particular for the marginal classes which will try to escape from absolute poverty by way of the easy money and by assuming the moral and ethical value of the new social class (the mafia).[50]*

Cano was right, of course, though few Colombians are brave enough to say this openly. His polemic also tells us that the chief threat posed by the cocaine kingpins is the destruction of the country's moral fabric and its embodiment, the legal system. "It's not an exaggeration to say that the legal system as we once knew it has broken down," an unidentified senior Colombian official told the *New York Times* in January 1988: "Even where there are honest judges, they are too scared to act," the anonymous official added.[51]

A year later it was disclosed that a Colombian judge had been

*Cano was assassinated outside the *El Espectador* building on December 17, 1989.

granted asylum in the United States. In fear of his life from drug traffickers and their guerrilla allies in the M-19, the magistrate, who remains anonymous, managed to avoid deportation from the United States in 1986 because he proved that he was living under a threat of death. The so-called roving magistrate had the power to investigate crimes anywhere in Colombia, as part of an elite corps of judges created to solve the problem of an intimidated judiciary; this, too, proved a failure. The judge in question argued persuasively that he could not trust his bodyguards, who may have had links with the drug traffickers. On top of that, he already had been kidnapped, shot at twice, and repeatedly threatened with death. His was hardly a unique case.

Granting the man asylum is unprecedented in American history. By doing so, the U.S. government in effect confers on the drug traffickers the powers of the state. Normally, protection is only granted to foreigners when they are subject to abuse by their own governments. Thus, the drug lords' reign of terror has set off a chain reaction within Colombia's political and legal institutions. All evade the issue to avoid the problem. For example, having been physically intimidated after the M-19 massacre, the Colombian Supreme Court ruled in June 1987 that the U.S.-Colombian extradition treaty was invalid. Why?

The Colombian Supreme Court argued that the implementing legislation had been improperly drafted. It has blocked the transfer of drug-trafficking cases from civilian to the less easily intimidated military tribunals, although the court has permitted a change of venue for terrorist cases, and has charged that the criminal element in Colombia is most feared. Colombia's legalism has been turned inside out to protect the narcotics traffickers, which effectively stymies any effort to combat the menace, an unfortunate domestic situation that seems to prevent any real changes. Due to public pressure the high court subsequently proceeded to hand the problem back to Colombia's executive and legislative branches by suggesting that new legislation could be drafted to put the extradition treaty once more into effect. Its congress has refused to consider any such thing, knowing full well that extradition to America is the one thing that the narco-traffickers fear most.

The Supreme Court recently passed off another "hot potato" by ruling that proper extraditions to the United States could take place under an earlier treaty signed in 1888, which could be done without separate rulings for each case by the judiciary. The court, pleased by its clever (but slightly warped) ruling, avoided biting the bullet by passing it on to the executive branch—but the president and his men were not impressed. In a pas de deux, then Attorney General Enrique Low Murta passed once more by insisting that the earlier 1888 treaty was null and void, having been superseded by the 1979 convention.

All of this must have amused the narco-traffickers, sitting in their Medellín and Cali palaces; they know that none of these legalistic maneuverings mean anything, in spite of President Barco's public statements to the contrary. For one thing, before this particular ruling *less than one percent* of the drug-smuggling cases had ever reached the courts for a verdict. What is worse, between 1976 and 1981 more than thirty drug traffickers "escaped" from jail with the complete cooperation of prison officials. In Colombia, getting out of the slammer is easy if you are rich and very dangerous. One such "escape"—that of Jorge Luis Ochoa, a true kingpin of cocaine—set off a bitter row between Washington and Bogotá. Yet after all of the diplomatic fireworks, which included an unprecedented close inspection of Colombian imports into the U.S. by the customs service, it came to nothing. Ochoa was free once again, ending any hope of the man's extradition through regular or irregular channels. The Ochoa affair, however, convinced many in the American government that Colombia was not on our side in the war against drugs. It was a sobering experience for bureaucrats who previously had made the drug issue a lesser priority.

The breakdown of the legal system with regard to drug trafficking has many more implications than the comings and goings

of one *narco-traficante*. The implications of institutional disintegration were captured perfectly by the State Department's
human rights report on Colombia in 1987:

[V]arious guerrilla groups, drug traffickers, organized bands of hired
killers, paramilitary "death squads," and independent elements of
the police and military acting outside the scope of their official duties
escalated the already high level of violence, directly challenging the
Government's ability to maintain order and preserve democratic institutions.[52]

The report concluded:

The failure of judicial institutions to investigate and resolve violent
crime encourages individuals to use violence as a means of resolving
conflict. Death squads, so-called civic "clean-up" operations, and
personal vendettas fueled by the ready cash of narcotics trafficking
all contribute to the progressive weakening of law enforcement and
judicial institutions and result in the generalized disintegration of
law and order.[53]

Vendettas? Colombians could teach Sicilians something on this
subject: On Easter Sunday in 1988, gunmen hired by the local
narco-traffickers attacked a peasant celebration of Christ's res-
urrection by killing forty-two men, women, and children in the
northwestern department of Cordoba. Why? To kill EPL guerrilla
leaders who were at the fiesta. Eight of them, in fact, were slain,
in reprisal for their extortion of narco-landholders in the area.
   The tearing of the country's moral fabric by drug lords has
affected even the Roman Catholic church. In February 1987, two
Colombian bishops informed the press that the church should
act as a mediator between the government and the narcotics
traffickers. One of them, Archbishop Samuel Buitrago of Popyan,
said that drug profits actually "invigorated" the Colombian econ-

omy. Although these statements were quickly repudiated by Cardinal Alfonso Lopez, it should be noted that the other would-be mediator, Dario Castrillon, bishop of Pereira, has admitted in the past to accepting trafficker alms—all in the name of the poor and our dear Lord, of course.

Although drug traffickers may take credit for accelerating the disintegration of Colombia's system of justice, they cannot be said to have begun the process. "Corruption," as Professor Peter Lupsha has observed, "has a long history in Colombia, along with contraband and violence. . . . [They] are parts of the foundation and infrastructure within Colombia that have so firmly supported the political economy of narcotics trafficking."[54] He is right. Smuggling has played an especially important role in the country's north coastal economy. Its particular geographic placement on both the Caribbean and Pacific coasts make contraband supremely profitable—and easy, in a country where the central government exercises little or no authority in the provinces. This tendency has been reinforced by Colombia's geography, where high mountains and rolling savannah have isolated communities for centuries.

By the time twentieth-century transportation came to South America, the pattern of local independence in Colombia, the first country to have scheduled air service, already had been firmly established for legal and illegal activities. This pattern also laid the basis for the country's many civil conflicts. Even now, a sense of nationhood—of one people—escapes many Colombians, who often think of the national government as the enemy or irrelevant to their lives, or sometimes as both. This attitude, of course, provides fertile soil for the guerrilla armies and the swarms of drug traffickers that plague the country not only to its profound harm, but to our own as well.[55]

Historically, Colombian earnings in illegal trade exceed even normal Latin American unlawful profits through smuggling. As a result, illegitimate always has competed with legitimate commerce, and throughout the years assumed at least a quasi-legitimate status in the popular imagination.* Colombia's long history of unlawful enterprise laid the foundations for the narcotics trade as well. But the narcotics industry could not flourish as it has without one other critical factor, and that is the drug traffickers' alliance with the guerrillas of Colombia.

That alliance is the basis for narco-terrorism. Without it, the problem could not have existed in this hemisphere, or would be very limited in scope. It has two fundamental characteristics. First, the economic incentive: Colombia's guerrilla armies have learned through long experience that drug money can provide them critically needed resources to carry out their revolution, and thus prolong the violence. Neither the Soviets nor the Cubans can supply the amount of aid that it would take to win, and the guerrillas can expect even less in the future as the Soviet bloc heads toward inevitable economic disintegration. As a result of that understanding, it now is estimated that of FARC's "fronts," its cadres collect "taxes"—that is, they receive protection money for guarding the illegal plots growing coca. They also protect the secret cocaine-processing laboratories and the landing strips that dot the Colombian countryside, and provide safe journey for aircraft bearing drugs to American customers.[56]

Second, the ideological incentive: there are now direct working links forged between the terrorist-guerrilla groups and the narco-traffickers to carry out acts of terrorism. The motives may be different, but their one goal is to destabilize and undermine the government. The evidence often is scattered and easily exaggerated, but what already is known is deadly and devastating. In the early 1980s, the FARC and the M-19 made agreements with at least several prominent narcotics traffickers. The deal was simple,

---

*In a meeting with Colombian academics in New York City in April 1990, Americans had a hard time explaining to the Colombians that the U.S., like many other countries, does not support second economies and black markets. At the end of the meeting, it was clear to all present that the Colombians were not persuaded.

straightforward, and mutually profitable. In exchange for guerrilla protection, the cartel would allocate a percentage of its drug profits to be spent on arms for the insurgents. Thus, while the drug lords had their gunmen enabling them to carry out their business, the guerrillas used the monies paid by the cartel to escalate their war.

Here in fact is where the Cubans came in again. As we have seen, the activities of the Colombian, Jaime Guillot-Lara, throws a bright spotlight on this fundamental arrangement. Already in the spring of 1982, then Assistant Secretary of State for Inter-American Affairs Thomas O. Enders told the Senate Subcommittee on Security and Terrorism that Colombian traffickers and communist guerrillas had come to a solemn agreement that also involved top officials of the Cuban government. According to Enders:

Since 1980, the Castro regime has been using a Colombian narcotics ring to funnel arms as well as funds to Colombian M-19 guerrillas. This narcotics ring was led by Jaime Guillot Lara, a Colombian drug-trafficker now in custody in Mexico. He has admitted to working for Havana in purchasing arms for the M-19. We have information that Guillot travelled twice to Cuba since October 1981 and that on the second visit he received $700,000 from the Cuban government to purchase arms for the M-19 guerrillas.[57]

Enders then explained how Guillot-Lara played a leading part in transferring arms from a ship to a Colombian plane that the industrious M-19 had hijacked, a skill that the group had perfected over the years with Cuban assistance. Providing security at the airstrip were five M-19 gunmen. In exchange, Guillot-Lara also supplied the M-19 with money by means of a bank in Panama. All of this, which by now should come as no surprise, was coordinated with the Cuban embassy in Bogotá.

That one deal is small change compared to the M-19's later involvement in the drug trade. I have already mentioned its attack on the Colombian Supreme Court. Here are the gruesome details of narco-terrorism in action:

The November 1985 assault on the downtown Bogotá Colombian Palace of Justice, within blocks of the presidential offices, took the lives of eleven members of the Supreme Court. Even more important, the terrorists from the M-19 destroyed thousands of records, which many believe was the original objective, making the prosecution of no less than *two hundred* key drug traffickers completely impossible. It was the kind of firepower and tactical skill that the Medellin cartel simply did not possess. It was also the deathblow to Colombia's system of justice.

In the four years that followed the attack, not one judge in Colombia has signed a single order of extradition to the United States for a known narco-trafficker. And why should anyone? If the government cannot protect the highest tribunal in the country, then it cannot save poor Juez Juan de Fulano of Pasto, who is poorly paid and carries little prestige in Colombia.

Recent evidence suggests that the M-19's relations with the Medellin cartel remain very close. This is particularly interesting, since the M-19 have now become a legitimate political organization. One Colombian-based American diplomat reported that after a week of army raids in Medellin on trafficker safe houses several years ago, a number of suspected members of the M-19 were captured by the military. According to the Fourth Brigade's commanding officer, General Jaime Ruiz, the arrested individuals "apparently served as liaison between the terrorists and the *narco-traficantes* in Medellin."[58] Having liaison officers does suggest a rather cozy relationship. And yet, the extent and permanency of the alliance is open to question. Unfortunately, the evidence is hazy at times and analysts have difficulty penetrating the levels of deception and misunderstanding. It would appear that the closeness of the drug traffickers' and the terrorists' relationship is not altogether perfect. Because the profits from the drug business are huge, the associations among these groups shift. If at times the right wing was targeted and massacred by both guerrillas and drug traffickers, at other times the left became the target. Since fall of 1989, it appears that so-called right-wing paramilitary groups were after "left-wing" terrorists and other organizations. But one cannot be too sure whether this is so, and if so, why or for how long.

The March 1990 *International Narcotics Control Strategy Report* issued by the State Department concluded: "There is now much greater awareness that the narco-guerrilla relationship runs the gamut from conflict to coexistence to cooperation, depending upon the location and groups involved. However, even in areas where traffickers and guerrillas are at war with each other, the guerrilla presence facilitates trafficker operations by weakening government control."[59]

Some of the strain may come from the fact that drug consumption is now a problem in Colombia. Only a few years ago, most Colombians thought of the cocaine trade as a North American disease from which Colombia profited, because most coca-leaf by-products ended up in North America. This is no longer the case. An increasing number of cocaine addicts are middle- and upper-middle-class Colombians. Far more serious, some 400,000 poor Colombians have become smokers of *basuco,* according to a 1987 Colombian ministry of health report. In the intervening time, the estimated number has climbed another 100,000. These figures have to be placed in context. The United States has a population eight times larger than that of Colombia. The former has "only" 875,000 regular users of cocaine and 500,000 heroin addicts; in Colombian terms, this means that the U.S. would have an equivalent of 4 million crack addicts among its marginal classes. As in Colombia, where the poor turn to crime to support their habits, such a total number would, of course, accelerate the already soaring crime rate astronomically. Thus, the introduction of drug consumption into Colombia has quickly turned that country into a jungle, as anyone can attest who has strolled the streets of Bogotá recently.

What, exactly, is *basuco?*

Basuco is from the residue of inferior coca base low in alkaloid, processed with gasoline. It is highly addictive, inexpensive, and very damaging to the brain. Like crack, *basuco* is something of an accident. The coca paste from which *basuco* is derived is from low-quality coca leaves grown only in Colombia. In the beginning, the Colombian drug traffickers wished to be independent from their Bolivian and Peruvian suppliers; as a consequence, they began to plant their own coca. Production soon rose from 6,000 acres in 1981 to 60,000 in 1988.[60]* Unfortunately for Medellin, the leaf grown is not of export quality, and as a result the narco-traffickers use it for local consumption in the form of *basuco*. With it came crack, which also is being increasingly consumed in Colombia's larger cities.

The prospect of dealing with a drug-addicted society apparently has promoted some rethinking on the part of the M-19. The use of crack and *basuco* by Colombia's urban poor, supposedly M-19's base of support, may be a contributing factor. While it is perfectly proper and ideologically sound to poison the population of the main enemy, the United States, destroying one's own is more difficult to accept. As Rensselaer Lee has observed:

Yet even if they do collaborate, narcotics traffickers and subversives do not share a common political or ideological agenda. Common sense suggests that guerrillas and drug operators have basically different goals: the former attempt to overthrow the government and to transform society, but the latter seek above all to be left alone, aspiring to a sort of quasi-legality within the political status quo.[62]

That makes good logic; unfortunately, while there is some truth in it, the proposition that in the distant future such interests might clash are not what now motivates most narco-traffickers and terrorists. The truth is, aside from past patterns of cooper-

*The available information about how much cocaine is being produced in Latin America is rather confusing. According to the State Department's March 1990 report, Colombia's cocaine crop reached only 105,000 acres in 1989.[61]

ation, the M-19 continued to provide the drug traffickers with badly needed kidnapping and killing services. The FARC also maintains its symbiotic on and off relationship with the cocaine cartel.[63] In April 1990, at the time of this writing, it seems to be off again. One of the reasons for the recent clash between the FARC and the traffickers may be FARC's involvement in the drug business.[64]

There is one final element in this extremely complicated mix and that concerns the death-squad activity of the *Muerte a Secuestadores* (MAS)—the "death to kidnappers" movement formed in the early 1980s by two drug traffickers. Their motives were simple. They were tired of their family members being held for ransom by various guerrilla groups, the FARC in particular. Soon the MAS included retired military officers in its ranks, and began a murder campaign of its own. Moreover, some drug dealers who became wealthy landowners have taken to hiring their own gunmen to protect them against guerrilla extortion. They have not been passive in their defense; private armies have cleared out insurgents in the Magdalena, Medio, Meta, and Cordoba provinces.[65]

There is also a hint of internecine activity among the traffickers themselves. This is particularly true for the so-called Medellin and Cali mafias. That conflict was demonstrated vividly when in March 1988, the Colombian army's intelligence arm released a series of letters and tapes indicating that a plot had been hatched by Pablo Escobar of the Medellin cartel to liquidate his rival, Gilberto Orejuela of Cali. The purpose? To take over the lucrative New York cocaine market, second only to that of Hollywood—Los Angeles, which the *cacenos* had been monopolizing profitably for years. The *New York Times* reported recently that the rivalry already cost the lives of 150 people, a toll which las led to a truce. Today both cartels are reported to have a share of the New York market, while cooperating on European ventures as well.[66] Although some observers once believed that the cross-city rivalry was only Colombian military "black propaganda" designed to create more divisions among the narco-traffickers, it is almost certain that the struggle has been for real and could resume in the future.[67]

Despite the strains between guerrillas and traffickers and within the ranks of the traffickers themselves, they continue to share one thing: a violent anti-Americanism. One is based ideologically in Marxism-Leninism, a view some traffickers, incidentally, claim to share; but all traffickers hate the United States, partly for deeply rooted cultural reasons, and also, in part, because of their fear and loathing of spending the rest of their lives in an American jail.[68]

Both fear and loathing are powerful motivators for the narco-traffickers. While they have bent Colombian governmental institutions to their will, they also have made themselves as indispensable as possible to the country's economy. In other words, Colombia could not do without cocaine-produced billions, a view not universally shared, however.

Richard Craig argues the reverse—that the drug trade incurs considerable costs. He lists six of them: (1) Craig estimates that the traffic is responsible for one fifth of the country's annual rate of inflation, which typically runs at 30 percent per year; (2) the trade swallows an increasingly large portion of the national budget in efforts to suppress the trade; (3) narco-trafficking contributes "substantially" to the illegal importing of some $300 million a year in luxury goods; (4) it has helped Colombia become a net importer of food because crops have been converted to the more profitable cultivation of marijuana and coca; (5) the narcotics industry has created a truly bizarre situation in which Colombia is the only country in the world where the black-market dollar sells for less than the official rate of exchange; (6) it has distorted Colombia's trade figures. Although many of the dollars earned in cocaine and marijuana remain abroad, some of the money filters back into the economy through the Central Bank's so-called *ventanilla siniestra* (side window)—where dollars are accepted and no questions asked.[69]

The "little window" was opened in 1976, after the Colombian government attempted to cash in on high coffee prices by placing new taxes on earnings. The inevitable result was that a major portion of Juan Valdez's coffee crop was smuggled out of the country, via the porous Venezuelan border. The "window" was a government effort to corral some of those lost dollars that were leaking out by government fiat in the first place.[70] This sort of Alice-in-Wonderland approach is common to the statist economies that are found everywhere in Latin America; Bogotá has kept its little window open even as we speak, and an increasing dollar flow is coming through—it has to, if Colombia is to keep its perfect record of servicing its foreign debt. In this regard, thanks in part to the narco billions, Colombia will continue to earn the admiration of the banks and the rest of the international financial institutions.

By 1985, in one year alone nearly a billion dollars crossed the counter, most of which is believed to have come from the sale of narcotics. For a $26-billion economy in 1987, that is not an insignificant portion of the whole.[71]* Yet whatever the economic cost, it is small in comparison to the damage done to the country's political and legal institutions. The reality is that in less than two decades the narcotics traffickers steadily have built a network of economic dependents. More than 100,000 peasants, for example, now make a better living growing coca leaf than they once did with subsistence food crops. The chain of loyalty down through the various stages of narcotics processing, of course, adds hundreds of thousands to the number of those who benefit from the drug industry economically.[72]

Can the Colombian government cope with such a formidable machine of crime and terror? Does the American government have the ability to help? The answer to both questions, at present, is no. For one reason, Colombian security forces never have been

---

*By 1988, the drug trade in Colombia represented an income of approximately $2 billion. Cocaine trafficking has increased and so, presumably, have the profits.

capable of suppressing either narcotics trafficking or guerrilla/ terrorist attacks, much less both. Worse, Colombia's security forces have deteriorated over the last decade. Another reason is that the defense budget was slashed by more than one half under former President Betancur, a sum only recently and partially restored by the present chief executive, Virgilio Barco, which hardly takes care of the problem. Here are a few of the problems the military and the police face: (1) Colombia's air force lacks trained pilots. In a country where much of the narcotics traffic travels by air, such a deficiency needs no further comment. (2) Aside from a lack of pilots, air mobility also is grossly deficient. The equipment simply does not exist in the quantity necessary to cover a country of Colombia's size, which is double that of France. (3) The central government's refusal to confront the issue of narco-terrorism has sapped the morale of officers and men alike. So, too, has its policy of pursuing a dialogue with the guerrillas when it is perfectly apparent that the latter use truces to strengthen their forces for the next round. (4) The weaponry of the armed forces is pathetically obsolete. It is a mixed armory from various countries and epochs—all of which make maintenance and replacement nearly a hopeless task. (5) Corruption has become a serious problem within the security forces. It is most apparent in the national police and local army commanders, who have been bought off either by the narcos or the guerrillas or both. The fear of infecting the rest of the army has led its top commanders to stay away from the job of fighting the narco-trafficker. The occasional exception is the Medellin-based Fourth Brigade.

As a result, Colombia possesses an ill-equipped army of 60,000, approximately the same size as that of Sandinista Nicaragua. It is supposed to carry on a two-front war. It does neither, of course. (The Nicaraguan armed forces, however, have more firepower than the Colombian general staff could ever imagine.) Of the total number of men available to Bogotá, perhaps only 25,000 are available for combat. And they face, according to one conservative

U.S. estimate, a total of 7,000 armed guerrillas and an unknown number of *narco-traficante* gunmen.[73] This ratio of little more than three and a half to one does not come close to the figure needed to defeat an entrenched narco-guerrilla force spread over inhospitable terrain that is double the size of France.

It is a very thin glaze of security. The vast FARC-dominated area of Colombia's southeast, for example, comprising one third of the country, is still protected by only a lightly armed, largely immobile brigade of 4,500 men. According to one estimate, the troop/guerrilla ratio in that region is no more than one to one, a fatal formula if ever there were one. Colombia's problems hardly end with this unfavorable count, however; consider the matter of armament. The army's weapons inventory reads like a *Jane's* of yesteryear. For the most part, soldiers still carry German G-3 rifles—the same worn-out weapons that the Salvadoran army got rid of in 1982. Artillery units have vintage U.S. 120-mm mortars, last seen in the Korean war where, incidentally, a Colombian battalion fought. They also have 105-mm howitzers and even pre–World War II Czech 75-mm "manpack" howitzers, designed for use in the mountains of Bohemia—not the Andes. The armor (such as it is) consists of 128 Brazilian Cascavel reconnaissance vehicles and 50 Urutu personnel carriers also from Brazil, of no use whatsoever in Colombia's jungles and trackless sierra. At least they have the virtue of being almost new. Now, the Colombian army would like to form a mechanized infantry battalion within each brigade. There is no money for this improvement in capability.

The actual upgrade plan (as opposed to the military's wish list) is far more modest. The G-3 eventually will be replaced with the Israeli Galil assault rifle and the U.S. M-60 machine gun, improvements that even if successful will only enhance the scrambled inventory problem. The maintenance and repair nightmare currently experienced by the Colombian armed forces should go on through the next generation of weapons acquisition, assuming, of course, that the regime survives another generation. The national police primarily are responsible for the war on drugs and they, too, complain about the lack of adequate equipment and training,[74] while the military lacks nearly everything else that distinguishes it from a casually armed mob. Spare parts, boots, canteens, first-aid kits, food, and ammunition are all in short supply. Regarding the last, one U.S. analyst estimates the army has a three-day supply of bullets. This makes any coordinated attack on Colombia's multiple guerrilla armies an impossibility. To rebuild an army into an effective counterinsurgency force means that Colombia must begin virtually from scratch. This is what El Salvador had to do in 1981, although San Salvador and Washington did it on a much smaller scale.

But these military defects hardly catalogue the government's weaknesses against the guerrilla and the narco-trafficker. Air mobility, critical in a large, mountainous country like Colombia, is almost totally lacking. The air force, a 6,200-man service, is no more than a flying club. It has well-trained pilots and excellent technicians, but there are not nearly enough of them. In fact, in terms of matériel the Colombian air force is worse off than the army, a situation also created by the Betancur budget cuts. Of all the services the air force suffered most from this misguided effort at making peace.

As of summer 1989, the Colombian air force has less than 300 craft, including such museum pieces as the French Mirage M-5 and A-37 Dragonflies (all of which have been grounded since the summer of 1986), and a handful of equally vintage T-33 Trainers. Jet aircraft, even ground-attack planes like the A-37, have a limited or even nonexistent role in effective counterguerrilla warfare; one needs helicopters to accomplish this. Colombia has few of these, and they are a mixed bag. The lack of spare parts keeps most of them on the ground, and maintenance problems are multiplied by the sheer diversity of the inventory. The Colombian air force owns no less than *seven* different types of helicopters, although at present all are U.S. made. Still, Colombia has fewer working choppers than El Salvador, even though the country is ten times larger in size and is fighting a two-front war against the guerrilla and the narco-trafficker. As a result, the Colombian air force is heavily dependent on confiscated aircraft, a situation perhaps unique in the world.

Currently, one sixth of Colombia's air force consists of up-to-date Cessnas and Pipers taken from the drug kingpins of Cali and Medellin. But if the military has problems, the first line of defense against both guerrilla and narcotics trafficker—the national police—are in far worse shape. Budget constraints are compounded by the fact that the police are a voluntary service. In short, there are not nearly enough of them to begin policing this vast South American country. They lack almost everything else; thus they are able to maintain permanent posts in only one half of the country's cities and villages. What they do have in matériel is wholly obsolete. Police still carry the M-1 carbine, a relic from World War II. Their enemies carry AK-47s and M-16s.

The police have another, even more serious problem, however. The drug lords have been highly successful in corrupting them. In that regard, retired General Jose Joaquin Matallana, former head of the Department of Administrative Security (DAS, Colombia's equivalent to the FBI), told the *Washington Post* that the national police are "profoundly corrupted," including the 1,800-man special antidrug unit.[75] The center of police corruption is Medellin, where two police chiefs and another 100 officers were dismissed in 1987 alone. This should not surprise anyone. Like all Latin American police, Colombia's "finest" are low paid and have no prestige. Working conditions are abominable. No wonder that when reviewing the state of Colombia's security forces one U.S. analyst concluded they are "stuck in a reactive mode . . . playing catch-up with the guerrillas." He added that "their response has been piecemeal, reflecting the absence of a national strategy or framework."[76]

Finally, it is difficult to disagree with another American government conclusion that the Colombian military (and police) are in worse shape than the Salvadoran army in 1979. That is perhaps the bleakest estimate of all.[77] Can the United States be of any help? It could be said that Washington has done enough already. In 1988, the U.S. Congress nearly eliminated the modest American military aid program.

The virtual elimination of U.S. military aid to Colombia is harmful in a number of ways, some obvious, some not so obvious. To begin with, it has reduced the amount of resources available to the Colombian security forces. Specifically, this will have an effect on key areas such as the purchase of helicopter spare parts. Since budget restrictions prohibit the Colombian armed forces from diverting funds from one program to another, the loss of U.S. aid will cut deeply into that crucial area. In addition, by withholding foreign military sales credits, the United States has forced Colombia to shop in other countries where state-owned arms industries are willing to finance Bogotá's purchases. This means the mixed-bag inventory problem will continue to worsen. The program reduction also undercuts our own credibility with the Colombians in arguing the seriousness of the problems they face from guerrilla and narco alike, all of which leaves us with one overriding conclusion: that Colombia's drug-trafficking problem and the guerrilla threat that goes with it are insoluble at the present time.

If the estimates are correct that the cartel(s) command at least $4 billion per year in revenue, then the problem is insurmountable because the central government has nothing to match it. If the *narco-traficantes* are to be beaten at all at some time in the future, their incomes must be radically reduced. How is that likely? The arrest of dealers and interdiction of drugs in this country have helped. The U.S. government claims to have seized $1.5 billion in drugs, equipment, and weapons, but this is merely a fraction of the total. It still remains a demand-side problem. Unless the appetite for illicit drugs lessens in the United States and Western Europe, the problem will perpetuate itself. In the meantime, narco-terrorism is an ongoing nightmare in Colombia, with all the consequences that has for the rest of us.

One one outside wall of Colombia's Palace of Justice are chiseled the words of Santander: "Arms have given us independence, Laws will give us freedom." It was, of course, the same Palace of Justice that the M-19, on orders from the lords of Medellin, hit in late 1985. No greater sacrilege of Colombia's institutions can be imagined. It was a direct declaration of war against everything Colombia and its founder, Santander, stood for. And it was as deliberately and cold-bloodedly done as the Japanese attack on Pearl Harbor in 1941. But President Betancur, unlike President Roosevelt, did not seize the initiative and rally the nation behind him. Instead, he is reported to have considered the M-19s' demand for negotiations while its *pistoleros* held the palace at gunpoint. Colombia's president was deterred only by the minister of war, who told Betancur if he did consider negotiating then the army would take over and he would be out of a job. Only at this point were the soldiers ordered to recapture the Palace of Justice, which today remains a blackened ruin, a standing mockery of Santander's *pronunciamento* on independence and freedom.

Toward the end of 1989, President Barco had a minor victory in his war on drugs—with a lack of popular support, because the Colombians seem to be fed up with the continuing violence that reached its height in December with the bombing of DAS headquarters in Bogotá. The half-ton dynamite bomb that created a thirty-foot-deep crater and damaged buildings forty blocks away killed fifty-two people and injured at least 1,000.[78] Jose Gonzalo Rodriquez Gacha, rumored to be behind the bombing, was killed in a shoot-out with Colombian forces in the seaside town of Covenas, not far from Cartagena. It was believed that Gacha was in this part of Colombia planning the assassination of President Bush during his participation in the drug summit in Cartagena in February 1990. Unfortunately for President Barco and the Colombian people, Gacha's death will have little effect in the overall control exercised by the drug cartel in Colombia.

The price Colombia is paying to fight what is considered by

many to be the United States's war on drugs seems to be too high for the Colombians. Both the outgoing President Barco and the incoming President César Gaviria had warned that the Colombian people have difficulties in understanding their sacrifice. As for U.S. help, "there have been more words than results," stated President Barco on June 3, 1990, before leaving Bogotá on a business trip to Washington, D.C. Colombia's minister of economic development followed, "If President Bush is offering cooperation, why doesn't it filter down to the bureaucracy?"[79]

In his inauguration speech, President Gaviria promised to fight terrorism, the terror that stemmed from drug trafficking, and the power of the drug cartels. M-19 is no longer a terrorist organization but a legitimate party with representatives in the government. On June 19, the Constitutional Assembly dismissed the Congress, and new elections were called for the end of the year. In the meantime President Gaviria was presiding by decree. He appeared to be in control of the country and the economy, but the reality was quite different. The power of drugs was behind the changes in the Constitution, the dismissal of Congress, and the abolition of extradition to the United States. Proof of this was evident when Pablo Escobar surrendered to the government the very same day extradition to the United States was abolished. Escobar and several of his associates now pass their time in a hacienda built by Escobar and guarded by his own men. The judicial process, we are told, will be secret in order to protect the judges. There has been no outcry from the U.S. government about these changes in Colombia. These events signal the legitimization of drug production and drug trafficking as the major commodity of Colombia. Recently Pablo Escobar and Jorge Ochoa have been declared the two wealthiest individuals in the world.

5

Peru and Bolivia: The Spreading of the Empire

——————— ▌▌▌▌▌ ———————

The home of narco-terrorism may be Colombia, but its neighbors in South America are hardly immune to its effects. Indeed, the process is a fluid and dynamic one, and for the present the momentum is on the side of the cocaine traffickers and their guerrilla associates. As a result, far more than Colombian legal and political institutions are in danger. In fact, it is not inconceivable that in another decade much of South America could be faced with similar and unprecedented problems of corruption and violence *assuming present trends continue* and little or no effective action is carried out. Then, maybe, politicians in Washington would realize that the threat to the national security of the U.S. had really materialized. How would this affect the United States? Colombia and Peru seem to provide a very good example of that future.

Before examining the truly dismal narco-terrorist picture in Colombia's neighbor, Peru, let us look briefly at two other countries where the record so far has been relatively encouraging: namely, Venezuela and Ecuador. I say relatively because the picture could change drastically at any moment. Moreover, neither are without problems in the drug field, and these could grow quickly if there is any relaxation of current efforts. But compared to Colombia or Peru, or Bolivia for that matter, these two bordering republics have put up a pretty good fight.

First, Venezuela. The country of Simón Bolívar's birthplace is no stranger to violence, although narcotics trafficking and its terrorist connection have been kept at a relatively low level so far. Venezuela has been a democracy for over thirty years. This is a dramatic reversal of form in a country that knew little but the rule of the strongman for a century and a half. Juan Vicente Gómez, who ran the country with an iron hand for a generation until 1935, was the model of Venezuela's darker past.

Democracy did not come easy. Shortly after the election of President Rómulo Betancourt in 1959, the beginning of Venezuela's turn to democracy, Fidel Castro targeted the country and specifically Betancourt himself for guerrilla and terrorist violence. Despite (or more likely because of) its democratic character, the Cuban *caudillo* threw everything he had into the battle against the embattled regime in Caracas. The climax of Castro's bloody assault on Venezuelan democracy was Venezuela's December 1963 presidential election. As in the case of El Salvador nearly twenty years later, the Cuban dictator was determined to wreck it. As a consequence, his Venezuelan followers, who made up the so-called *Fuerzas Armadas de Liberacion Nacional* (FALN), unleashed a wave of terror up to election day itself. The FALN modestly proposed to shoot anyone who turned out to vote, a fine example of moral degradation in the whole, sad history of Cuban-sponsored terrorism in this hemisphere. With civic defiance, the Venezuelan electorate ignored the threats. Havana's bloody fingerprints were all over this intended massacre of innocents when a cache of Cuban arms was found on a Venezuelan beach weeks before the election.

After its failure to wreck the elections, the FALN was put on the defensive by a revitalized army and national police supported by a people sick of the Castroite gunmen. Venezuela's determined and decisive action served it in good stead. Unlike Colombia, where the communist guerrilla armies were never put completely out of action, Venezuela has made sure that they would not be revived by maintaining its democratic institutions, by economic reform and growth, and by keeping its security forces intact, all of which has kept narco-terrorism from thriving.

But not all is well by a long shot, and Venezuelan authorities are keenly aware that the shadow is growing larger. Already, large amounts of marijuana (at least 3,700 acres) are grown in western Venezuela near the Colombian border. As far as officials in Caracas know, coca leaf is not. But cocaine traffic through Venezuela is growing rapidly. Early 1990 DEA figures estimate that as many as eighty tons of cocaine are moved through Venezuela annually.[1] Furthermore, Colombian guerrillas are said to be providing the growers the same kind of protection they provide in Colombia.

The Colombian cocaine is shipped across the porous two-thousand-kilometer border following age-old routes established by earlier generations of smugglers, who moved everything from coffee to cattle. With the Colombian drugs have come wandering bands of Colombian guerrillas who when caught have been dealt with harshly by the Venezuelan army. Unlike Bogotá, Caracas was not long in throwing the military into the fight against both guerrillas and traffickers—largely because of their foreign origin, and because they are difficult to tell apart. The Venezuelans tend to shoot first and then go through the formalities. There is also another reason. They have no intention of repeating their experience in the 1960s, nor do they want to go the way of their Colombian brothers. As these incursions have increased in recent years, Caracas has strengthened its presence in the area. Regular army troops reinforced National Guard units assigned to protect the border. This changed when the pro-Castro Colombian guerrilla group, the ELN, attacked Venezuelan border outposts killing seven Guardsmen in 1987.

Since the Colombian army has been stretched thin to the point of invisibility, the Venezuelans have not hesitated to engage in hot pursuit of traffickers and guerrillas who also on occasion have kidnapped Venezuelan ranchers. Their troops have crossed into

Colombian territory on a number of occasions at least with the tacit consent of Bogotá. In fact, the Venezuelan side of the border is considered so secure by the Colombians that Bogotá has proposed to reroute its oft-attacked oil pipeline, vital for foreign exchange, through Venezuela. The proposal, however, has drawn little interest in Caracas.

Still, Venezuela's problems with narcotics do exist, and they are getting worse. Narcotics trafficking through Venezuela is increasing steadily, and its large consumer-minded middle class has developed a taste for drugs.[2] Even worse, money laundering through Venezuela's wide-open banking system is already a serious problem and corruption has been on the rise.[3] These problems are not likely to be corrected in the near future. Venezuela suffers from the Colombian spillover despite the tough measures taken, although it has not yet reached disastrous proportions.

The same can be also said for Ecuador. But like Venezuela, this small Andean republic sandwiched between Peru and Colombia has its share of problems and they, too, could grow worse in a very short period of time. Fortunately for Ecuador, the country has never been high on Fidel Castro's list of priorities. The tiny would-be guerrilla grouplets of the 1960s got nowhere. One little band of university students, would-be Che Guevaras, hiked about the sierra for two entire days, then promptly surrendered to the police, tired, footsore, and anxious for a warm bed.[4]

Neither Castro nor Che Guevara were idolized in Ecuador, in contrast to other Latin American countries, although the country has its usual share of parlor revolutionaries. The Andean peace and quiet, however, was rudely shattered after the 1979 Sandinista victory in Nicaragua and the nearly coincident emergence of the M-19 in Colombia. Both, in fact, have been instrumental in training, supplying, and even directing a new Ecuadoran terrorist organization, the *¡Alfaro Vive Carajo!* (AVC), which first appeared in 1981.

Like the M-19, AVC first attracted attention and publicity by

Robin Hood gestures. Like the M-19 and the earlier *Tupamaros* of Uruguay, the AVC soon turned violent with a wave of kidnappings, bank robberies, and assassinations. At its peak in the early 1980s, AVC may have had as many as 3,000 cadres plus thousands more as sympathizers and supporters. AVC's relationship with the Colombian M-19 appears to be close. "They are the same thing," said then Ecuadoran President Leon Febres Cordero in early 1986, who also stated that AVC members were caught with narcotics in their possession.[5]

Indeed, when four AVC terrorists were shot and killed by police rescuing a prominent banker who the AVC had abducted, three of the four kidnappers killed turned out to be Colombian, and members of the M-19 to boot. Quito's officials also have charged that the Colombian terrorists in fact planned and helped execute the kidnapping, an operation apparently beyond the capability of the Ecuadoran AVC.[6] In addition, according to American intelligence AVC's top cadre received training in Nicaragua and El Salvador, where they fought with FMLN units for "live fire" training.[7] AVC has been involved in drugs as well, once again copying its M-19 mentors. But the extent of its involvement in drug trafficking is still unknown. What is known is that the Ecuadoran government under its conservative President Febres launched a successful attack on the AVC, putting it virtually out of business by 1988.

The government has pressed narcotics traffickers hard as well. Unlike other South American republics, its officials were convinced that narco-traffickers were not just an American problem. Ecuador has the problem under better control than most. Whether that situation will last under the new government of President Rodrigo Borja, which is much further to the left and less eager to cooperate with the United States, is a different question entirely. In any case, Ecuador is far from the kind of problems that are bringing devastation to Colombia and, as we shall see, Peru.

Peru: Are the Bad Guys Winning?

Peru is the world's leading producer of coca, and narco-terrorism has now reached regime-threatening proportions. In Colombia *only* the legal system has been smashed; the government in Bogotá staggers on, at least for the near future. The Medellín cartel and the guerrilla armies may have achieved a strategic stalemate, and their presence is considered now a permanent fact of life in the country. In Peru, on the other hand, the entire political system is now at risk. If the Shining Path is not stopped, it will be no exaggeration to say that Peru may become the first South American country to be ruled by a Marxist-Leninist government that took power through violence and financed its victory through narcotics trafficking. Whether Mario Vargas Llosa or Alberto Fujimori wins the upcoming presidential elections, the survival of Peru as a democracy depends on the ability of the Peruvian government to dismantle Shining Path.

How could such a probable outcome develop with so little notice? For one thing, South America is not a high priority for many Western governments. As for the United States, with its decade-long preoccupation with Central America, even a moment's thought about Peru had, for a long time, proved to be too much effort. Perhaps the attack on the DEA's Santa Lucía base at the Upper Huallaga Valley on April 10, 1990 will change this.[8] Yet Peru's dire straits are hardly exclusively the result of American neglect. The burden of blame must fall largely on the Peruvian political class. The administration of Fernando Belaunde Terry, for example, virtually ignored Peru's drug problem despite repeated warnings from U.S. officials and diplomats. The succeeding government of Alan Garcia not only ignored the warnings at first, but also plunged Peru into ruinous economic policies that have made its fight against narco-terrorism a feeble and unwinnable affair.

There is more, however. Narco-terrorism in Peru began as a
small problem, occurring in stages, and only developed fully in
the last few years. In the beginning, narcotics and terrorism were
two separate streams, largely ignored by Lima when both were
mere trickles. Narcotics were an American problem, and the terrorists hardly more than backland bandits, or so the Lima authorities thought. The terrorist stream, now a wild and roaring
river, no longer can be ignored. Its most important element is
the so-called Shining Path (*Sendero Luminoso*) guerrilla movement. The drug stream is composed of mostly small landholders,
growers of high-quality coca leaf, who began supplying the Colombian cocaine producers in the early 1970s. Peru's coca-leaf
industry, which had grown coca for centuries in relatively small
amounts for local consumption (as in Bolivia), thus suddenly
mushroomed when Colombian narco-traffickers found a bonanza
in the seemingly insatiable American craving for new stimulants.

At first, Peru's guerrilla groups, principally the *Senderos*, had
little to do with the drug trade. Founded in 1970, the Shining
Path is as ambitious politically as its name is pretentious.* Its
major goal is to promote socialism à la Mao and to eliminate so-
called Yankee imperialism. Through the years, the *Senderos* have
lacked neither ambition nor pretension. Nor can they be matched
anywhere in the region for sheer brutality, no small achievement
in a place where multiple communist insurrections over the last
thirty years or more have led to the loss of several hundred thousand lives. In the last eight years, some 14,000 lives have been
snuffed out, with the death toll rising steadily each year.[10]

Unlike most Latin American guerrilla and terrorist groups in-
variably led by upper-class white radicals (Fidel Castro himself
being the role model for the *caudillo blanco*), the *senderos* are

---

*José Carlos Mariátegui founded the Peruvian Communist party in 1978. His
essay "Seven Essays about the Peruvian Reality," had an impact far beyond Peru.
Mariátegui, who died at the age of thirty-five, was also a brilliant polemicist
indicting the many ills of present-day Peruvian society while celebrating in lyrical
terms a mythical Inca communal past. Marxism became his tool of analysis.[9]

something quite different. Gabriela Tarazona-Sevillano, one of the few Peruvian scholars tracking the movement, observes:

Shining Path's recruits are the sons and daughters of the Indian (Quechua-speaking) inhabitants, who have had access to education. Their leaders are university students and graduates who are highly intelligent and well educated in the arts and sciences. Sendero has also recruited from white middle class families . . . although not as extensively as from the Indian-Mestizo population.[11]*

The *Senderos* thus sank their roots in the Indian and mestizo community from the beginning, in sharp contrast to, say, Che Guevara's disastrous experiment in revolution without a local native base, which occurred in Bolivia in 1967.

The *Sendero* movement was founded by Abimael Guzman, a professor of philosophy enamored with the teachings of Mao Tse-tung, who taught and recruited at the University of San Cristobal de Huamanga in Ayacucho, the southern Peruvian stronghold of the ancient Incas with a still largely Indian population. However, unlike nearly every other revolutionary leader in Latin America, Guzman has cultivated an aura of mystery, including the recurring rumor that he is dead. Most intelligence reports say that Guzman—also known as Comrade Gonzalo—is very much alive, directing an increasingly successful insurgency.

In fact, Guzman's success has fed on the radically two-dimensional nature of Peruvian society. A small, white, middle and upper class still commands most of the country's resources. The mestizo and Indian majority—the latter in particular—for centuries have been either shunned or exploited by the descendants

---

*There is one more Peruvian narco-terrorist group that is worth mentioning, the so-called Tupac Amaru Revolutionary Movement. Unlike the Shining Path, Tupac Amaru is not rooted in the Indian community, but resembles closely the Castro-style urban-based revolutionary terrorist movements of the 1960s and 1970s. Indeed, it does have the support of Havana (and Managua). Smaller than the *Sendero*, it, too, has attempted to cash in on the drug trade, although with less success.[12]

of the Spanish conquistadors. Left-wing reforms carried out by a largely mestizo military in the 1960s and 1970s made matters worse by raising expectations while the economy slowed down even further because of state-driven experiments that failed to work, leaving less for everyone.

Although the military-imposed "revolution" failed and civilians were allowed to return to power through elections in 1980, the steady stream of propaganda promoting *campesino* and Indian rights (not to mention the inciting of class envy) had a deadly effect on this bifurcated society. According to Tarazona-Sevillano:

What is remarkable about this period of time is the pervasive indoctrination throughout the countryside, where slogans were used such as "The Landowner will never eat from your work again," and "The Land is for the ones who work it." Deep human feelings of revenge and hatred were exacerbated, and indeed, in many parts of the territory, the process of agrarian reform was cruel and bloody.[13]

But the matter did not end with the growing frustrations of oppressed and impoverished Indian and mestizo peasants. Tarazona-Sevillano explains:

Important in this historical context was the "consciousness raising" of the youth in the universities, especially in the University of Huamanga. In that institution, which particularly served the Indian community, students were required to do the "mita," field work in the villages around the area. This field work was an effective way to form the new moral consciousness at the grass roots. Additionally, in the University of Huamanga there were extra-curricular activities . . . where Marxism-Leninism-Maoism was discussed.[14]

All of this ferment led to something that was not just talk. In May of 1980 the leaders of the *Sendero Luminoso* launched the "armed fight" by burning ballot boxes during a national election in one small village in the sierra. Six months later, *Sendero* activists were stringing up dead dogs on lampposts in the posh suburbs of Lima. The dogs, symbols of what Peru's white rulers could expect, became the gruesome trademark of a revolution that played by no other rules but its own.[15]

Although the *Senderos* remained active in the capital and other major cities by blowing up electric-line pylons (causing extensive blackouts) and by assassinating major political figures, the guerrillas always have made their major effort in the countryside, in good Maoist fashion. The Shining Path gradually has extended its influence in rural areas beginning in the south and spreading to the north. The tactics are always the same: *Sendero* units move into a new village where they indoctrinate the Indians; attendance of these classes in revolutionary thought is mandatory. Shirkers are murdered, usually in the most grisly fashion possible. Local officials, including police, are killed out of hand. This combination of cruelty and the fact that *Sendero* recruiters speak Quechua—something that no Peruvian revolutionary of the 1960s would ever have done (Hugo Blanco and Luis de la Puente Uceda come to mind)—have made the Shining Path a formidable if not unconquerable enemy in less than a decade. By the mid-1980s, *Sendero Luminoso* had become a national movement. Guerrillas operated in each of the six zones into which the country had been divided, and the *Senderos* did so apparently without Soviet-bloc support. Even more remarkably, they fought their war with primitive weapons, ancient rifles and dynamite acquired from either the ill-equipped and dispirited police or from Peru's many mining centers, where explosives are available in abundant supply. One report estimates that by 1986 the *Senderos* had over 400,000 sticks of dynamite.[16]

Noteworthy, too, is that the *Senderos* have built their movement without any aid from Peru's active but more conventional left. The main parties in the United Left coalition led by a former mayor of Lima, Alfonso Barrantes, consider the Shining Path as "sectarian and authoritarian" (!), and armed tactics unjustified, although as Marxists the UL have warned the government that its response to the *Senderos* was equally illegitimate.[17] Having it both ways, of course, is nothing new for noncombatant Marxists, but it is unlikely that they will have any influence whatsoever on the *Senderos*. Although Shining Path is a growing movement, it is still a matter of debate as to how many guerrillas it can field. One expert gives the following estimate:

Judging from the presence of Sendero not just in the Department of Ayacucho but in 15 departments out of 24 in Peru, we can conclude that their numbers are growing and they now have "bases of support." Intelligence sources indicate that militants of the party are estimated to be around 5,000, and activists around 20,000. But still in every shanty town of Lima, and in the rural population not integrated into the productive process, of the city or the countryside, there are potential Senderistas.[18]

That estimate almost surely is a cautious understatement. With the Peruvian economy disintegrating with negative growth rates of 10 percent or more and 8,000-percent inflation as of mid-1989 thanks to the relentlessly foolish Alan Garcia, the *Senderos* as never before are recruiting throughout the country in both the *campo* and the densely populated cities with their teeming slums and desperately unemployed millions. But sheer numbers and a revolutionary ideology form only a part of the terrorist threat in Peru; what has placed that country in even deadlier danger is the relatively recent marriage of this Marxist-Maoist movement with narcotics trafficking.

Peru long has been the globe's biggest producer of coca leaf. With Bolivia, the two grow about 90 percent of the world's supply. Moreover, half of America's cocaine comes from Peruvian coca. And much of the leaf is concentrated in the immensely fertile, 150-mile-long Upper Huallaga Valley that lies about 400 miles north of Lima. Production has been rising rapidly: it more than quadrupled between 1980 and 1986, with a present area of illicit coca-leaf cultivation now estimated at somewhere between 350,000 and 420,000 acres.[19]

In short, the Upper Huallaga has become the principal artery of the Colombian drug empire. If severed, it would make the Medellin cartel's ability to maintain the level of narcotics flow out of their laboratories difficult indeed. Needless to say, this is not presently happening. In fact, the area of cultivation still appears to be expanding, with an estimated 80 percent of the farmers now in the coca-leaf business.* No wonder. The local growers, often impoverished peasants who have migrated to the region, have cultivated and sold their product with little effort at good prices to Colombian narco-traffickers. In return for the leaf to be processed into cocaine in Colombia, the traffickers supply cash and police protection through either bribery or murder.

Yet relations between the Colombian narcos and the Peruvian peasants have not been all that amiable in the past. As Professor Tarazona-Sevillano explains:

[T]he peasant growers bear the risk of getting caught by the police: they have a strong need to organize because the traffickers pay them in advance and it is up to them to deliver the coca leaf and to confront the police. . . . If they do not deliver, the consequence is certain death. The peasant growers organize in order to defend their economic interest by negotiating better prices for their crop and to fight the forces that would interdict their trade. The daily experience of open corruption on the part of government officials reinforces this perception.[20]

Conveniently, the *Senderos* began appearing in the valley in strength after several years of reconnaissance and propagandizing, activities that started in 1983. The Shining Path cadre were able to offer peasant growers "protection" against narco-traffickers from Colombia as well as the police. In response, although the alliance remains uneasy and at times unwanted, the drug smug-

---

*As stated by Alberto Fujimori, one of Peru's presidential candidates, April 14, 1990.

glers have accepted the *Senderos*, especially in their joint confrontation against the police and the army.

President Garcia recently summed up the situation best:

[The Huallaga] is a strategic zone for the country's future. It is strategic because what the subversives want to do here is block all roads and prevent the Huallaga region from being connected to the rest of the country. This is how subversion has a direct connection abroad. Colombian airplanes and drug traffickers have direct connections abroad, while the Huallaga Valley is isolated from the country. Large amounts of money are taken from this valley. Subversives also obtain weapons, which are probably brought in by those planes. Young men are probably also recruited here.[21]

Strip that statement of the "probablies" and one has an accurate picture of what his administration and future governments face in Peru. That relationship continues up to the present moment, but the *Senderos* are not sitting still. According to Tarazona-Sevillano:

Since April 1987, Sendero has started to take control of each town in the Upper Huallaga Valley and to make them "Liberated Zones," expelling the police and reestablishing order:—ending prostitution, killing homosexuals, administering justice in their unique way. They govern the towns, even to the extent of charging tolls for entry. They attack police stations and burn them, kill police and confiscate their weapons.[22]

Virtual control of the Upper Huallaga has been a major step forward for the *Senderos*. With their hands on the drug trade, the guerrillas have now increased their resources enormously. Previously, they had scraped along with what little they could collect from the impoverished Indian and mestizo populations living in the bleak sierra. Now, the lush Huallaga guarantees them far more.

One conservative estimate: the valley generates some $700

million each year. Assuming the *Senderos* collect a tax of 5 percent, revenues would amount to $35 million annually, a figure that surely underestimates the Shining Path's bonanza. Others believe that the drug trade alone generates some $500 million and that the guerrillas take the lion's share of that amount;[23] some calculate that earnings from coca leaf production in Peru vary from $500 million to $1 billion.[24] With a rapidly building war chest, it is not difficult to imagine that the *Senderos* soon will be purchasing far more sophisticated war material to continue their attack on an increasingly beleaguered regime. Nor is that the end of it; in the last three years, the Shining Path has initiated a similar pattern in the Lower Huallaga Valley, an immense jungle area that the guerrillas are fast consolidating as one more base of support.

But their supreme demonstration of power to date occurred in mid-May of 1988, when the Shining Path issued an "armed strike" order to cease work for three days in Peru's heartland. An estimated one million Peruvians obeyed that order, which effectively cut off food, energy, and export minerals from three provinces to Lima, the capital—a reassurance from the *Senderos* that their Maoist-style strategy to encircle the capital while controlling the countryside was very much on schedule.[25] The government in reaction did nothing. At the same time, the Shining Path ordered the 500,000 citizens of Huancayo to give the visiting President Alan Garcia the cold shoulder. By day, the president saw only a few sullen people on the streets. The night was punctuated with dynamite explosions.

If this is an insurgency out of control, what is the Peruvian government doing about it? The answer seems to be, very little. Whatever is done is too late and at times utterly contradictory in nature. Here is a representative sample:

• It took the Peruvian government until May of 1989 to declare a "total war" on the Shining Path. To do so it appropriated the miserly sum of $21 million to carry on the struggle. This amount is smaller than is currently available to the *Senderos* each year from its non-narcotics revenue alone.

- In the Upper Huallaga, police and army units rarely venture from their garrisons. Those who do are consistently ambushed. At present, ten policemen a month are murdered in the valley. Meanwhile, forty employees of Peru's Coca Reduction Agency have been killed—a toll that caused Lima to suspend the manual coca eradication program in February 1989.
- After approving the use of herbicide on the Huallaga's coca crop President Garcia reversed himself and banned air-borne weed-killers three months later, effectively eliminating any real attempt to combat the problem.[26]

None of this comes as good news. But the situation is in fact worse than that. Consider the U.S. efforts to help Peru combat its growing narco-terrorist problem. Because of congressional cut-backs in Washington's security assistance programs and because of priorities in the Middle East and Central America, Peru gets next to nothing in military assistance. The chief supplier for Lima's armed forces has been the Soviet Union, which for decades has cheerfully supplied heavy tanks and supersonic air-craft—anything, that is, expensive and wholly inappropriate to wage war against narco-terrorists—to the mostly conventionally minded Peruvian armed forces. To this day the military still believes the main enemy remains Chile and not the *Sendero Luminoso*, much less the Tupac Amaru. Moreover, even if the military were to fully engage itself in the narco-terrorism war, it has virtually no resources to spend on the needed equipment; and Peru is unlikely to produce those resources, at least in the foreseeable future. Still, the question is largely moot considering the army's diffidence to that which it considers a police matter. Thus the burden of American aid has fallen on the Drug Enforcement Administration.

Undermanned and underresourced, the DEA has zeroed in on the Upper Huallaga as the center of its effort. The fight has not gone well; in fact, it had been going badly for the past year, until the successful defense of the DEA base in Santa Lucía when it was attacked by Shining Path in April 1990. For example, by mid-1989, of the nine helicopters that the agency had loaned Peru's embattled narcotics police, only three were still function-ing. All were riddled with bullets, although none had been shot down. At the beginning of 1989, the forty Americans engaged in the antinarcotics drive, including a contingent of DEA agents, were forced to move their headquarters out of Tingo María, the Upper Huallaga's principal city. Their safety no longer could be guaranteed, which forced a daily commute from distant Lima, thus cutting into their effective time on duty, occasionally with disastrous results.[27]

But worse was yet to come. Another operation, dubbed "Snow-cap," in which DEA agents were assigned to accompany para-military strikes on narco-traffickers in the Upper Huallaga, also had been suspended. The reason? Too dangerous.[28] Ironically, when the program was initiated, critics of the operation warned that the risks involved would result in a withdrawal—the kind of retreat that would only encourage both the traffickers and their *Sendero* allies. DEA spokesmen dismissed the warnings at the time as "hyperbole."[29] United States authorities drew in their horns even further after an American-owned Cessna airplane crashed on its way to Lima from the valley. On board were five State Department contract employees and the chief of Peru's Coca Reduction Agency. Though neither Lima nor Washington ever came to any conclusion regarding the cause of the crash, sabotage was never eliminated as a possibility.[30]

That left the Bush administration with one last turn of the card in regard to Upper Huallaga. With U.S. assistance, in mid-1989 the Peruvian police began constructing a fortified base in the center of the valley. According to a *New York Times* report: "From the base, helicopters equipped with machine guns are to carry eradication teams to coca fields at the surrounding Upper Hual-laga Valley. Moving along within tight defensive perimeters set up by the Peruvian police, workers are to cut down coca plants with American-supplied gas-powered pruning saws."[31] The actual clearing work is supposed to be done by a small, 150-man police unit trained and paid for by the United States. Cost: $10 million.

There are several problems with this proposed effort aside from its relatively modest size. First, operations were not to begin until 1990, leaving the *Senderos* and their erstwhile allies from Colombia ample time to expand the range of operations. Second, the strategy is aimed at clearing, but not holding. After the coca plants are cut down, the police will return to Santa Lucía, leaving a thoroughly enraged peasantry more dependent on the guerrillas than ever before. Moreover, there is nothing to prevent the coca crop from being replanted at a greater distance from the police camp. Rapid cultivation of coca is taking place with or without police action, and it greatly exceeds the present eradication effort. In the meantime it is not very likely that this one operation can even keep up with the expanded production. In the peak year of eradication, 1988, some 11,000 acres of mature plants were cut down, a fraction of the 250,000 to 350,000 acres estimated under cultivation.[32]

In short, the prospects for both reducing the supply of coca from Peru and eliminating the *Sendero* presence in the Upper Huallaga are very dim indeed; and what is true for that one valley applies to the rest of this much-battered Andean nation. No one in Lima or Washington yet has summoned up the will or the resources even remotely close to matching the narco-terrorist effort in Peru. Without either, in time it is almost certain that the wrong side will win. On June 10, 1990, Alberto Fujimori was selected as Peru's new president. Unknown before the election, this engineer, the son of Japanese immigrants, faces a country on the verge of catastrophe. Mr. Fujimori's plans to resolve his country's problems were designed by *Instituto Libertad y Democracia* (ILD), headed by Hernando de Soto. Its focus is to improve Peru's economic situation and to fight terrorism. In order to obtain U.S. financial support for this plan, it had to include a program to eliminate the production of coca. In 1991, Peru was plagued by a cholera epidemic and by an increase in terrorist bombing, murder, and kidnappings that have brought the economy to the verge of collapse. The bilateral antidrug accord between the United States and Peru was signed on May 14, 1991. The United States committed itself to help persuade the *campesinos* to switch from coca to other crops and to assist financially. In July 1991 the UN joined in and agreed to supervise Peru's antidrug campaign. Unfortunately, narco-terrorism has distorted the Peruvian economy to the extent that it will be impossible to implement Fujimori's plans without taking the necessary steps to change the social and economic infrastructure of Peru. The Shining Path, under the pretense that this is a goal of theirs, has gained control of the drug trade and, over an eleven-year period, has claimed the lives of over 22,000 Peruvians, mostly peasants. In the first nine months of Fujimori's administration, 2,129 deaths were recorded from terrorist violence.

Bolivia: The Good Guys Fight Back

Bolivia, in many ways, is Peru's poor relation in the narcotics industry. Like Peru, it is a major supplier of high-quality coca leaf and coca paste for the Medellin cartel, although it takes second place to its mountain neighbor. As in Peru, Indian peasants have been growing and chewing the leaf for thousands of years to relieve hunger, cold, and other misery. Bolivia in particular is ideally suited for growing the coca bush. According to *Miami Herald* reporters Guy Gugliotta and Jeff Leen, "Cocaine production begins . . . between 1,500 and 6,000 feet above sea level in the mist-filled valleys on the eastern slope of the Andes. There water vapor from the Amazon rain forest rises upward, providing the warmth and wetness for the shrubs that bear the coca leaf."[33] It is on tiny, terraced plots that the plants grow to twelve feet in height, as many as 7,000 per acre, producing leaves up to four times a year.

When Americans began discovering cocaine en masse in the early 1970s, the industrious Bolivian peasants helped meet the demand as entire families collected the harvest—and why not? These poor Indians were quadrupling their income with no greater effort, and Bolivian coca leaf replaced tin as the country's leading earner of foreign exchange.[34] In fact, the cocaine industry today employs as many as 300,000 people in a total population of seven million, in a country that still has an unemployment rate of at least 20 percent. Moreover, it also is responsible for approximately one quarter of the country's foreign exchange earnings, some $250 million by one estimate.[35]

Because of this ancient tradition, Bolivia became corrupted early in the era of mass cocaine consumption, before even Colombia and Peru. By the late 1970s, its unstable, numerous, and usually military-run governments were penetrated thoroughly by the country's major drug dealers. In exchange for official protection, even assistance in the transporting of the paste, government officials (including at least one president and his minister of the interior) were compensated liberally in millions of American dollars. By the beginning of the Reagan administration the Bolivian example had become so flagrant that on a bipartisan basis U.S. officials targeted the Andean nation as a special project for coca-leaf eradication and drug control before such programs were even attempted, much less allowed, in Colombia and Peru.

As a result, the Drug Enforcement Administration sent more agents to Bolivia than anywhere else in South America, including Colombia, as did the Coast Guard, the Border Patrol, and U.S. special forces, in a remarkable display of interagency cooperation. Funds were quickly (or comparatively so) appropriated by the U.S. Congress for drug-eradication and crop-replacement purposes. The sum has increased steadily to $50 million for such programs in fiscal year 1989, more than any other country received, until the escalation of the war on drugs in Colombia in the summer of 1989 changed the picture.[36]

Most dramatically, in mid-1986, 170 American troops and their equipment, including Blackhawk helicopters, were sent at the invitation of President Victor Paz Estenssoro to Bolivia to participate in quick strike missions against narcotics traffickers and their jungle processing labs.[37] Moreover, two years later the Bolivian Congress passed a coca-eradication law that set out to radically reduce the estimated 192,000 acres to 30,000, the level believed necessary for traditional domestic consumption.[38] The strategy was to work on several levels: first, it assumed that the goal of eliminating coca-product exports would take from eight to ten years; second, it would take a double-barreled approach. First, the peasant growers were to be persuaded to do something else through a one-time-only cash payment of $2,000 and technical assistance for every hectare (two and a half acres) withdrawn from production. If persuasion did not work, more coercive measures would be employed. The accent was on persuasion since many feared, particularly in the Bolivian government, that an attack on the *campesinos* would set off a guerrilla war. After all, Bolivian peasants were at the forefront of Bolivia's 1952 revolution that placed Paz Estenssoro in power for the first time. The second barrel was to be an all-out attack on the industry's infrastructure—the processing centers and airplanes that take the paste out of the country. In 1988, forty-five jungle-based labs were destroyed and eleven aircraft seized. Officials from both countries hoped such efforts would reduce the demand for the coca leaf, thus driving down prices for the crop.[39]

Despite this unprecedented cooperation, however, the antidrug effort at best has been a mixed success. Here are some of the highlights:

- After a few months of effort in the 1986 operation, the American troops left and the flimsily built processing labs quickly were rebuilt.
- So far the new reduction program has made little progress despite high hopes for a quick cut in producing acres. Only

1,500 in fact have been taken out of use, although the Bolivian government argues it is triple that number.

- At the same time, actual production of coca leaf has increased by as much as 20 percent in Bolivia, thanks to higher yields on existing acres caused by modern agricultural techniques, including pesticides.

- Despite an aggressive and honest Bolivian leadership—a dramatic change from a decade ago—lower-ranking officials in the army, police, and judiciary remain on the payroll of the traffickers who, in turn, are routinely informed of pending raids.

- Perhaps as a result, the number of arrests fell from 904 in 1987 to 509 in 1988—although U.S. officials insist the *quality* of the arrested has risen considerably.[40]

Despite the official face-saving optimism, there are internal doubts about the effectiveness of the program, judging by one memorandum written by a visiting State Department official from its narcotics bureau. The inspection trip to Bolivia took place in November 1989, and what he saw was not an overwhelming success; indeed, there was little success to report at all. For example, the memorandum declares that coca-reduction and intelligence operations were flat-out failures. So was public diplomacy—convincing Bolivians that the war against drugs was in their interest—as well as interdiction. Only "infrastructure support" received a partially successful rating, barely.[41] What happened?

To begin with, the program to reduce coca acreage was not on schedule, and the Bolivian government had done little or nothing to help replace coca with other cash crops. In addition, intelligence collection had been a near-complete failure and "needs to be completely revamped." According to the memo: "This project is in serious trouble due to a complete lack of adequate tactical intelligence and the absence of a professional response capability were such intelligence available."[42] A lack of intelligence in turn has severely hampered the interdiction effort. If the police do not know where the traffickers are working or when they are shipping, drug busts become very difficult indeed. Public diplomacy, especially regarding the use of herbicides against the coca bush, has convinced few in Bolivia that herbicides can be safe. Least of all was La Paz convinced and the legislation remains on the books forbidding the use of them.

But the problems are even more basic than that. For example, coca-leaf production figures vary widely. Since the area under cultivation varies by 100 percent, how can anyone tell if real progress is being made in reduction? Even the new eradication law has severe defects, according to the memorandum: it does not specify a deadline for peasants to give up coca production voluntarily; it also refuses to divide production areas into legal and illegal zones, and instead favors a murky three-part system, including a "transitional" zone of crop production.[43] All in all, despite greater efforts made in Bolivia than in either Colombia or Peru, the net effect is that this Andean country remains a major producer and exporter of coca-leaf by-products. What once was seen as a slow, decade-long effort to eliminate the drug industry in Bolivia is changed; administration officials are in fact wildly optimistic.[44]

What about the vital link of narcotics trafficking with terrorism?

Bolivia is another kind of story from that of Colombia or Peru; recent developments add another dimension of concern. The United States drug effort in Bolivia has the highest profile in Latin America, which in turn has inspired a nationalist backlash, inevitably fed by men and women of the left. Cries of "Honduranization" have been heard, the latest catchword of the anti-American element in Bolivia, which translates into the following charge: that the U.S. is turning Bolivia into a military base in South America as it did Honduras in Central America to help stanch revolutionary forces in neighboring states.[45]

The accusation that echoes widely throughout the country conveniently ignores the antinarcotics thrust of this effort, but it has had a dampening effect on the program and its expansion, even though widespread popular resentment has to be stirred up. In this atmosphere other problems can be created. Bolivia has not been free of guerrilla violence in the past. Che Guevara's attempt at guerrilla warfare was not the only effort at promoting political violence in the country; however, in recent years such activity declined, especially in the first half of the 1980s. Yet the potential exists, and in recent months there have been disturbing signs that it is far from dead. In August 1988, a visit of Secretary of State George Shultz nearly came to an abrupt end when his caravan was bombed by left-wing terrorists. In May 1989, two American missionaries of the Mormon Church were murdered by left-wing extremists who specifically linked the killings to retaliation against the "Yankee murderers who come to massacre our fellow farmers," a crystal-clear reference to the American-sponsored eradication effort.[46] In case anyone believes that these acts were simply the work of disgruntled anti-Americans, the same group carried out a dynamite attack against the Bolivian Congress in December 1988. This group calls itself the Zarate Willca Armed Forces of Liberation, and so far has eluded the police and the military. Is it the future *Sendero Luminoso*? Possibly, and the parallel is worrisome.[47] It takes little imagination to foresee a surge in left-wing violence if and when the coca-reduction effort becomes serious in Bolivia. In other words, we may now be witnessing the start of a full-fledged narco-terrorism in Bolivia as well, an assessment reinforced by the sociological fact that Bolivia has a large and impoverished Indian population that despite the 1952 revolution has remained largely outside the small, modern economy. A Bolivian equivalent to the Peruvian Shining Path might well find fertile soil to launch a similar effort.

Since 1990 government clashes in Colombia have disrupted some of its cocaine production. One of the results has been a major increase all over Bolivia in the number of laboratories that refine cocaine. The transfer of this activity to Bolivia sets the stage for the local drug cartels and terrorist groups to take over economic and government institutions.

6

The Other America: From Grass to Crack

———————— ▮▮▮▮▮ ————————

It was the summer of 1989, and not the best of times in America. A New York tabloid's front-page headline possibly summarized the mood: GUNS OF AUGUST, it screamed, in fifty-point type. The *Post* was not talking about the opening month of World War I, but rather of another conflict, the battle against drugs being conducted in the mean streets of New York City. The subleads ran:

BLOODSHED IN CITY, L.I. & NEW JERSEY

UNDERCOVER COP SHOT IN BACK

FOUR SLAIN IN MOB RUB-OUTS

BULLETS FLY ON BLEECKER ST.

DRUG WIDOWER: I'LL FIGHT ON [1]

Was this media hype, as some have suggested, or was the war on narcotics finally coming home to America—home meaning the inner cities and, most surprising of all, its rural backwaters as well? For those who have followed our story so far, it is decidedly the latter. Suddenly the scourge of imported narcotics from Asia, the Middle East, and Latin America, with its attendant mayhem and corruption, was beginning to have its effect on Americans at large.

136

They were scared, and with good reason. The inner cities, the ghettos of the 1960s, were not the only battlegrounds being lost in this war—increasingly, America's heartland, too, became involved. When hard drugs began to show up in Wyoming and in all-American towns like Fort Wayne—once dubbed the city of churches and now called the "crack capital of Indiana"—the problem then became much larger than Harlem or Anacostia or Liberty City.[2] In the very same month of August 1989, the drug war in the South American republic of Colombia made the headlines and the lead stories on the nightly news for the first time and continued for weeks. The story exploded when a prominent Liberal party politician and presidential candidate was gunned down by drug-linked assassins during an election rally. The drug lords had almost casually killed all perceived enemies: hundreds of politicians, police, judges, and journalists had been liquidated over the years.[3]

But when the government of President Virgilio Barco began a crackdown on the narco-mafia by arresting more than 11,000 persons in less than a week, confiscating the property of leading Medellin drug lords and finally, and most important of all, issuing a presidential decree that permitted summary extradition of the cartel's criminals to the United States for trial, "the extraditables" (or some of their minions) struck back with an unprecedented declaration of war of their own against both Colombian and American officials.

This rush of events in turn triggered a response from the Bush administration that included a package of assistance worth $65 million that went far beyond the hopes of antidrug hardliners in Washington only a few weeks earlier. The evil of narco-terrorism suddenly was beginning to get close and uncomfortable, which greatly disturbed otherwise isolationist Americans. Consider the remarkable results of two opinion polls that came out that summer of 1989, even before the Colombian crisis emerged: The first, sponsored by the new "drug czar" William J. Bennett but carried out by the Gallup organization, found that drugs were the chief worry of the American public. Twenty-seven percent believed this to be the country's leading problem, which vastly exceeded all the other problems that had been proclaimed by the American media for years, including homelessness, poverty, and the budget deficit. Abortion rights did not register at all. For George Gallup, Jr., it was a jolt: "In the 50 years that the U.S. public has been asked to name the most important problem facing the nation, it is virtually unprecedented for any social issue to appear at the top of the list. . . . The American people are in a war-time mode [on the issue]."[4]*

Even more fascinating was the even stronger stand taken by 500 teenagers who were polled in a separate survey: Thirty-two percent registered drugs as their chief concern; 60 percent thought it was the most difficult problem facing people their age; and they were very tough on both users and sellers, tougher, in fact, than the adults sampled. They were tougher on themselves: Eighty percent wanted high-school students to be tested for drug use, and 84 percent wanted their teachers tested as well. These figures, compared to the adult survey, favored the testing of teenagers on the part of 68 percent sampled.[6] Most remarkable of all, these figures were triple those of a similar Gallup poll on drug concerns conducted only two years previously. A few years before that, illegal drugs as a problem was not even on the American public's radar screen.[7]† The Gallup poll also showed that Americans not only were scared, but angry, too. Eighty percent surveyed wanted tougher laws against *users*. Ninety percent demanded the same thing for drug pushers.[9]

Those skeptics who would rejoin that a poll instigated by an antidrug bureaucrat could never be honest—the integrity of the Gallup organization aside—had better consider the results of

*Republican pollster Richard Wirthlin found narcotics to be Americans' chief concern in thirteen of fourteen monthly polls as of August 1989.[5]
†The sample size was 1,000 adults and 500 teenagers contacted by phone. The margin of error for the adult survey is plus or minus 4 percent, for teens, 6 percent.[8]

another poll, conducted shortly afterward by ABC and the *Washington Post*: The ABC-*Post* poll found that more than 40 percent of those sampled felt drug abuse to be the nation's top worry—double the number of only a few months before; as in the Gallup poll, illegal drugs scored far ahead of any other concern, foreign or domestic. In fact, narcotics with its 44 percent ran well ahead of the second category, "poverty, hunger, homeless," which registered only 8 percent. Pollution and the disease AIDS registered 4 and 3 percent respectively; unspecified foreign policy questions, 3 percent. For blacks, more often the victims of neighborhoods infested by crack and heroin peddlers, the figure was an astounding 70 percent, compared to only 19 percent in January of that year and 20 percent in September 1988.[10]

The ABC-*Post* survey registered that 76 percent of Americans wanted more money spent on federal antidrug programs; half wanted substantially more money allocated for the effort.[11] Of course, the public has a habit of changing its mind when the pollsters take the nation's pulse. Only a few years ago the concern over nuclear war and its disarmament handmaiden, the nuclear freeze, registered high on the worry list, only to disappear in the wake of "neo-detente" international arms agreements; and at least one pollster believes that were the U.S. to experience an economic downturn, the concern about narcotics would be "probably cut in half."[12] The rising concern over drugs in America is likely to last awhile. For one thing, it is featured on the network and local news nearly every night, and there is no relief in sight. The Bush administration, with the president's September speech, has made it a high profile issue. This incessant media attention should not be dismissed lightly, however. There is evidence that some segments of the public merely are reflecting what they absorb from the media, rather than expressing personal experience. The question is worth asking, aside from impression and anecdote, is the drug crisis worse now in America than it once was?

As is often the case, the data show some contradictory trends.

For example, the National Institute of Drug Abuse reported in August 1989 that casual consumption of marijuana and cocaine had declined between 1985 and 1988. In fact, a third of Americans using these drugs had stopped.[13]* That data was cited widely in the media and while probably accurate is very misleading; for one thing, accurate and comparable data don't exist. Drugs now may be perceived as the nation's leading problem, but no one knows how big the problem truly is. Law enforcement officers and analysts are almost totally in the dark on that score. The only widespread impression is that the drug menace is bad and getting worse.

So how much worse? While no one really knows for sure, there have been some attempts to light a few candles and lessen the darkness. There is little cause for optimism about what is emerging from the shadows. For example, one recent study that showed a decline in the use of cocaine, as presumably health-conscious middle-class Americans rediscovered what was known about it almost a century ago, fails nevertheless to mention how cocaine only recently had been casually consumed in this country. At its peak there were an estimated six million *regular* users of cocaine, not to mention eighteen million habitual users of marijuana, and a heroin-using population of one half million.[15] Compared to twenty years ago, only the number of heroin addicts remains about the same; most other illegal drugs have ballooned in importance. Some, like crack, which was invented in Jamaica and first came to the United States in the early 1980s, were not available during the flowering of America's drug era that began in the mid-1960s.

The estimated earnings from illegal drugs reflect an increase as well. It is estimated that in 1966 the American consumption of heroin, which had the lion's share of the market, came to $600

---

*Perhaps. There is new evidence that contradicts this. The National Institute of Drug Abuse (NIDA) survey suggests that cocaine use is once more on the rise among college graduates. According to NIDA: "The survey of 500 consecutive callers to the national hot line found that 30 percent had a college education, compared with only 16 percent in 1987." The year 1987 was indeed a low for the more affluent. In 1985, 50 percent of cocaine users were college graduates.[14]

million. Illegal drugs now represent an industry worth at least $100 billion, with heroin falling to fourth place as the drug of choice, preceded by cocaine/crack, marijuana, and PCP (street name, angel dust; a powerful stimulant).[16]* The earnings from the cocaine trade also reflect the increased production of coca leaf, which is processed into cocaine and crack, and as political economist Jean-Baptiste Say (1767–1832) said, supply creates its own demand. If the supply of drugs reflects demand, then we are indeed in trouble. According to the *International Narcotics Control Strategy Report* submitted to the U.S. Congress, production of coca jumped from 1985's estimated 150–162,700 metric tons to 185–213,650 metric tons in 1988; twenty years ago it was only a fraction of that, mostly for local use.[18]

Drug arrests are way up as well: between 1983 and 1987 arrests have increased in Atlanta by 40 percent; in Chicago, 40 percent; in Cleveland, 54 percent; Detroit, nearly 55 percent; Miami, 147 percent; New York, 68 percent; and Washington, D.C., 61 percent. Only a handful of cities, such as Cincinnati, Dallas, and Denver report small decreases.[19] In fact, the total number of drug arrests has increased from 768,000 in 1984 to 1.1 million in 1988,[20] but this has not diminished the scope of the drug problem. For one thing, the number of police officers killed by the drug kingpins is rising dramatically. From virtually zero ten years ago, 1988 saw fourteen officers killed; of course, this is only the beginning. In the words of Lawrence Sherman, head of the Crime Control Institute, which tracks the deaths of policemen: "The record levels of drug enforcement, combined with rising risk levels per arrest, suggest that the total murders of police in drug enforcement will increase in future years."[21]

Establishing neat patterns of cause and effect when dealing with human as opposed to physical phenomena is never easy. Philosophers who have been concerned with the eternal myster-

*One early 1970s estimate by the Bureau of Narcotics and Dangerous Drugs listed 559,000 heroin addicts, half of them in New York.[17]

ies of epistemology have known for centuries that cause-and-effect relationships cannot be scientifically determined. They express probabilities. That is why guesswork is always involved, but a rough idea of the problem can be gathered by looking at some recent crime statistics: according to the FBI, violent crimes increased by 5.5 percent in 1988, establishing an all-time record; in the sub-categories, robberies were up 4.9 percent; aggravated assault, 6.4 percent, and murder 2.9 percent. In the cities, homicides in fact were increasing by 4 percent while declining in suburban and rural areas by 2 percent.[22] The grim figures prompted William Sessions, the bureau's new director, to tell the Associated Press: "While violent crime known to law enforcement reached an unprecedented high in 1988, there is currently no way to measure accurately drug involvement in these unwelcome statistics."[23] Epistemologically sound, if cautious, but this is hardly the end of the question. There is, for example, the murder rate in Washington, D.C., which currently leads the country. Only a few years ago, Washington did not even rank in the top ten; since the Nixon administration began pouring money into law enforcement after the disastrous 1968 riots, and the heroin epidemic wound down in the early 1970s, Washington had become a relatively safe city to live in. The high honor of leading the nation in homicides always had belonged to cities with high rates of unemployment, like Detroit, and booming economies, like Atlanta.

Two years ago, in 1988, that all changed; there were 369 people killed (372 by another count) in the nation's capital, 59.5 per 100,000 inhabitants. The national average was 8.4. In 1989, the rate for D.C. homicides was even higher. Some experts said it would top 500 by the end of the year, despite drug czar William J. Bennett designating Washington, D.C., as a model for crime and drug control.[24]* On April 14, 1990, a year after Washington

*Homicides passed the 300 mark in Washington on August 29, 1989, and at the present rate the total should be close to 500—another record. Few police expect the murder rate to decline any time soon, and their commanders expressed uncertainty as to how to combat it. No wonder. Despite the recent efforts of the

became Bennett's war on drugs "test case," an admission of failure was announced: "War on drugs . . . is a failure."[26] Had Washingtonians suddenly become more murderous? The answer, of course, is no. Indeed, the only independent variable that explains such a geometrical increase in the homicide rate is the flood of new drugs that poured into the area—crack and PCP especially—over the last several years.

With the narcotics came, for the first time, organized gangs that systematically recruit customers and eliminate rivals as well as those who are disloyal within their ranks. Police estimated that 60 percent of Washington's murders in fact were drug related, an estimate considered to be conservative at best.* Other factors include a large, upscale income group of recreational druggies; a large welfare class with time and money on its hands; a woefully lax city government led by a man himself suspected of drug use, all of which contribute to and accelerate the problem's pace, but hardly can be considered the basic cause.

Washington's crime and drug crisis is only an exaggerated version of what other cities, large and small, are facing going into the 1990s. Take New York, for example. Elaine Shannon has snapped a very revealing photograph of a city in deep trouble:

Crack abuse created enormous problems for city police departments as addicts turned to theft to satisfy their habits. In contrast to the limp, withdrawn heroin addicts that the cops used to encounter, cocaine addicts thought they were supermen; they gave a new meaning to the cliche "crime spree." By the middle of 1986, half the drug cases handled by the U.S. Attorney's Office in Manhattan involved crack. A study conducted by the National Institute of Justice found that of four hundred people charged with crimes in Manhattan in

---

federal government, the corrupt and incompetent city government led by Mayor Marion Barry, who himself has been accused of taking drugs, continues to show, as it has in the past, a nearly unbelievable inability to function.[25]

*Neighboring Arlington County in northern Virginia registered no murders in 1988 and the first seven months of 1989.[27]

September and October 1986, more than 80 percent tested positive for cocaine, compared with 42 percent in 1984. The study showed that between 59 percent and 92 percent of persons charged with robbery in Manhattan in 1986 tested positive for cocaine; in the same period, more than 70 percent of those charged with burglary were high on cocaine.[28]

What is even more remarkable, it was not supposed to be this way. As James Q. Wilson and John J. DiIulio, Jr., observed in *The New Republic:*

According to the projections, crime was supposed to be under control by now. The postwar baby-boom generation, which moved into its crime-prone years during the early 1960's, has grown up (or dead or in jail), yielding its place to the (proportionately) less numerous baby-bust generation. With relatively fewer 18-year-olds around, we should all be walking safer streets.[29]

We're not, of course, but why not? Wilson and DiIulio have the answer: "In south central Los Angeles, in much of Newark, in and around the housing projects of Chicago, in the South Bronx and Bedford-Stuyvesant sections of New York, and in parts of Washington, D.C., conditions are not much better than they are in Beirut on a bad day."[30] This is the effect. What about the cause? Drugs, especially crack, are sold openly on street corners; rival gangs shoot at each other from moving automobiles; automatic weapons are carried by teenagers onto school playgrounds; innocent people hide behind double-locked doors and shuttered windows. In Los Angeles there is at least one gang murder every day, Sundays included. "A ten-foot-high concrete wall is being built around the junior high school one of us attended, in order, the principal explained, to keep stray bullets from hitting children on the playground."[31] Somehow the image of Beirut does not seem so exaggerated. But, as the authors explain, it is far worse than that: "The problem is drugs and the brutal struggles among competing gangs for control of the lucrative drug markets. The drug of choice is crack. . . . The crack craze has led to conditions far worse than were found in these same neighborhoods a decade or so ago when heroin was the preferred drug."[32] And speaking of heroin, in the "good old days" of the 1960s and 1970s the market was controlled in the United States by well-established, highly centralized monopolies run by what euphemistically is known as "organized crime," the Mafia. They had the power to make sure those monopolies were retained. Entry into this market was difficult; rivalries were kept to a minimum, and hence random violence remained low.[33]

With crack (and PCP) this is no longer the case, as Wilson and DiIulio well know. Crack is marketed by competitive distribution systems, some of whose members are literally fighting to establish monopolistic control.[34] Depending on the situation, rival or sometimes cooperative groups of Colombians, Jamaicans, Haitians, Salvadorans (in Los Angeles), and a few Americans still are far from carving up stable fiefdoms, as attested by the gunfire in Washington's northeast and southeast districts. Observers of the drug scene predict more cooperation between the different gangs domestically as well as internationally. Already home-grown gangs like the Los Angeles–based Crips that have reputedly close ties with Medellin and Cali have spread to Baltimore, Philadelphia, and other places. "Gang" does not refer to small groups of disadvantaged youths, as sentimentally portrayed in Leonard Bernstein's *West Side Story;* the Crips are not the Jets and Sharks of storyland but an organization with an estimated membership of 10,000 to 15,000.

The Colombian drug cartels responsible for at least 80 percent of the cocaine brought to the United States annually have at least 300 different groups operating all over the country, each of them headed by a Colombian representing his home-base cartel. The gangs themselves are composed of immigrant Colombians with family ties to Colombia. Law-enforcement agencies in the United States estimate that there are at least 22,000 Colombians currently responsible for marketing and distributing drugs here.[35] Because the market in the United States has grown, the cartels have become more sophisticated and have virtually eliminated local middlemen.

The Jamaican gangs, known as posses, are an interrelated network of forty organizations spread through the country with another 10,000 estimated members. They are by all accounts the most violent of the drug gangs.[36] They themselves soon may have the power to form cartels. One Philadelphia police captain quoted recently by the *Washington Times* foresaw a war between the new, largely black gangs and the more established white mafia. According to this source, it is only a matter of time before the heads of the black organizations sit down and say, "We are going to whack out the 24 families."[37]

Just what are they peddling? Until recently it was mainly crack, which is relatively cheap compared to cocaine; but the newest drug on the block is "ice," the effects of which are more addicting than crack and create much more violence than anything we have seen thus far.* Crack has become the drug of preference for the poor and the young, affecting all: black, white, and Hispanic.† Unlike heroin, both crack and PCP are big and fast rush

---

*According to the New York State Division of Substance Abuse,

Ice is a common street term for Methamphetamine, a powerful synthetic stimulant. Methamphetamine normally comes in a white powder. When sold as the street drug "Ice," it resembles clear rock candy, rock salt or shaved glass slivers. The substance is also known by other names—"Rock Candy" and "Hawaiian Salt." Methamphetamine is considered a Schedule II Controlled Substance indicating there is a high potential for abuse. It can be snorted, injected or taken orally. However, when Methamphetamine is processed into Ice, the substance can also be smoked like crack. Ice is a central nervous system stimulant. It impairs mental faculties, produces elevated blood pressure, tachycardia and palpitations. The drug is associated with dizziness, dysphoria, insomnia, tremors, irritability, restlessness and headaches. Prolonged use leads to tolerance, extreme psychological dependence, and severe social disabilities— anxiety, delirium, panic states and paranoid ideation. The exact method for producing Ice is unknown. Ice was developed in the Far East and it is relatively expensive. One gram sells for $250–$400.[38]

†"Crack" or "rock" is hydrochloride powder boiled with baking soda. The result is a white crystal-like substance. In December 1989, a vial of crack could be

stimulants, which accounts for the penchant for violence by those under their spell. If William Bennett is correct, the crack epidemic is not ebbing, it is getting worse.[40]

And the latest menace? After years of comparative stability, the heroin market has begun to expand. Crack addicts (the drug is smoked and is more addictive than cocaine) are developing a taste for heroin either with the cocaine derivative or separately. The reason? Heroin is a sedative, which helps relieve the severe depression that follows the first feelings of euphoria induced by crack.* In the last year, very large supplies of much purer heroin have begun arriving in the United States, specifically New York, most of it coming from Asia, with the market controlled in New York by Chinese tongs.[41]† According to Melvyn Levitsky, Assistant Secretary of State for International Narcotics Matters, the opium crop in Burma alone is expected to be close to 3,000 tons, producing 300 tons of pure heroin. This amount is less than half the opium and heroin production in the world.[44] All of this means that "phenomenal quantities" of the drug now are pouring into the country. It is also cheaper and thus more readily available to the young and the poor. Furthermore, the increased purity means that it can be smoked, often in combination with crack, and that has torn down a barrier that kept many from trying heroin: the fear of intravenous injections.[45]

Is the problem restricted to the confines of the inner cities?

---

purchased in New York for $2. Its effects last for about ten minutes. It is highly addictive. It creates a short-lasting "violent high" with depression afterwards. Frequently, crack smokers move on to "moon rock," which is crack impregnated with heroin in order to diminish the severe depressive state associated with crack use.[39]

*Addiction, to be sure, is a loaded term, and the limits of our understanding of chemical dependency will be explored later in the chapter. See pp. 150–51.

†The new heroin, called "black tar," is from Mexico and first appeared in the U.S. West Coast cities. Because of its relative purity, black tar in Seattle has resulted in an increase of overdose deaths and emergency-room visits.[42] Washington police in the late summer of 1989 reported that a potent mixture of crack and heroin was being "test marketed" by local dealers "to coincide with the opening of area schools." The new mixture goes by various names, including moon rock, parachute, and speedball.[43]

Not likely. Crack began there, but it won't end there. The rapid spread of drugs all over the country shows this to be the case. The intellectual problem for analysts is a recurring error: believing that the present will continue unaltered into the future. Extrapolating from a single point in time is highly misleading and dangerous. Already there are signs that those who believe the crack epidemic is confined to the poor and black and brown are very badly mistaken. One survey that suggested cocaine use to be on the rise once again among the more affluent also shows that 59 percent of them were using crack. According to Mark Gold, director of research at Fair Oaks Hospital in Summit, New Jersey: "It looks like crack is starting to overcome its stereo-type as a drug for inner-city youth, and is beginning to enter suburban and rural areas as a drug for the middle class."[46] We must mention middle-sized cities of the Midwest as well, such as Columbus, Dayton, and Toledo, Ohio; Fort Wayne and Richmond, Indiana; Charleston and Wheeling, West Virginia, and even smaller communities in Colorado, Iowa, Louisiana, and Oklahoma. Crack has become a major problem in these places only three years after it hit the major East Coast cities. As usual, local law-enforcement officials in the smaller cities were and are slow to react. In Columbus, Ohio, the police have hit back with over 300 raids on crack houses in the last sixteen months, although it took them eight to ten months before they realized they had a problem.[47] Others take longer. Even in Columbus, where a fight is being put up, the chief result so far is that the crack gangs from the East Coast and Detroit have become more mobile, dealing out of rented motel rooms rather than houses, although 200 crack houses are still in operation—and crack consumption is still going up.

The pattern of the spread is almost always the same: crack gangs in search of new markets move into a new area, their couriers bringing the drugs in from Detroit or eastern cities by bus, plane, and rented automobile; the potential markets to be targeted by the gangs as they expand are the inner cities. After giving out free samples, initial prices in the new areas can reach $20 to $25 compared to $2 or $3 in New York or $6 in Detroit (in summer 1989).[48] When the market reaches saturation, the prices usually go down.*

With smaller populations, seepage into more affluent areas, especially among the young, is inevitable, and is probably already happening. Thus, according to one DEA internal report, crack cocaine remains a predominantly inner-city urban phenomenon that is mainly confined to minority sections. Large-scale interstate networks controlled by Jamaicans, Haitians, and black street gangs dominate the manufacture and distribution of crack.[49]† By the time the next yearly report is issued by the DEA, the agency no doubt will discover that crack and the pleasure it affords is no longer confined to the minorities, or even the urban-suburban areas. The Justice Department reported recently that largely rural states like Iowa and Wyoming are now being targeted by dealers. In rural Georgia that old 1960s favorite, LSD, was showing up. In South Carolina the latest drug of choice is amphetamines.[51]

What is even more disturbing is the increasing sophistication of the drug-marketing network, which federal officials believe the Medellin and Cali cartels have worked hard to establish. First, the Colombians established regional distribution centers: Houston, Los Angeles, Miami, and New York. Couriers fan out from these points transporting narcotics to all parts of the country. As *New York Times* reporter Richard L. Berke discovered:

*Couriers come in all shapes and sizes, including teenagers rented out by their parents. If caught, owing to their juvenile status they rarely are held. In June 1990, crack prices were reported by the media to be on the increase and the quality to be on the decline. Whether this indicates that government efforts are beginning to show results, or whether this is due to some temporary shortage, only time will tell.

†Washington, D.C., in fact was the model followed by the gangs. Since it is not a major seaport and has only middling sized international airports nearby, the City has had its drugs funnelled in by courier from New York and Miami. Nor was Washington dominated by organized crime, which meant that ease of entry into the local drug market was fairly simple. The lessons learned there were easily transferred to places like Cincinnati and Toledo.[50]

Whether stuffed in teddy bears or buried on hot days in truckloads
of refrigerated but potentially very smelly fish, whether stowed in
Federal Express packages or merely tossed into the trunk of a car,
cocaine crack, marijuana and heroin are making their way to retail
markets on airplanes, automobiles, trucks, boats, buses and trains
all across the nation. Drugs are found on anything that moves.[52]

After years of dealing with Americans, the Colombian cartels
are tightening control by putting in their own countrymen as
national and regional supervisors with a strict chain of command.
As many as 5,000 Colombians representing the Medellin and Cali
cartels are operating in the United States.[53] With improving drug
networks such as the 300 identified Colombian groups now operating in the United States,[54] the battle is nationwide, but so far
it looks as if only one side is waging it; and where narcotics go,
violent crime is found also, despite the changing demographics.
In fact, in comparison to the sluggish response of federal, state,
and local authorities, the narco-traffickers and their terrorist allies
have proved quite adaptive. When cocaine use was slowing down
or even declining, a new market was opened for its derivative,
crack. Moreover, the Colombian cartels have discovered that heroin can be combined with crack and cocaine, and thus have
attempted to move into that market as well, despite heavy competition from the traditional heroin establishment.[55] As a result,
despite all the upheavals and promises of new antidrug programs,
the narco-empire, overall, is not in retreat, and American demand
continues to supply the dollars that keep the narco-terrorists alive
and active, undercutting Western interests for the indefinite
future.

Is there hope?

Some, as we shall see; little unless there is a radical change
in attitudes and beliefs, along with policies and programs that
flow from these attitudes. How far Americans have to go is the
theme for the remainder of this chapter.

To begin with, the very notion of addiction is, admittedly, subject to wide interpretation. The truth is that little is known about it: An addict is someone who is physically and psychologically dependent on a chemical substance, the lack of which causes excruciating agony, or even death; yet the experts cannot tell us what, exactly, separates physical from psychological addiction. Experience with heroin addicts in the 1960s and 1970s showed that complete withdrawal (known as "cold turkey") even without methadone (yet another drug, also addictive) is possible without serious side effects to the addict, or not as serious as often portrayed. Indeed, as Mona Charen has observed: "[W]ithdrawal from the drug [heroin], far from the hellish torments he had expected, was actually very much like a bout of flu—definitely not pleasant, but endurable. So endurable, in fact, that addicts would voluntarily undergo withdrawal on a regular basis to regulate their need for the drug as the price fluctuated."[56] As Charen points out, much of the evidence for physical addiction comes from tests on laboratory animals where, for example, monkeys would inject themselves with cocaine repeatedly, stopping for neither food nor water; they would not do the same for heroin. But simple transference from monkey to man in many cases often proves misleading, leaving us without a precise idea of physical addiction.[57] In the case of cocaine and crack, we still don't know everything about how they work, although it is clear that crack is more physically addictive and acts more quickly than cocaine. As for psychological dependence, less is known. Psychotherapy has a poor record in separating the psychological and physiological aspects of addiction.[58]*

What eventually may prove to be more important is the realization some researchers are only just coming to, that culture plays a bigger role than thought, either reinforcing drug use or discouraging it. A culture can change in its attitudes and beliefs toward a range of things, including drugs. In the case of the latter

---

*One new drug, flupenthixol, in trial runs has reduced cravings for crack in nine of ten addicts tested.[59]

it can turn decidedly negative, though it may be a long process. We know this to be true. It has happened before.

One case in particular is cocaine. Cocaine was produced in the late nineteenth century by German chemists looking for a local anesthetic for eye surgery. It also was prescribed for alcoholism and morphine addiction. During the American Civil War, this drug was considered a miracle painkiller for men in utter agony. Cocaine's therapeutic value was championed enthusiastically by Sigmund Freud.[60]* Heroin, too, would be turned out by German labs as another miracle drug, and as in the case of cocaine it would take twenty years for its dangerous side effects and consequences to be recognized.[61]

Soon, on both sides of the Atlantic the well-to-do acquired a taste for the stuff. But as its use spread to the middle class, and its addictive as well as other nasty side effects became better known (increased pulmonary infections, hard to cure in those days, for there were no antibiotics), the drug ceased to have its allure, and cocaine consumption virtually disappeared from this class by the 1930s. How long did that cycle last?

Almost fifty years. What was the result? Elaine Shannon explains:

In the 1930's and 1940's, the American establishment regarded drug abuse—which by now meant heroin addiction—an imminent hazard to society, a cause of predatory crime and degradation, but a habit confined to the underclass. "We will use any method we can to 'get' dope smugglers, dope peddlers, and bootleggers," Henry Morganthau, Jr., President Franklin Roosevelt's secretary of the treasury, declared in 1934. "We've got to go after them with every weapon at our command—not in a sissy manner."[62]

---

*There is, of course, the nineteenth century's famous fictional character, Sherlock Holmes, who injected cocaine in a seven-percent solution to relieve the tedium of having no problems to solve. Dr. Watson only mildly disapproved in the stories and quite probably represents the point of view of the author, Sir Arthur Conan Doyle.

Morganthau's hard-line stand was popular at the time and enjoyed the support of the then rather primitive media—and illegal drug consumption went down.

You may take what comfort you can; there are factors at play that suggest it won't be as easy this time. For one thing, the number of users was far smaller. Since a wealthy few enjoyed the experience, they kept it pretty much to themselves. It did not take long before the popular press would make unflattering and persistent references to "cocaine fiends," reducing even further the allure of cocaine to the upper and middle classes. Only pockets of ethnics such as Chinese immigrants, Mexican itinerant workers, and poor blacks were consuming narcotics, which only reinforced white middle-class revulsion for drugs. Of course, at that time there were no powerful foreign and ruthless cartels to manufacture, market, and promote the products; and crack was not around for the poor and underprivileged to sample on a continuous basis in their low-rent public housing apartments. But above all, in the early twentieth century there was no supportive culture that openly advocated the use of drugs. They were glamorized mainly in the 1960s and 1970s, in a culture that still remains latently powerful.

The importance of cultural attitudes and how they are formed is largely and conveniently overlooked by most experts on drugs, critics who appear frequently on the op-ed page of the *New York Times*. It is a major underlying cause of America's feeble and much-delayed response to the problem. As the libertarian *Wall Street Journal* aptly put it in a recent editorial:

Twenty years ago, liberals agitated for the effective decriminalization of drugs and weakened the tools of law enforcement; now the wheel has come full circle. The law is coming down on drug *users*. Despite this progress, the ACLU and others are in agony. "Assault on the Constitution," wails Rep. Don Edwards. Really? We frankly doubt that any court will discover a right to use drugs.[63]

Only occasionally does the openly prodrug attitude fostered at one time by many of this country's bohemians, intelligentsia in the academy, and their counterparts in the media ever reveal itself nowadays; but it does manifest itelf now and then. For example, in the days and weeks surrounding the twentieth anniversary of Woodstock, the central myth of the nation's youth revolt was sentimentally celebrated over and over again. As might be expected, the nostalgia for the music festival served as a rite of celebration that was mixed with pain at the loss of the dream (or illusion) of perpetual innocence in a world unable to achieve peace and stability, gone mad and materialistic.

Virtually no one suggested that Woodstock also had been a celebration of unrestricted drug use by performers and audience alike, until William Bennett reminded a television audience of the number of entertainers who had appeared at Woodstock and who could not make any appearances in 1989 because they died from an overdose of drugs. Jimmy Hendrix and Janis Joplin were the most prominent. Underneath the mud and raunch of Woodstock was a much larger, and more complicated problem than the sound system or the kids thinking they were having a good time, or even pretending that they were the advance guard of a new just and moral order.*

Permeating the whole Woodstock event that long-ago August in upstate New York was an already well-formed cluster of feelings that had become widespread by the mid-1960s: it was called a revolution, a brotherhood, a love of fellow man, and peace, but in fact it was a revolt; a revolt fed in part by peer-group pressure and the Vietnam War against which many were protesting. In the end, it was directed against traditional attitudes, beliefs, and values that had seen the United States through two world wars

---

*The sentimentalists celebrating Woodstock two decades later, would, quite naturally, conveniently forget other follow-up events like the drug and music festival held in Altamont, California. In full view of the drug generation's prototype, Mick Jagger of the Rolling Stones, an obese male who, laced with illegal substances, apparently tried to assassinate Jagger, was brutally knifed to death by a posse of local Hell's Angels motorcyclists.

and the Great Depression. These values were perceived to be grossly deficient by those young men and young women who had experienced neither.

That revolt was not carried out by an entire generation of youth—a lie that would form the central myth typical of the era—but was created by a minority of activists. Some of them were not so young. There were a few leftovers from an earlier radical tradition referred to as the new Left (as opposed to the youthful "New Left" beginning to emerge in 1959–60) and a handful of in-betweens who, generationally, belonged to neither. They nearly all were lionized and celebrated by the media; the Marxist Herbert Marcuse found glory in the press. The radical press such as the *Village Voice* and *Rolling Stone* decided who was in or out, and promoted these personalities to the society at large. These personalities were largely self-selected and by definition a small minority within American society. Those few were ready, willing, and able to question society's values and recommended remedies such as the use of drugs and communal living to cure its many ills. They were well paid for their efforts into the bargain.[64]

In fact, the underlying ethic was disregard of all traditional morals and values; and even backward-looking films like *The Big Chill* seem to argue the sordid present is a betrayal of a good past.[65] It will be difficult to argue today that the dominant spokesmen were the best or brightest or even the particularly able. In fact, most were not. Reviewing the painfully bad writing on a counterculture that for the most part was one vast cultural wasteland reveals an almost total lack of knowledge of history, philosophy, sociology and, of course, economics. The science and the scientific method were not needed in the Age of Aquarius.

Nevertheless, the sophists of the 1960s were influential. The tone and feeling of that era continued through much of the 1970s and is with us today, although it may be in retreat for the moment. The feeling is captured by Fay Weldon in her novel *The Hearts and Lives of Men,* and cited by Joseph Adelson:

Back in the Sixties! What a time that was! When everyone wanted everything, and thought they could have it and what's more had a *right* to it. Marriage and freedom within it. Sex without babies. Revolution without poverty. Careers without selfishness. Art without effort. Knowledge without learning by rote. A dinner, in other words, and no dishes to clean up afterwards.[66]

That's how a good novelist put it. A sociologist like Edward Shils would give it an even richer perspective. Shils spelled out the consequences of what he called "the antinomian temptation," the reigning credo of America's elite, nearly a generation ago:

The highest ideal of antinomianism is a life of complete self-determination, free of the burden of tradition and conventions, free of the constraints imposed by institutional rules and laws and of the stipulations of authority operating within the setting of institutions. . . . All human beings . . . are entitled to whatever an individual is entitled to. All human beings are entitled to be gratified as the promptings of the self require it.[67]*

It is interesting to note that neither novelist nor sociologist suggested that the real problem was Americans' apparently unique gift for demanding instant gratification, America's social critics' all-purpose explanation for everything that goes wrong in the United States. Instant gratification also is linked to consumerism and capitalism—the latter being anathema to the radical left social commentators; the radical right follows closely, only their gist is the complete opposite argument. Needless to say, there is no serious evidence for such an assertion. Why are Americans driven by instant gratification any more than Canadians or Chileans or Mongolians, assuming that whatever can gratify is close at hand? Self-indulgence is not a unique American problem or a product of twentieth-century affluence. Nor, of course, is

---

*Later, deep thinkers would contrast the "idealism" of the 1960s generation with the selfishness of the "me" generation.

the United States the only wealthy country in the world; some nations have by now a higher per capita income. As for self-indulgence, it is a pity that our social critics never visited, say, Venezuela during the oil bubble.

The problem is that Americans in general and the social critics of American society in particular (on the right or the left) nearly always are conversant with only one society (namely ours) and thus have no real basis for comparison with any other. Nevertheless, they continue to pronounce their conclusions with the airy and careless grace resembling that of a trapeze artist doing a triple somersault without a net. But unlike a trapeze artist, who works extremely hard to achieve grace in performance and to prevent any injury or pain, Americans, in addition to the need for instant gratification, try to pursue life without pain—and to achieve this instantaneously, of course, they learn to lean on crutches (chemical or otherwise) to relieve any pain; for the ideal in America always has been to appear young, success-ful, healthy, and happy. Instant gratification and a painless life are clearly only a symptom; they do not explain why people demand immediate pleasure through drugs. That question, of course, was not perplexing America's deepest thinkers on social questions.

Those who giddily embraced these notions that spurred on the counterculture believed that they were on to something entirely new and they did not want to have anything to do with the past. In fact, human beings have periodically deluded themselves in similar fashion from the time they sat around their cave camp fires. Those Christians who embraced the original version of an-tinomianism, the assertion that faith alone was necessary for personal salvation negating the need for obedience to the moral law, had at least a belief in something other than themselves. The devout Woodstockians did not. Their radical attack on in-stitutions, restraints, limits, and the law, of course, blended per-fectly with the notion that drugs were a part of the rebellion; if authority forbade them, all the more reason to use them. Whether they were "mind expanders" (actually, dangerous hallucinogens) like LSD, peyote, and mescaline, drugs that made you feel good before, during, and after exam week (marijuana and cocaine came later), the lid was off. In Adelson's able analysis: "there is little question that it [the 1960s rebellion] rationalized (the drug epidemic's) early stages and beyond that helped undo the immune system which had kept drugs—and much else—at bay."[68] Who would object? Certainly not authorities like college presidents, who were grateful if they could enter and leave their offices without being harassed with yet another list of nonnegotiable demands.

Everything from high-school dress codes to required courses at the universities were pitched overboard.* We have yet to recover. This is why some of America's elite schools are among the great consumer frauds of the century. Meanwhile, respect for institutions—particularly the American government, mired in a war it did not and could not win—was definitely lost on the part of America's youth in revolt.

Why? Because restraint means limits, and that keeps the human spirit from its development and fulfillment; it was a profoundly optimistic reading of human nature, not unprecedented. It was mistaken, however, and led to very unpleasant surprises for those who believed, as did Timothy Leary, that drugs were the key that would unlock the door to human perfection.

They were wrong, but they were influential. At first, these doctrines that naturally led to a taste for drugs were confined to the university population, graduate students and faculty at selected schools. Quite rapidly drug use spread to America's equivalent of Britain's red brick schools, and from there filtered down to the undergraduates, then beyond to an even wider circle of

---

*This is not to say that experiments with education are always bad; throwing everything familiar away for the sake of change is bad. The results of those changes are felt in America now more than ever. The "educational summit" convened by President Bush at the later part of 1989 demonstrates the desperate need for improving the education that has been ruined during the radical changes of the 1960s and 1970s.

believers in the New Age. This happened with an able assist from the media, eager to spot and propagate a trend—any trend, especially if it smacked of revolt against the gray and uncreative years of the Eisenhower era.

It was as unstoppable as a tidal wave. Although now it is conveniently overlooked or minimized, the cues for tuning in and dropping out were everywhere; not just from hopelessly muddled Harvard professors of psychology, but from all points of the compass, if one were literate or able to turn on a radio or television. There were, of course, the bands: the Beatles, the Rolling Stones, The Who, America's own Grateful Dead and all of their myriad imitators, ingesting drugs when they could and often in full view of their admirers. And there was the fawning press, led by *Rolling Stone,* but quickly imitated by the major mass media, whose editors and reporters largely approved of every nuance of the drug, rock-and-roll, piss-on-America revolution.

Hollywood was not far behind, and few films portrayed the nasty reality of heroin addiction like *Panic in Needle Park* which, to say the least, was no box office hit. Indeed, drug celebration movies are still being made, as long as the insufferable and monumentally unfunny Cheech and Chong are still good box office. And for those who just stayed in on weekends, there was always NBC's *Saturday Night Live,* possibly the most satirical piece of avant garde prodrug entertainment that commercial television ever produced—and with satisfying profits to the network's stockholders. Today's *Saturday Night Live* is pale in comparison to the evenings when John Belushi and Dan Ackroyd reigned supreme; Belushi unfortunately died of a drug overdose, but the celebration of drugs goes on nonetheless.

How powerful was the prodrug cultural elite in the United States at the end of the 1960s and the beginning of the 1970s? Very. The straight-and-narrows within even the most conservative end of the political spectrum duly took note. In fact, they fell over backwards to avoid any sort of confrontation, and law enforcement soon got the message—Richard Nixon, for one. The

President and his supposedly law-and-order Attorney General John Mitchell at the beginning of their administration sent a bill to Capitol Hill that radically changed the official attitude toward drugs. Elaine Shannon got the tone right:

[The legislation] drew sharp distinctions between so-called professional traffickers, especially those involved in the heroin trade, and people arrested for possessing small quantities of marijuana. The hundred page proposal known as the Comprehensive Drug Abuse Prevention and Control Act of 1970 streamlined and stiffened criminal penalties against wholesale drug dealing but reduced the penalty for simple possession of marijuana to a misdemeanor. Henceforward, youthful first offenders found with small amounts—and in some cases, significant amounts—of marijuana and other "soft" drugs would be shunted to treatment-and-education programs.[69]

The Nixonian political wisdom of 1969 is still the conventional belief of many, judging from even the latest opinion polls, which do not support the punishment of casual users of so-called soft drugs.

Of course, the apparently neat equity of being tolerant toward consumers while hard on suppliers got lost in the translation. The druggies in fact had no interest in such establishment distinctions. They were only too happy for a sign of tolerance from the much-despised conservative administration for any drug. Quite naturally, that was interpreted as proof that they were right in all matters dealing with illegal substances, the predictable effect of which was the demoralization of antidrug government agencies. No wonder that in the popular media they had become the bad guys while pushers, in Elaine Shannon's perfectly tuned phrase, had become "dealers" who served "clients": "A particularly ingratiating salesman, who anticipated a customer's needs like a solicitous wine merchant, acquired the honorific title of 'my dealer,' as in 'my doctor,' 'my broker,' 'my lawyer.' He was courted with tips, tickets, and invitations.""⁷⁰* While the elite held out a glad hand to the criminal, the much-despised "narcs" were of course the enemy, as Shannon describes: "Narcotics investigators . . . were not even welcome in neighborhood beer joints; bartenders complained that they made the other customers nervous. Many DEA agents would not tell their neighbors what they did for a living, for fear their children would be teased or bullied by their playmates."⁷¹ This was no exaggeration, as America's politicos, Republican and Democrats alike, knew full well. Much more will be said on the loyal opposition.

In respect to the cultural pacesetters the Nixon firebreak not only did not work, it failed to hold with the blue-suit crowd as well. A hard drug like heroin may have been considered bad; but the rest of the drugstore soon would be safe even from official pronouncement, much less punishment. In September 1975, a typical establishment entity called the Domestic Council Drug Abuse Task Force, led by Vice President Nelson Rockefeller, wrote a white paper that essentially condoned the use of both marijuana and cocaine. The blue ribbon, blue-suited personages that sat around the meetings did not actually write the report; a younger, more with-it staff did that. Predictably, the conclusions were that marijuana was a nonproblem and cocaine was not physically addictive.† One of the major conclusions was that U.S. drug agencies must pay less attention to marijuana and cocaine smuggling (which had only just begun in Colombia) and concentrate on heroin—the establishment's fixed idea of ultimate drug evil, even though at the time consumption of smack already had peaked.⁷²

It was the perfect conventional wisdom, managing to miss the point and at the same time failing to anticipate a much larger problem that was already taking shape. The *Washington Post*

---

*The almost nauseatingly precise description of this sick junky-pusher relationship, of course, is now quite conveniently forgotten.
†At the time the actual physiological and psychological effects of both marijuana and cocaine were not known.

found it "common sense" and a welcome break from a past where all illegal drugs were considered a threat to the society.[73] But the Nixon-Ford years were hardly the low point in dealing with a spreading drug problem.

Jimmy Carter's administration sank lower. The Southern born-again Baptist might have been expected to take a strong stand against drugs. But he didn't; in fact, his administration was a total sellout to those it avidly courted, including drug-using rock-and-roll bands that performed for the candidate at fundraising concerts. Suddenly, the White House staff and much of the government bureaucracy was taken over by relatively young Democrats who brought with them every feelgood cliché of the Woodstock generation. The Hill, already dominated by liberal Democrats, had long gone to pot—Carter's sons, for example, were casual drug users. One was expelled from the Navy for marijuana use. But that was hardly the Carter administration's only absurdity on the drug front; this distinction was reserved for Jimmy Carter's adviser on drugs, Peter Bourne, a psychiatrist who finally lost his job for writing an illegal prescription for one of his aides. But before he even entered the White House office, Bourne made his feelings on drugs quite clear.

At least as strong a case could probably be made for legalizing [cocaine] as for legalizing marijuana. Short acting—about 15 minutes—*not physically addicting,* and acutely pleasurable, cocaine has found increasing favor at all socioeconomic levels in the last year. Although it is capable of producing psychosis with heavy, repeated use, and chronic inhalers can suffer eventual erosion of the nasal membrane and cartilage, the number of people seeking treatment as a result of cocaine use is for all practical purposes zero. . . . One must ask what possible justification there can be for the obsession which DEA officials have with it, and what criteria they use to determine the interdiction of a drug if it is not the degree of harm which it causes the user. [Italics added.][74]

It is an utterly remarkable passage. It deserves to be sealed in a time capsule to give future generations a notion of the myths surrounding drug use of that decade. Bourne, of course, was at best telling half-truths about the properties of cocaine. He also apparently had his own carefully hidden agenda about his own use, later revealed when he reached the goldfish bowl of the White House.

There was contempt for those working at the DEA as well, for those who could not appreciate his "knowledge" when it came to commenting on drugs and their supposed dangers. Needless to say, Dr. Bourne was too preoccupied with his own pursuits to be interested in tracking the Colombian cocaine cartel that was establishing a clear and present danger at the time of his comments. An expert on drugs should have known about this. Bourne's boss, James Earl Carter, was hardly any better. Elaine Shannon recounts a particularly revealing story:

In the fall of 1980 [!], a DEA agent was invited to join a small group of politicians and White House aides who were making small talk with Carter between campaign stops. Carter noticed the large stranger and asked where he worked. "I work for you, sir," the agent said proudly, puffing out his chest. "For me? Where?" Carter asked. "For the DEA," the agent said. Carter stared at him blankly. "DEA," the agent prompted. "Drug Enforcement." Carter's expression changed from puzzlement to boredom. He turned away and began to chat with other guests about politics.[75]

Carter's "boredom" was understandable. The administration was rife with apologists for and consumers of all kinds of drugs. The Carter years, in short, were America's maximum tolerance for drugs. It was an invaluable four years' breathing space for the Colombian cartel and their allies to build the kind of infrastructure that has defied latter-day attempts to tear it apart. But it allowed the myth of the drug culture to deepen, rooting itself even further into all levels of American society. This is the legacy from an administration that only wanted a government as good as the American people; one searches in vain the platforms of the Democrat party in the 1970s and 1980s to find even the least awareness of the drug problem. The Republicans meanwhile fussed and fumed and unimaginatively attacked heroin users, a safe target because they were believed to be anything but Republican. From the Democrats there was nothing but a wink, a nudge, and a knowing smile, asserting that certain drugs were harmless.

Not much has changed. In the 1988 campaign, liberal Democrat Michael Dukakis could bring himself to address drugs only in the context of condemning Panama's strongman Manuel Antonio Noriega and his drug dealings, and the Reagan administration's inability to rid the world of him. At the same time, Governor Dukakis had nothing to say about how drugs in the United States had become such a problem. No one in the media bothered to ask. Only lately has one Democrat pollster, Tubby Harrison of Boston, suggested that the party had lost the battle with the Republicans over "values and symbols." To recoup, Harrison suggested that the Democrats, among other things, "[get] tough on crime and drugs."[76]

Can a culture be changed with these leaders? Only with great difficulty. This is why the United States is far from a serious attack on the problem. Though far from hopeful, the situation is not totally hopeless. The corrosion and corruption of America goes on. The physical effects of drug-related behavior, such as AIDS, violence, and crime are only part of the story; there is another matter I call the Colombianization of America. When Americans think of Colombia, some no doubt imagine a criminal conspiracy having wrecked the legal institutions in one country, yet the United States is hardly immune. What is known already is frightening. What can be anticipated is far worse.* There are reports

*Richard Foster described this advancing phenomenon as follows:

> The enormous profits from drugs create a new dimension of corruption—of police, the courts, prosecutors, mayors, city councilman, and the entire political legal system

of local police in south Texas, for example, who are on the payroll of narcotics smugglers; in South Florida, the Miami police force is riddled with bought and paid officers; and recently, seven Los Angeles DEA agents were suspended on suspicion that they diverted for their own use cash seized from arrested drug dealers, while the DEA's supervisor of internal investigations commented, "If somebody wants to go bad, there's nothing you can do to stop it."[78]

None of this should come as a surprise. The Colombian cartel, in particular, with its long experience in buying off police and judges, can hardly be expected to change its pattern once here in America. In its view, every man has his price, and the odds are in the cartel's favor. After all, if a teenage crack pusher in Washington, D.C., can earn as much as $1,000 a day tax free, how much would the payoff be for a federal judge?[79] It hardly stops with the cops and the courts. Take the pathetic example of a Georgia Republican congressman, Patrick Swindall, convicted last August and sentenced to a year in jail. His crime? Lying to a federal grand jury about a money-laundering scheme that would have netted him an $850,000 loan to build a luxury home. He had negotiated with an undercover federal agent over plans to launder money generated from the sale of illicit drugs.[80]

Drugs are not doing the legal profession any good, either. Lawyers—some of whom are former state and federal attorneys—are specializing in defending drug-connected criminals, a pattern that faithfully copies what happens in Colombia. Can it happen here? Listen to Michael Abbell, former chief of the Justice Department's office of international affairs and now a Washington lawyer representing Gilberto Rodriguez Orejuela, a Cali drug kingpin: "My impression of them is they are legitimate busi-

---

of cities and local government generally. A "double corruption" phenomenon takes place: the corrupt official may become a user and has a double stake in protecting the drug traffickers. The scope of corruption is international; one has only to examine Panama's General Noriega for a prime example.[77]

nessmen. I've never seen any cocaine or drugs whenever I've been with them."[81] Why would Abbell and others spout such nonsense? Simple: it pays well; and with courts and jails already overburdened with drug cases, a good lawyer can easily get a reduced sentence for his client.[82]*

Better known is the story of a DEA agent (and a highly decorated one, at that), Edward K. O'Brien, who has admitted to carrying cocaine from Florida to Boston on two occasions for $147,000. On the second trip he was arrested with sixty-two pounds of cocaine in his possession. For the Colombian cartel, what could be better than having its product transported under the protection of a federal officer? The reason for O'Brien providing the service was simple: he needed the money.[84]† Not surprisingly, DEA agents have been caught before in similar schemes; hundreds of investigations are carried out each year by the DEA after allegations surface—and O'Brien was the fourth agent arrested in 1989 alone.[85]‡ What made the O'Brien case particularly frightening is DEA's fear that the arrested agent may have compromised plans and operations on a global basis. Since May 1988, O'Brien had been staff coordinator overseeing agency operations in Europe and the Middle East, which meant that he had access to all information about major drug investigations there and in this country. The possibility of a well-placed cartel

---

*The drug-lawyer phenomenon has its own grim humor. In December 1988, one hundred of them gathered in Key West, Florida, to commiserate and exchange techniques for defending their clients. According to the *Wall Street Journal,* "a significant purpose of the meeting seemed to be to lift the lawyers' spirits a bit. 'Practicing drug law is like beating your head against a wall,' says lawyer John Wesley Hall, Jr., cradling an empty beer. 'Then you come here and talk to these guys and you realize you are not alone out there.' " What the *Journal* reporter left out was the money made from their highly specialized practice.[83]

†O'Brien's younger brother is also charged with being involved in the drug-running operation. O'Brien had been decorated by both the American and French governments for his work in breaking the French connection, a ring of heroin smugglers headquartered in Marseilles.

‡The charges against the three formerly Los Angeles–based agents were formidable: theft of seized drugs, money laundering, and dealing in major quantities of heroin and cocaine.

mole has alarmed DEA officials and prompted a top-to-bottom investigation. In the words of David Westrate, assistant DEA administrator in charge of the operations division, "It's a damage assessment. It's extremely serious."[86]

Another form of the Colombianization of America is prosecutors who are having an increasingly difficult time finding witnesses willing to give evidence. Reason? They are being intimidated. On the streets of Washington, D.C., for example, bystanders who see the killings are threatened by the gunmen on the spot if they report anything to the police. To retain any credibility, the cops have stopped making reassurances that giving evidence will not be fatal.[87] Those who want to organize and combat drug dealers on the local level face many difficulties. The *Washington Post* describes what often happens: "Organizational meetings are often tense because of wide-spread fears that dealers are in attendance. After the meetings, many participants speak of getting veiled threats. At its most extreme, residents watch their own neighbors work in tandem with the drug trade."[88] In fact, community organizers like the brave Martha Hernandez of Brooklyn are threatened and then killed if they persist. In Hernandez's case, she was to testify before a grand jury. Usually, like Hernandez, they have little support from their neighbors who either are afraid or benefit themselves from the drug trade.[89] As in Colombia, the smarter drug dealers win the hearts and minds of local residents by doling out small amounts of cash. They become the local Robin Hood. It is effective and it frustrates the police. As a result: "Doors are open to dealers being chased by police, allowing them in some cases to disappear in a maze of houses or apartments without anyone seemingly seeing anything, hindering further investigations."[90]

That is not all, as Roscoe Howard, an assistant U.S. attorney in Richmond, Virginia, learned. After cracking a major cocaine distribution ring in rural Caroline County, a few of the seventeen defendants were willing to turn state's evidence. They were, that is, until they were told by a stranger: "We know where your family is." It was straight from the Medellin threat manual—and it worked.[91] A Prince George's County, Maryland, defense attorney described how it has all changed in the last few years: "I remember when I first got into the business, the attitude [about cooperating witnesses] would be that that's their problem; they're going to have to live with the guilt [of informing on their associates]. Nowadays, they're able to blow their house up, kill them and take their firstborn."[92] The lawyer knows what he is talking about. According to the *Washington Post:* "Witness intimidation got so bad in Prince George's County this year [1989] that State's Attorney Alex Williams said in March he would ask the Maryland legislature to change the crime of witness intimidation from a misdemeanor to a felony."[93] Maryland is no different from many other states ill-prepared to thwart the intimidation of witnesses; and since drug cases depend on this form of evidence, state and even federal courts will be hard-pressed to gather it. Thus, bit by bit the American legal system is being challenged, corrupted, and changed, just as society and its culture is being corrupted under the impact of illegal drugs.

One other institution needs to be mentioned, the banking system. Until three years ago, money laundering was not even against the law. As a consequence, many banks never bothered to check very closely large infusions of cash that suddenly appeared. This is especially true among Florida's and California's financial institutions. Even now, despite the new law, many banks are reluctant to look too closely. To be sure, they argue that their only purpose is to protect the privacy of their legitimate clients; but it is a convenient excuse. The recent federally run Operation Polar Cap that caught the Panamanian-based Banco de Occidente red-handed is only the tip of a large iceberg.[94]* In the long run, it is an open question of whether the U.S. can regain the integrity of its institutions or simply go the way of

---

*At least two American banks are being investigated from this particular affair, the Continental Bank in New York and the Guarantee International Bank of Stamford, Connecticut.

Colombia. This benefits not only the drug cartels worldwide, but America's ideological enemies as well.

So what can be done?

The *Economist,* in a recent leading article, called war on drugs "Mission Impossible." That is to say, the United States, much less Colombia, cannot solve its drug problem by present methods, meaning law enforcement. "Repression," it said, "however vigorous, cannot win the war against drugs." People with a craving for drugs are going to do them no matter what. They always have and will.[95] The editors instead prefer legalization (presumably all drugs, no matter how dangerous) and detailed regulation: taxes, purity checks, health warnings, and the like. It is a familiar argument and has had a growing number of adherents. Political libertarians, of course, who believe the solution to all human misery is open and free markets for everything; liberals like Hodding Carter III, and conservative William F. Buckley, Jr., have long advocated legalization because, as Carter put it recently, "We are losing the drug war because prohibition never works, [p]rohibition can't work, won't work and has never worked."[96]

The argument has its appeal, aside from the assurance that "prohibition" is no more practical than the Volstead Act banning the manufacture, distribution, and sale of alcoholic beverages in 1919. Furthermore, it contends that a vast amount of government spending could be saved if the legal apparatus were turned toward something else. Corruption, too, would be halted. Moreover, the price of drugs would go down, making it far less profitable for the gangs and the cartels. Presumably some of them would find other forms of employment.

But is this a solution? Most experts doubt it. They do so in spite of the bad news coming in from the various fronts of the drug war. For one thing, precedent for legalization is not very encouraging. When Britain legalized heroin through prescription, the system worked for awhile—until lower-class youngsters discovered the narcotic. Heroin consumption in the U.K. increased forty times, until the system had to be abandoned.[97]

If legalization were tried not just on heroin, but a whole range of drugs, what might happen? Without the law, the moral authority against taking drugs would be drastically undercut, especially for the young. "Why can't I, dad? After all, it is legal" is something that would be heard in quite a few American homes were we to go the route of legalization. Even among the libertarians, not many argue for legalization without regulation; but regulation would have to be enforced, and the costs would not be cheap. How much would we save in the end? How much of the problem would we actually decriminalize? Who will profit from the new legitimate drug business; and what about the ethical implications?

It is likely that legalization would cause a drop in the price of drugs, at least in the beginning. The first effect, however, would be to increase consumption, including crack and its designer-drug equivalents. In time, the additional demand would again drive up the price. Meanwhile, society will pay severely for the increased usage. Along with crack and all the future chemicals that promise nirvana there undoubtedly will be some very nasty side effects. Crack, in addition to sudden death, causes pathological levels of sexual activity and violence that stimulates the addict's brain. The combination of crack, the AIDS virus, and a sharp rise in the syphilis rate and other sexually transmitted diseases (in the U.S.) is leading experts to fear that AIDS increasingly is spreading through heterosexual contact.[98] Violence pales in comparison.

The greatest difficulty with legalization is that consumption no doubt will go up. The criminal element will not simply fade away, as most legalizers casually assume. Mark Kleiman, a drug-policy expert formerly with the Justice Department, commented recently, "No one should ever assume that the future cannot be worse than the present: In a singing contest never award the prize to the second soprano until you have heard her sing, even if the first one was awful."[99] This is precisely where the analogy to America's experience with Prohibition breaks down. It is assumed that the criminals will remove themselves from the drug business just as the Al Capone crowd got out of illicit alcohol. Organized crime did not go away. The mafia gangs made their profits elsewhere, and the crime families continue to flourish today. Will the Colombian cartels and their American allies abandon narcotics if they are made legal? Hardly. When Prohibition ended in 1934, there were already large and legal entities, distilleries and breweries, ready to step in and slake the thirst of Americans. The same will happen with the legalization of illicit drugs. In the beginning, the "shift of profits from illegal dealers to legitimate firms"[100] will make the private sector in America very happy; the total impact of unprohibited drug consumption in time would devastate all the foundations on which this country is built.

There is no exact counterpart with illegal drugs; cocaine does not have its equivalent of an Anheuser-Busch or a Seagram's, which brings us to another problem that economists understand very well, even if some liberal social thinkers do not. It is called *ease of entry*. That means that getting started with some products and services is easier than with others, owing to start-up costs and a variety of other factors. With the manufacture and distribution of illicit drugs ease of entry will not be simple, because even a loosely grouped criminal cartel will resist, violently if necessary, the loss of markets to legitimate dealers. They will continue to fight over turf among themselves, unless they are accepted as the legitimate supplier. Meanwhile, as the British experience proved after every drug law was repealed—a utopian legislative notion—there soon would be massive leaks of drugs from legal suppliers to the black market. Why? Because it would be immensely profitable for individuals.[101]

In short, a realistic knowledge of human nature and the laws of the marketplace is not the legalizer's strongest suit. Moreover, the thought that the Colombian and Syrian-Lebanese narcotraffickers and their American gang allies will see the handwriting on the wall and enter another line of business is hopelessly naive. In fact, it is laughable; street gang members are not suddenly going to become realtors or earn Harvard MBAs. They will fight, and fight hard, to hold on to what they have gotten. This time, the police will not be able to touch them unless the gangs are violating the new set of regulations that accompany legalization. In that case, of course, we are back to where we started: except that drug consumption has suddenly shot upward.

Another small matter the legalizers tend to overlook is the reality of the streets. In the ghettos in particular, consumers will stick to their own rather than the "legitimate" drugstore. Most people continue to place bets with their known bookies rather than a state betting agency; even the white middle-class drug user also earns psychic income by participating in a demi-monde activity. Buying drugs at an ABC store simply does not have the same allure as having one's own dealer. In the end, nothing would really change, except that a layer of bureaucracy would be added to the top, something that would probably be abolished in time, as it was in Britain. But there would be differences. The moral underpinnings to any antidrug effort in the future would be knocked away. We thus would be at least one more generation away from controlling, but not eliminating this tangible evil. As we have stated, any antidrug effort without an accompanying change in the basic cultural attitudes and beliefs of the society stands small chance of success. As long as the idea that it is okay to use a few drugs recreationally continues to be accepted by many leading policy and public-opinion makers, there is no "war on drugs"; and as long as opinions are considered as facts replacing the real hard data based on scientific studies in pharmacology, epidemiology, physiology, and psychology, opinions that reach the public through the media, there will be no "war on drugs," because the public fails to understand the reasons for this war or the danger of losing it.

Finally, a quote from the drug czar William Bennett's speech at Harvard's Kennedy School of Government. The consensus about the legalization of drugs has a political dimension . . . the far right has a tendency to assert that the drug problem is essentially a problem of the inner city . . . if those people want to kill themselves off with drugs, let them kill themselves off with drugs, would be a crude but not too inaccurate way of summarizing this position. . . . On the left, it is something else . . . the problem facing us isn't drugs at all they say, it's poverty or racism or some other equally large and intractable social phenomenon. If we want to eliminate the drug problem these people say, we must "eliminate the root causes of drugs."[102]

Bennett went on to compare racism with drugs and said that racism in the United States was dealt with through education, prevention, the media and, not least of all, the law: "so too with drugs." According to Bennett, those favoring legalization who claim that there is a "debate," surrounding the issue are doing so to suggest that there is indeed an argument, and a serious one. "More sober minds recognize the recipe (legalization or decriminalization) for a public policy disaster."[103] It must be said that behind many of the arguments for legalization is the hidden agenda of the majority (if not all) of advocates. Legalization would justify their own use of drugs, a throwback of course to the 1960s. What they want are chemical pleasures brought to them without risk and, more important, without moral stigma.

Can anything be done to halt the undermining of American society?

This is a very large topic indeed, but before we launch into a real (as opposed to rhetorical) war on drugs, certain structural problems must be understood. As we have seen, drug arrests have increased enormously in most cities in the last few years. That trend is likely to continue. But the District of Columbia provides a good example of the effect on the system: in Washington, while arrests are up 43 percent, prosecutions for drug offenses have increased no less than 500 percent; convictions, *700 percent*. But, as Wilson and DiIulio explain, that is hardly the end of the problem:

Clearly judges and prosecutors were starting to get tough. But until very recently, the toughness stopped at the jailhouse door. As recently as 1986, only seven percent of the adults arrested on drug charges—and only 20 percent of those convicted on such charges— were sent to the city's principal correctional facility at Lorton.[104]

Which was already crowded. In short, the problem won't be relieved, because there isn't any more jail room.

On April 4, 1990, Bush administration officials concluded that Mr. Bennett's special test case, winning the war on drugs in Washington, D.C., has failed. D.C. remains the nation's "murder capital" and drugs are more available everywhere in the city. "We haven't had a drug war. We've played some foolish games," concluded D.C. police chief Isaac Fulwood.[105] Following these statements, it is reasonable to assume that accusations for this failure will fly, and the efforts to contain the drug problem will be pushed aside.

In New York it is hardly any better. Those arrested stood only a 50-percent chance of being indicted; a 38-percent chance of being convicted; and only a 15-percent chance of going to prison. In the opinion of the *Wall Street Journal*: "In other words, the overwhelming percentage of those arrested are in the street and smirking within days."[106] As a result, the cost to dealers is slight. Plea bargaining for shorter sentences is a relatively easy affair, and the profits earned from drug dealing are so great that short stretches in jail become only one more business cost.*

But jail capacity is not the only problem. There are not enough prosecutors and judges. There is no shortage, however, of defense lawyers to handle the present caseload, but we can anticipate one if we were to fully enforce present (not to mention future) laws. Of course, Washington, D.C., is not unique. In New York,

---

*Provided, of course, the criminal is dealing with state and local courts. The 1986 antidrug legislation provides immutable and mandatory sentencing for drug dealers—and the penalties are harsh, provoking some criticism by judges as to the law's inflexibility.[107]

the number of convicted drug felons in jail has increased 500 percent since 1989, compared to 200 percent for the rest of the prison population. As for federal prisons, no less than 44 percent of the population are there for drug offenses—and these same prisons are 58 percent over "planned capacity."[108] In Florida, it is estimated that forty to fifty new prisons in that state alone will be necessary to deal with the *known* backlog of drug offenders.[109]

There are other structural problems in waging any kind of real war against drugs, and the federal government provides several outstanding examples. A real war, of course, will require new legislation and appropriations from the Congress. But the Senate and House have no less than seventeen full committees and thirty-six subcommittees with jurisdiction over illegal-drug issues. Everything from Senate Agriculture to House Ways and Means has had and will have a piece of the action.* Thus, no matter how well thought out any administration's plan may be when introduced, how long will it take to put through, and how coherent will be the result? Precedent is not encouraging when one talks about controversial ideas like tax reform and trade matters; drugs will prove no less difficult.

This is only the beginning: the executive branch has no less than thirty-three agencies and departments involved in the drug effort, among them the FBI, the DEA, Customs, the CIA, the Coast Guard (nonsensically located in the Department of Transportation), the Pentagon, and so on. All approach the problem from their unique perspective, and turf battles and jealousies are no secret, nor are they confined to any one administration. The military is very reluctant to be involved in the fight, even though

---

*Not that certain congressmen don't have peculiar ideas on the subject. Representative Charles B. Rangel, a prominent New York Democrat and (to his credit) a strong opponent of drug use nevertheless has recently criticized the Bush administration for not cooperating with Fidel Castro on stopping the drug flow. "After all, it is drugs, not communists, that are killing our kids." The problem with this is that the communists, Castro included, *are* helping kill the kids. Castro, as described in chapter 2, for years has aided and abetted narco-traffickers and narco-terrorists.[110]

it is now carrying out some interdiction and training chores. Most of the interagency conflict seldom is seen by the public—although once in awhile it does emerge. For example, when the Commissioner of Customs William von Raab sent in his letter of resignation to President Bush in July 1989, it was no two-paragraph note praising his boss for allowing him the privilege of serving the American people; instead, it settled some old scores: "The political jockeying, back stabbing and malaise that has crept into the current effort have frustrated me, and are threatening the anti-drug efforts and successes of the past years."[111] Who was involved? William von Raab was not about to avoid mentioning names, and the State Department was at top of the list: "[State] has objected to every effort to control foreign drug production; thus earning the title, the 'conscientious objectors' in the war on drugs. . . . Many senior officials want to negotiate and compromise on policies, rather than take strong, tough actions."[112] The Justice Department was hardly treated better in von Raab's letter; the Coast Guard was in the wrong department, the Department of Transportation; Treasury officials, his home department, "have shown at best a distinct lack of interest in the drug efforts of the Customs service, and at worst an outright demotion of Customs in relation to other Treasury priorities."[113] Criticism about von Raab ran just as deep within the agencies and departments he criticized. "Loose cannon" were probably the kindest words said about him—this from an anonymous State Department official.[114]

Of course, this conflict and backbiting will not make any drug policy easier to carry out, even if one were to emerge from both ends of Pennsylvania Avenue. The appointed "drug czar," William Bennett (incidentally, a title he loathes), is in a difficult if not impossible position. His job gives him no real line authority over the antidrug forces. He cannot tell any agency how to deploy its agents or spend its money. Suggestions only, please. That means he is largely left with coordinating its work—but coordination depends on exerting some form of authority; that his suggestions count when it comes to the White House, the Congress, and budget time, is the one thing that does concentrate the minds of bureaucrats quite wonderfully.[115]

What does Bennett have? It seems very little, beyond his own abilities and convictions. President Bush did not give him cabinet rank, and he is not a member of the NSC—which alone sends the inadvertent signal that drug use is not a national security problem. That leaves Bennett's association with the president. In the busy world of Washington this is at best a difficult relationship.[116]

Another problem is the uncertain foundation laid on the drug front during the Reagan administration. To be sure, there was a corrective shift in rhetoric and action from the darker days of Carterian tolerance; in terms of real programs during the first five years, there were only the interdiction of drugs in the form of a vice-presidential South Florida task force, and Mrs. Reagan's "Just Say No."[117] Nor should that be surprising; Ronald Reagan was and is an astute politician. In the early 1980s there still was no perceived drug problem in the U.S., and had the president moved, chances are that he would have failed.

By 1986, however, that all changed. The catalyst: crack. It was a new drug, it was dangerous, and it was associated with violence. Also, the favorite recreational drug of the upper-middle class, cocaine, was proving surprisingly lethal, as Maryland basketball star Len Bias found out too late. Almost like thunderstorm on the prairie, the major media discovered the downside of drugs. The national newspapers, *Time, Newsweek, Life,* and such relative journalist lightweights as *People* and *Sports Illustrated,* were doing major features on drug abuse and its awful consequences— almost as if they were making up for lost time.[118]*

Suddenly, politicians were falling all over themselves in a rush to deal with the problem. The result? A hastily put together "Anti-Drug Abuse Act of 1986." Elaine Shannon captures its flavor:

*CBS's "Forty-eight Hours on Crack Street" had the highest Nielsen rating of any television documentary in the last five years.

"[I]t consumed fifty-six pages of the *Congressional Record* and touched on every conceivable aspect of substance abuse, from marijuana eradication in the national forests to alcoholism on Indian reservations."[119] In other words, a little something for everyone.

Now it was George Bush's turn. To be sure, he did not wait long to announce his own view on drugs. In his inaugural address, the new president made clear the fight would be a priority. Bush's early appointment of William Bennett and his orders to the drug czar to produce a plan within six months were steps in the right direction—though the deadline approach smacked of Jimmy Carter's ill-conceived energy legislation of 1977. Still, there were worries; even Republicans feared that the president and his largely upper-class, business-oriented cabinet were unable to understand the devastating effect of drugs on American society. To be blunt about it, the precise worry was that the president and his men truly believed drugs to be simply one more inner-city problem, and nothing more. Whether this is the case or not will be seen in the coming months. If drugs do have a priority, Bennett will get the necessary backing, and other matters (such as diplomatic relations with Syria, for example) will genuinely take second place. Only the White House can decide that; if it were up to the State Department, the outcome would be different. Some signs are not encouraging: the issue of drugs did come up at the Group of Seven economic summit held in Paris in 1989, and appeared in the communiqué—well down among the list of concerns, along with international cooperation against AIDS.[120]

William Bennett is no stranger to the problem. He also understands that there is no one magic bullet to take care of the problem. Even more important, he understands the fundamental need for a wholesale change in attitudes and beliefs that must be deeply held among the nation's elite in particular. One idea (that soon fell by the wayside) is the use of so-called drug bonds, pushed by Democrats and Republicans alike: the U.S. Treasury would sell bonds at market rates to help finance the war on drugs. The money raised is secondary, however, according to its supporters; Representative Jerry Lewis, a Republican from California, explains: "Bonds will unite the American people in the war on drugs. No war has ever been won without the support of the American people. And no one can doubt that in combating today's drug crisis we are fighting for the lives of our children and our nation."[121] Stirring words, and true ones at that. But despite a favorable nod from Bennett and a hundred congressional co-sponsors on Capitol Hill, the White House poured cold water on the idea, citing budgetary difficulties.[122]

Still, Bennett has persisted. Clearly, the new $7.8 billion program announced by President Bush on national television on September 5, 1989, is an eclectic one, and instantly drew fire from many—particularly Democrats—who heretofore had little or nothing to say about America's drug crisis; yet this is not entirely more of the same old thing, as some analysts would have it. The Bush administration has made drugs a moral problem, stressing individual accountability. "Doing your own thing" is no longer acceptable in America, and after having wandered in the wilderness for twenty years or so, this is the start of a new direction.[123]

There also has been a shift away from a nearly exclusive emphasis on interdiction, and with all the money and effort expended, American enforcement agencies, Customs, the Border Patrol, and even military units still intercept as little as 10 percent of all drugs smuggled into this country. Busts are at an all-time high; unfortunately, so are imports. Thus, while federal officials seized over 27 metric tons of cocaine in 1986 (compared to 1.7 tons in 1981), exports jumped from an estimated 68 metric tons in 1981 to at least 153 tons in 1985.[124] As a result, the interdiction efforts of the Reagan administration that once consumed 80 percent of the federal antidrug budget will be somewhat deemphasized. The budget increases for the new program for the Coast Guard and Customs amount to only $73 million.[125*]

But enforcement has a new look: new federal prisons are to be built, increasing capacity by 85 percent; state and local authorities will be encouraged to toughen up against the druggies; and money will be provided to back up the inevitable consequences (i.e., more arrests): up to $350 million.[127] The other relatively new approach is to punish the fancy dan users, the well-heeled casual consumers of cocaine and hashish who are the mainstay of the narco-trafficker's and terrorist's income. Recreational users, now clearly recognized by law enforcement as criminals, can expect heavy fines, including confiscation of their beloved BMWs, and they also now run the risk of spending time in a military boot camp. For the draft-dodging generation this should have an especially poignant bite to it. (Of course, this is reserved for first-time offenders; a second offense will result in something more serious.) "That should cut across nerve ends from coast to coast," A. M. Rosenthal, legendary editor of the *New York Times*, drily observed.[128] For a gutless group of pleasure mongers, a whiff of grapeshot would be more than enough to convince them their little vices are no longer tolerated—provided that well-publicized and consistent punishment does, in fact, take place.

The penalties have caused the inevitable outcry in the guise of concern for civil liberties, and as a result may never be fully applied. The American elite has a way of rationalizing its illicit pleasures,† and has the political and legal muscle to protect itself

*Criticism of Bennett's interdiction program is voiced also by those who call for the legalization of drugs. "Bennett, to the extent he promotes drug interdiction, is promoting higher drug profits."[126]

†But more often, they use economic rationales such as: "the captains of the cocaine economy are no different from the producers of beer, wine, liquor, semi-automatic weapons, cigarettes, phone sex, MTV, fluorocarbons or dirt bikes. They all sell pleasurable consumption with varying degrees of alleged antisocial consequences. The cocaine economy is not an aberration in the national consumer economy but a microcosm of it."[129]

from the full extent of the law; but just possibly, for the first time it may not succeed. If it does not, it could be a major blow to the drug empire's income and to America's soft underbelly, its underclass of marginals who could never quite make up for the financial losses. [130]

Drug-treatment programs also would get more money; but the soft notion that people will come in willingly has been given some backbone: Bennett intends some treatment to be made compulsory—a red flag waved in front of civil libertarians. Experience with these programs suggests, however, that without an element of coercion it will be money largely wasted. [131] According to Wilson and DiIulio:

The advocates of treatment and prevention sometimes argue as if these programs can be made to work under wholly voluntary arrangements, provided enough treatment seem preferable to the callous toughness of law enforcement strategies. This is sometimes true, but for the majority of addicts it is a serious error, akin to thinking that alcoholics will follow their doctors' advice, if there are enough doctors around. Alcoholics need some measure of coercion; AA supplies it, through the peer pressure generated at regular meetings of other alcoholics. Cocaine users will require even more pressure because coke is far more pleasure-giving than alcohol. [132]

As with addiction, the problem is that very little is known about treatment: what works, what doesn't. Most studies on this subject are still under way.* New drugs, especially those that could help with crack withdrawal, are still in the experimental stage. The question is, how much money should be spent on various initiatives when no doubt much of it will be wasted? [134] No

---

*In his article "Little Is Known About Treatments," Kenneth Bacon is quoting Dr. Fredrick Goodwin, Director of the Federal Alcohol, Drug Abuse and Mental Health Administration, saying: "We simply don't have enough knowledge about what works." [133]

one knows for sure; possibly, no one will ever have a complete answer.

As for education and prevention, more money is to be spent: $392 million, an increase of over $35 million that had been previously allocated. But like the treatment portion of the program, there is a hard edge to education as well. Schools will be pushed to adopt tougher policies for students caught with drugs, including suspension of high-school students and loss of federally funded scholarships for college students.[135]

Finally, the Bush administration wants to spend more money investigating drug money laundering—the new budget line item for this would be $130 million, an increase of $11 million.[136] Is it enough? No. With budget restraints and the administration's commitment to refrain from any tax increases, its refusal even to consider drug bonds has prevented any further spending.

We have concentrated on Andean South America as if that spells out the whole problem now facing the United States with regard to the threat of narco-terrorism. It does not. Just as in the 1970s, when American politicians considered heroin to be the worst of the drug problem, we have become fixated on Colombia and, to a lesser extent, Peru and Bolivia. If such is the case, sooner than later we are in for a rude awakening. But that is hardly the only problem. Desperate Democrats are making drugs a partisan issue. With their power in the Congress, a reasonably coherent program already has turned into a fragmented, increasingly incoherent mess. In the meantime, complaints about President Bush's lack of oratorical flash miss the point. Churchillian prose won't solve the problem; absolute Churchillian stubbornness—the refusal to quit—is crucial if there is to be hope for any progress at all.

It very much remains to be seen whether the administration will stay the course, or simply abandon it for something more politically profitable. One thing is certain: unless Americans curb their appetite for drugs, they will continue to provide the funds that the world's drug traffickers and their terrorist allies need to continue their war against the United States and the West—and the price we finally pay will dwarf anything we are spending now. It is a cheerless future Americans are facing; the signs are that Americans do not yet fully understand it. This is equally true for most of America's political and cultural leaders.

Postscript

——————— ▐▌▌▌▐ ———————

The Bush administration's original program announced in September 1989, is an important step in the right direction, particularly in the domestic area. But it is not enough, as the failure of the "war on drugs" in Washington, D.C. proves. The foreign aspect of the problem barely has been touched upon. This is because the whole problem has yet to be acknowledged, much less defined.

The administration has defined only what is deemed to be an American drug-consumption problem; and it has defined this as a national security threat. What Washington has not yet done is to identify the sources of this threat in order to combat it. What has been neither acknowledged nor identified are the origins of what we now are forced to live with, the drug war in the streets of America. Government policy deals only with the problem as it exists from day to day, reacting to the current situation, but no solution can be found unless the root causes are identified.

State sponsorship of narco-terrorism has been ignored thus far because of other diplomatic priorities. If this continues it will result in further escalation. The past failure to acknowledge Marxist-Leninist state sponsorship of narco-terrorism has helped create the infrastructure operating so successfully and independently today. When we began the war on drugs we viewed ourselves as standing on the edge of a precipice, and in light of what is happening today, it seems that the only progress we have made is to take a giant leap forward. In other words, it's like taking aspirin for a headache caused by an infected tooth; the aspirin serves to fool us into thinking we have dealt with the problem.

The real enemy in this war on drugs is not the American people; it is those states and organizations who combine drugs with terror in a still largely clandestine war against Western societies, above all, the American one. Since the enemy has not been clearly defined he cannot be eliminated, and therefore the measures already proposed will be necessarily incomplete, sometimes misdirected, and the problem will not be solved. The narco-terrorist looking at the accumulating evidence of misdirected Western antidrug efforts finds reason to believe that he is winning the war of attrition. But even here the metaphor of conventional war is misleading: the narco-terrorist wins if he survives. What is to be done?

First, with acknowledgment of the problem comes concrete changes in our antidrug effort. This means changing intelligence priorities both in the collection and analysis of data. At the least it means identifying the risks and vulnerabilities of each country in the Western Hemisphere and their effect on U.S. security. Among other things, it means an examination of the international drug cartels' growing control over governmental institutions and our lessening ability to influence favorable antidrug activity. Second, much more investigation has to be done on the economic and financial implications of narcotics trafficking in all countries affected, particularly in the United States. We need to understand the effect on U.S. banks and other financial institutions of drug-derived profits that worldwide amount to hundreds of billions of dollars each year. Means and methods have to be devised to disrupt the flow of resources to the narco-terrorists through all financial institutions. For the United States, one crucial negotiating point will be the actual implementation of laws by signatory countries shutting down money-laundering operations in banks and financial institutions throughout the world. Third, we must learn from our efforts in the past. A country-by-country analysis of efforts to combat the drug menace, including laws, legal institutions, law enforcement (or its absence), successes, and failures is needed. Only on this basis can we at least begin to harmonize enforcement measures throughout the Western world.

But dealing with one's friends and allies is not enough. Narco-terrorism should become a major issue in bilateral discussions in the international community, including the Soviets and their explicit and implicit allies. Avoiding the problem may encourage those countries that until recently used drugs as a political weapon to continue to do so for economic benefits. Terrorist organizations and other subversive groups have witnessed the success of the drug business and the failure of democratic governments to deal with the problem; in all probability, this will embolden them to continue business as usual.

Indeed, one acid test of our commitment to combat narco-terrorism will be the reordering of our diplomatic priorities. Adding one more divisive issue to the East-West agenda is never popular in Western foreign ministries, much less in the west wing of the White House; but it is time to stop pretending that drug trafficking is exclusively a criminal enterprise. The source is ultimately political and should be dealt with as such. It should identify those outlaw states such as Syria and organizations such as the PLO and their involvement in the business. Failure to do so means the war will still be fought on the wrong front, in the wrong way, with little or no chance of victory.

Notes

———————— ▐▐▐▐▐ ————————

Introduction

1. Rowland Evans and Robert Novak, "Honecker as Pusher," *Washington Post,* 7 March 1990.
2. Elxos Konstantinidis, "Drug Traffickers in Cyprus Were PLO Representatives," *Yediot Aharnonot* (Tel Aviv), 4 February 1990 (in Hebrew).
3. Douglas Farah, "Colombian Political Violence Surges, with Renewal of Drug War Awaited," *Washington Post*, 8 March 1990.
4. Karen Payne, "Indictment Links Castro to Noriega, Drug Cartel," *Miami News,* 5 February 1988.
5. Ralph Cwerman, *Narco Terror: Lebanon and the Bloody Politics of Drugs* (typescript, 1987), p. 42.
6. Rick Bowers, "Smugglers Detail Nicaraguan Drug Role," *Miami Herald,* 20 April 1985.
7. Peter A. Lupsha, *Towards an Etiology of Drug Trafficking and Insurgent Relations: The Phenomenon of Narco-Terrorism* (typescript, 1989). Professor Lupsha suggests that " 'narco-terrorism' is currently a badly defined and politically contaminated term." (p. 1). See also Grant Wardlaw, "Linkages Between Illegal Drug Traffic and Terrorism," *Conflict Quarterly* 7 (3 [Summer 1988]): 7 and 24, as well as James Inciardi, "Narco-terrorism: A Perspective and Commentary," paper presented at the 1988 Annual meeting of

the Academy of Criminal Justice Sciences, Chicago, April 4–6, 1988, pp. 2 and 20. These critics object to the use of "narco-terrorism" as a definition because they consider it elusive.

8. U.S. Committee on the Judiciary, Senate Subcommittee on Security and Terrorism, "The Role of Cuba in International Terrorism and Subversion," 97th Cong., 2d. sess., 26 February, 4, 11, 12 March 1983 (Washington, D.C.: Government Printing Office, 23 April 1982), pp. 2–3.

9. See the transcript from the hearings before the Senate Drug Enforcement Caucus, the Senate Subcommittee on Security and Terrorism and the Senate Foreign Relations Subcommittee on Western Hemisphere Affairs, 30 April 1983: *The Cuban Government Involvement in Facilitating International Drug Traffic*. Further evidence relating to Cuba's involvement in narco-terrorism will be found in chapter 2.

10. *Sovetskaya Voyenna Entsiklopedia*, vol. 7 (Moscow: Voyenizdat, 1979), p. 493; S. Pope, "Diversion: An Unrecognized Element of Intelligence?" *Defense Analysis* 3 (2 [1987]): 133–151. See also Victor Suvorov, "Spetsnaz—The Soviet Union's Special Force," *International Defense Review* (September 1983): 1210. In addition, see Russian texts of the "Soviet Military Encyclopedic Dictionary" of 1986 wherein the definition of special reconnaissance remains the same.

11. As reported in the *New York Times,* 27 November 1989, p. A12.

12. As reported from Moscow, Mary Dejevsky, "Lenin article Boosts Gorbachev," *New York Times,* 8 March 1990.

13. Evans and Novak, "Honecker as Pusher."

14. Martin Fletcher, "Honecker Smuggled Cocaine," *New York Times*, 8 March 1990.

15. George P. Shultz, speaking before the Greater Miami Chamber of Commerce, 14 September 1984. See the *Miami Herald*, 15 September 1984.

Chapter 1. The Little Brothers from Bulgaria

1. For a concise analysis of Bulgaria's ties to and services on behalf of the Soviet Union, see Paul B. Henze, *The Plot to Kill the Pope* (New York: Charles Scribner's Sons, 1983), pp. 91–103.
2. Blaine Harden, "Bulgarians Oust Three from Politburo," *Washington Post,* 17 November 1989, p. A53.
3. For further reading about Bulgaria's relation to the USSR, see J. F. Brown, *Bulgaria Under Communist Rule* (New York and London: Praeger, 1970).
4. *Rabotnichesko Delo,* 28 May 1962, as cited in J. F. Brown, *Bulgaria Under Communist Rule,* p. 129.
5. Associated Press Wire Service, 24 October 1983.
6. U.S. Department of Justice, *Special Report,* "The Involvement of the People's Republic of Bulgaria in International Narcotics Trafficking," Drug Enforcement Administration, Office of Intelligence, May 1984, p. 5.
7. Nathan M. Adams, "Drugs for Guns: The Bulgarian Connection," *Reader's Digest* November 1983, p. 97.
8. U.S. Justice Department, *Special Report,* p. 2.
9. Ibid.
10. *Bottin International Business Register,* vol. 2, *Europe* (1983), p. 927.
11. As confirmed by the Justice Department, *Special Report,* p. 2.
12. Ibid.
13. Svirdlev quoted in Justice Department *Special Report.*
14. U.S. Justice Department, *Special Report,* appendix, p. 1.
15. For a vivid description of KINTEX and Sofia in the early 1970s, see *The Heroin Trail,* a 1974 Pulitzer prizewinner written by the staff and editors of *Newsday* (Holt, Rinehart and Winston: New York, 1973).
16. See Captain Robert B. Workman, U.S. Coast Guard (retired), *International Drug Trafficking: A Threat to National Security* (typescript, 1984).
17. See U.S. Justice Department, *Special Report,* p. 3.
18. Adams, "Drugs for Guns," p. 90.

19. Justice Department, *Special Report,* p. 6.
20. Ibid., appendix, p. 1.
21. Ibid., pp. 93–95.
22. Quoted in Workman, *International Drug Trafficking,* chap. 2, p. 7.
23. Reported by Justice Department, *Special Report,* p. 8.
24. Ibid., pp. 93–95.
25. Ibid., p. 10.
26. Ibid., p. 11.
27. Statement of John C. Lawn before the Foreign Affairs Committee Task Force on International Narcotics Control, U.S. House of Representatives, 3 May 1984, p. 4.
28. Quoted in Justice Department, *Special Report,* p. 4.
29. Ibid., p. 6.
30. Ibid., appendix, p. 2.
31. Testimony of Francis Mullen, hearings before Senate Subcommittee on Alcoholism and Drug Abuse, 2 August 1984, p. 22. See pp. 25 and 32, for Sofia's reaction to American concerns. Washington had supplied names and addresses of known traffickers living in the Bulgarian capital. Needless to say, they remained safely in place pursuing "openly flamboyant and free-spending lifestyles."
32. Ibid., p. 95, for testimony of Paul B. Henze.
33. DEA quoted in Justice Department, *Special Report,* p. 7.
34. Ibid., pp. 6–7.
35. Details are to be found in Peter Fuhrman, "The Bulgarian Connection," *Forbes,* 17 April 1989, p. 41.
36. Ibid., p. 42.
37. Ibid.
38. Ibid.
39. Justice Department, *Special Report,* appendix, pp. 2–3.
40. See Henze, *Plot to Kill the Pope,* pp. 91–103, for his chapter on "Bulgarians as Mercenaries."
41. Ibid., p. 97; see also Paul Seabury and Angelo Codevilla, *War: Ends and Means* (New York: Basic Books, 1989), p. 25.
42. Further details in John Barron, *KGB: The Secret Work of Soviet Secret Agents:* (New York: Reader's Digest Press, 1974), pp. 29–57.

43. Velichko Peitchev, a Bulgarian defector, in an interview in the *New York Times*, 23 March 1983.

44. Henze, hearings before Senate Subcommittee on Alcoholism and Drug Abuse, pp. 98–99; and Justice Department, *Special Report*, appendix, p. 8.

45. The best account of this sordid affair can be found in Claire Sterling, "The Plot to Murder the Pope," *Reader's Digest*, September 1982. Also a useful chronology of the events can be found in the Justice Department's *Special Report*, appendix, pp. 7–10.

46. Louis Freeh, quoted in U.S. Department of State, *International Narcotics Control Strategy Report*, (Washington, D.C.: Bureau of International Narcotics Matters, 1 March 1989), p. 159.

47. Freeh, quoted by Peter Samuel, "Senior Bulgarian Aides Linked to a Booming Trade in Heroin," *New York City Tribune*, 30 March 1989.

48. U.S. State Department BINM, *Strategy Report*, pp. 159–60.

49. The leak was first reported in Samuel, "Senior Bulgarian Aides." Peter Fuhrman followed with a lengthy article in *Forbes*, "The Bulgarian Connection," 17 April 1989.

50. Samuel, "Senior Bulgarian Aides."

51. Ibid.

52. See Foreign Broadcast Information Service, *Soviet Union Daily Report*, 25 April 1989, p. 15 (official use only).

Chapter 2. The Cuban Connection: Castro, Cocaine, and Terror

1. Quoted in Rolando E. Bonachea and Nelson P. Valdes, eds., *Revolutionary Struggle: The Selected Writings of Fidel Castro*, vol. 1 (Cambridge, Mass.: MIT Press, 1972), p. 379. This most revealing letter was not published in the official Cuban press until 27 August 1967, in *Granma Weekly Review* (Havana), p. 8, long after the myth had been established that the United States had pushed Castro into communism.

2. Interview in *Revolución* (Havana), 1 November 1964, as

cited in Theodore Draper, *Castroism, Theory and Practice* (New York: Praeger, 1965), p. 103.

3. For more on Cuba's economy before and after the revolution, see Claes Brundenius, *Revolutionary Cuba: The Challenge of Economic Growth with Equity* (London: Westview Press, 1984).

4. For details on Cuba's economic and social condition before Fidel's revolution, see Hugh Thomas, *The Cuban Revolution* (New York: Harper Torchbooks, 1977), p. 125; see pp. 311–398 for a thorough description of old Cuba. See also Draper, *Castroism,* pp. 97–103; and Camelo Mesa-Lago, *The Economy of Socialist Cuba: A Two Decade Appraisal* (Albuquerque: University of New Mexico Press, 1981), pp. 9–10.

5. Louis A. Pérez, Jr., *Cuba: Between Reform and Revolution* (New York: Oxford University Press, 1988), pp. 185–86. For more on the effects of the Platt amendment, see Thomas, *Cuban Revolution,* p. 641.

6. Staff and editors of *Newsday, The Heroin Trail* (New York: Holt, Rinehart and Winston, 1973), pp. 167–72.

7. Captain Robert B. Workman, U.S. Coast Guard (retired), *International Drug Trafficking: A Threat to National Security* (typescript,1984), p. 22. See also, U.S. Department of State, "Cuban Involvement in Narcotics Trafficking," 30 April 1984.

8. John Dorschner and Jim McGee, "The Case Against Cuba," *Tropic: Miami Herald Sunday Magazine,* 20 November 1983.

9. Drug Enforcement Administration, "Involvement in Drug Trafficking by the Government of Cuba," July 1971, declassified 31 March 1982, p. 3.

10. Letter from Sal Vizzini, then chief of police, South Miami, to Morley Safer, CBS, 27 February 1978. The Cubans who were arrested in 1962 and 1963 were Ramon Diaz and Jose Barrel.

11. For a thorough analysis of Cuban support of and involvement in international terrorism, see U.S. Department of State, "Cuba's Renewed Support for Violence in Latin America," *Spe-*

cial Report no. 90 (Washington, D.C.: Bureau of Public Affairs, 14 December 1981).

12. Raymond W. Duncan, *The Soviet Union and Cuba: Interests and Influence* (New York: Praeger, 1985), pp. 66–70.

13. For Soviet-Cuban relations, see "Cuba's Renewed Support for Violence in the Hemisphere," research paper presented by the Department of State to the Senate Foreign Relations Committee, Subcommittee on Western Hemisphere Affairs (Washington, D.C.: Government Printing Office, 14 December 1981), pp. 3, 6, and 8. See also Roger W. Fontaine, *Terrorism: The Cuban Connection* (New York: Crane Russak, 1988); and Timothy Ashby, *The Bear in the Backyard: Moscow's Caribbean Strategy* (Mass. and Toronto: Lexington Books, 1987).

14. Fontaine, *Terrorism,* p. 3.

15. Selwyn Raab, "A Defector Tells of Drug Dealing by Cuban Agents," *New York Times,* 4 April 1983.

16. Brian Ross, "The Cuban Connection," "NBC Nightly News," 29 September 1982.

17. For a full account of the DA and its widespread activities, see Rex A. Hudson, *Castro's America Department* (Washington, D.C.: Cuban American National Foundation, 1988).

18. Francis M. Mullen, Jr., in testimony before the House Committee on Foreign Affairs, Task Force on International Narcotics Control, "Cuban Government Involvement in Drug Trafficking," 21 February 1984, p. 3.

19. Ibid.

20. For reports on Cuba's early involvement in drug trafficking to the U.S., see DEA, "Involvement in Drug Trafficking"; see also, Joint hearings before the Senate Committee on Foreign Relations and the Committee on the Judiciary, *International Terrorism, Insurgency, and Drug Trafficking: Present Trends in Terrorist Activity,* 99th Cong., 13, 14, and 15 May, 1985 (Washington, D.C.: Government Printing Office, 1986), p. 130.

21. *La Habana,* 30 September 1977 (in Spanish).

22. DEA, "Involvement in Drug Trafficking," pp. 4, 5, 6.

23. Nathan M. Adams, "Havana's Drug Smuggling Connection," *Reader's Digest,* July 1982.

24. "NBC Nightly News," 29 September 1982.

25. Testimony of Thomas O. Enders, hearings before the Senate Committee on the Judiciary, Subcommittee on Security and Terrorism, "The Role of Cuba in International Terrorism and Subversion," 97th Cong., 2d sess., 26 February, 4, 11, 12 March 1982 (Washington, D.C.: Government Printing Office, 23 April 1982), pp. 2–3.

26. *Castro and the Narcotics Connection* (Washington, D.C.: Cuban-American National Foundation, 1983), p. 9.

27. Mullen, "Cuban Government Involvement," p. 4.

28. Joint hearing before the Senate Committee on the Judiciary, Subcommittee on Security and Terrorism and the Senate Foreign Relations Committee and the Drug Enforcement Caucus, Subcommittee on Western Hemisphere Affairs, "The Cuban Government's Involvement in Facilitating International Drug Traffic," 98th Cong., 1st sess., 30 April 1983, Serial J-98-36.

29. *U.S. Government Confidential Report,* as cited in "Narcotics: Terror's New Ally," *U.S. News and World Report,* 4 May 1987.

30. For more details on both David Lorenzo Pérez and Mário Estévez González activities see the District Court of the U.S. for the Southern District of Florida, 7 February 1983, no. 82-643-Cr-JE.

31. "Cuban Government Involvement in Facilitating International Drug Traffic," pp. 59–68.

32. Stanley Penn and Edward T. Pound, "Havana Haven," *Wall Street Journal,* 30 April 1984.

33. *U.S. Government Confidental Report,* p. 61.

34. Ibid.

35. U.S. Department of State and Department of Defense, *The Soviet-Cuban Connection in Central America and the Caribbean* (Washington, D.C.: Government Printing Office, March 1985), p. 38, cited by Rachel Ehrenfeld in "Narco-Terrorism and the Cuban Connection," *Strategic Review* 16 (3 [Summer 1988]): 60–61.

36. Joel Brinckley, "Panel Hears Details Linking Managua and Drugs," *New York Times,* 20 April 1985.

37. Susan Sachs, "Cuban Government Protecting Drug Runners, Smuggler Says," *Miami Herald,* 11 July 1985.

38. Bill Gertz, "Castro Runs a Resort for Narcotics Dealers," *Washington Times,* 23 March 1988.

39. Michael Isikoff, "Five Guilty in $10 Million Cocaine Run," *Washington Post,* 26 July 1988. Further details in Michael Hedges, "Videotapes Bind Cuba Officials to Cocaine Ring," *Washington Times,* 28 July 1988.

40. Quoted in *Washington Times,* (editorial), 22 June 1989.

41. Foreign Broadcast Information Service (FBIS Latin), 13 July 1989, pp. 1–26.

42. Ibid., 16 July 1989, p. 1.

43. Ibid., 19 June 1989, p. 1.

44. Robert Pear, "Cuban General and 3 Others Executed," *New York Times,* 14 July 1989.

45. Julia Preston, "Castro's 'Iron' Response on Drugs Masks Issues," *New York Times,* 1 August 1989, p. A14.

46. Julia Preston and Michael Isikoff, "Top Officer Arrested in Cuba," *Washington Post,* 17 June 1989; Robert Pear, "Cuba Arrests Top General on Corruption Charges," *New York Times,* 18 June 1989.

47. Tad Szulc, "Join with Castro to Fight Drugs," *New York Times,* 9 August 1989.

48. Rachel Ehrenfeld, "Castro is Shocked!! Shocked! to Find Drug Dealing Comrades," *Wall Street Journal,* 23 June 1989.

49. Michael Isikoff, "Drug Flights Unabated Over Cuba," *Washington Post,* 28 June 1989.

50. AP, 8 July 1989, cited in *Castro and the Narcotics Connection* (Washington, D.C.: Cuban-American National Foundation, 1989).

51. Rachel Ehrenfeld, "Narco-Terrorism and the Cuban Connection," p. 62.

52. For more information on Gorbachev's agenda, see Mikhail Gorbachev, *New Thinking for Our Country and the World* (New York: Harper & Row, Perennial Library ed., 1988).

53. Blandon's testimony before a grand jury in Miami, January

1988, and in hearings before the Senate Committee on Foreign Relations, Subcommittee on Terrorism, Narcotics, and International Communications, "Drugs, Law Enforcement, and Foreign Policy: Panama," 100th Cong., 2d sess., 8, 9, 10, and 11 February 1988 (Washington, D.C.: Government Printing Office, 1988), p. 104; and as reported by the *Washington Times,* 11 February 1988.

54. Senate Committee on Foreign Relations, "Panama," p. 108.
55. Ibid., pp. 106–8.
56. See U.S. intelligence sources, State Department.
57. Allan Gerson, Deputy Assistant Attorney General, Office of Legal Counsel, Department of Justice, in remarks made at the Central America Briefing at the White House, 14 March 1986, p. 3 (typescript).
58. Ibid.
59. For further details about Herring's credibility, see Commissioner von Raab's testimony before the Senate Committee on Labor and Human Resources, Subcommittee on Children, Family, Drugs and Alcoholism, "The Role of Nicaragua in Drug Trafficking," 99th Cong., 1st sess., 19 April 1985 (Washington, D.C.: Government Printing Office, 1985), pp. 26–37.
60. Carlton-Sherwood, "Undercover Agent Plans to Detail Vesco Drug Tie to Cuba, Managua," *Washington Times,* 19 April 1985.
61. "Cuban Government Involvement in Facilitating International Drug Traffic," pp. 45–46.
62. Gerson, Central America Briefing.
63. Ehrenfeld, "Narco-Terrorism and the Cuban Connection," p. 59.
64. Testimony of Alvaro Jose Baldizon Aviles, hearing before the Senate Committee on the Judiciary, Subcommittee on Security and Terrorism (Washington, D.C.: Government Printing Office, March 1985), pp. 24–35.
65. Ibid., p. 35.
66. Ibid.
67. "Cuba, Soviet Union Sign $14.7 Billion Trade Pact," *Wall Street Journal,* 19 April 1990.

68. The reports on Cuba's continuing involvement in drug trafficking and its continuing strategic importance were revealed
by a defector from the Cuban Ministry of the Interior. See
Bill Gertz, "Cuba Involved in Novel Drug-Smuggling Tech-
nique," *Washington Times,* 3 July 1991, p. 10; Jonas Bernstein, "A Cuban Trump Card," *Insight,* 1 July 1991, pp. 20–
22.

Chapter 3. The Lebanese Inferno: Drugs and Terror

1. Meir Zamir, *The Formation of Modern Lebanon* (Ithaca, New
York: Cornell University Press, 1985).
2. See "Lebanon's Slide," *Economist* (London), 5 August 1989,
p. 39.
3. Youssef M. Ibrahim, "Lebanon Slain Pact," *New York Times,*
23 November 1989.
4. Ali Jaber, "French Rightists Visit Lebanon to Support Ren-
egade General," *New York Times,* 30 November 1989.
5. Ibid.
6. Detailed information can be found in U.S. Department of
State, *International Narcotics Control Strategy Report*
(Washington, D.C.: Bureau of International Narcotics Matters, March, 1988), pp. 218–20.
7. "Lebanon's Slide," p. 39.
8. Thomas Hobbes, *The Leviathan: Or the Matter, Form and
Power of a Commonwealth, Ecclesiastical and Civil* (New
York: Collier Books, 1962), pp. 101–2.
9. Barbara Newman (with Barbara Rogan) *The Covenant: Love
and Death in Beirut* (New York: Crown, 1989), pp. 130–31,
211.
10. Ralph Cwerman, *Narco Terror: Lebanon and the Bloody Politics of Drugs* (typescript, 1987), p. 42.
11. Ibid., pp. 42–43.
12. In *An-Nahar,* 24 June 1985.
13. Cwerman, *Narco Terror,* p. 45.
14. See U.S. State Department, BINM, *Strategy Report,* pp.
221–22.
15. Cwerman, *Narco Terror,* p. 45.

16. Ibid., pp. 48–49.
17. U.S. State Department, BINM, *Strategy Report,* p. 221.
18. Cwerman, *Narco Terror,* p. 50.
19. Ibid., p. 52.
20. For the development of contemporary international terrorist organizations, see Roberta Goren, *The Soviet Union and Terrorism* (London: Allen & Unwin, 1984), quote on p. 109.
21. Newman, *The Covenant,* p. 211.
22. Cwerman, *Narco Terror,* pp. 55–56.
23. Jenney Chater, "Police Link Ex-President to Heroin Racket," *Sydney Morning Herald,* 19 November 1987.
24. U.S. State Department, BINM, *Strategy Report,* p. 221.
25. Jaber, "French Rightists Visit Lebanon."
26. Cwerman, *Narco Terror,* pp. 22, 49, 56. See also Newman, *The Covenant,* pp. 211–12.
27. More about Syria's support of terrorism in Daniel Pipes, "Terrorism: The Syrian Connection," *National Interest* (no. 15 [Spring 1989]): 15–28.
28. Rachel Ehrenfeld and Peter Samuel, "Drugs, DEA, and Damascus," *Australian Review* (25 August–7 September 1987): 4–5.
29. H.R. 2979, "To Impose an Embargo on Trade with Syria," 29 June 1989, p. 4.
30. Cwerman, *Narco Terror,* p. 62.
31. Ibid., p. 37.
32. Ibid., p. 23. For another detailed and well-documented account of the PLO's activities in Lebanon, see Raphael Israeli, ed., *PLO in Lebanon, Selected Documents* (London: Weidenfeld and Nicolson, 1983), especially pp. 1–7.
33. James Adams, *The Financing of Terror* (New York: Simon & Schuster, 1986), p. 233; See also "Terrorists Move Into Drug Trade," *Sunday Telegraph* (Sydney), 18 August 1985; and Athalie Thomas and Kent Acott, "Thirty-five Charged Over $40 Million Drug Racket," *West Australian* (Perth), 16 August 1985.
34. Ihsan A. Hijazi, "PLO Completes Buildup in Lebanon," *New York Times,* 2 April 1990.

35. Ran Dagoni, "Drug Traffickers in the U.S. Finance the PLO," *Maariv,* 9 March 1990 (in Hebrew).

36. For documentation on the Communist bloc–PLO connection, see Israeli, *PLO in Lebanon,* pp. 33–203.

37. *Sovetskaya Voyenna Entsiklopedia* (Moscow: Voyenizdat, 1979).

38. Ibid., vol. 7, p. 493; S. Pope, "Diversion: An Unrecognized Element of Intelligence?" *Defense Analysis* 3 (2 [1987]): 133–51; Victor Suvorov, "Spetsnaz—The Soviet Union's Special Force," *International Defense Review* (September 1983): 1210. In addition, see Russian texts of the *Soviet Military Encyclopedic Dictionary* of 1986, wherein the definition remains the same.

39. Goren, *Soviet Union and Terrorism,* p. 108.

40. See Damian J. Fernandez, *Cuba's Foreign Policy in the Middle East* (Boulder, Colo.: Westview Press, 1988), pp. 72–74, 91–92. See also Roger W. Fontaine, *Terrorism: The Cuban Connection* (New York: Crane Russak, 1988), pp. 113–18.

41. Goren, *Soviet Union and Terrorism,* p. 123.

42. This letter can be found in full in the *Congressional Record,* E2476, 12 July 1989, Washington, D.C.

43. See Israeli, *PLO in Lebanon,* ch. 5, "The Communist Bloc Connection" (documents 7–39), pp. 33–59.

44. Goren, *Soviet Union and Terrorism,* p. 140.

Chapter 4. Colombia: The Superstate of Narco-Terrorism

1. U.S General Accounting Office, "Drug Control, U.S.-Supported Efforts in Colombia and Bolivia," GAO-NSIAD-89-24, November 1988, p. 16.

2. Roger W. Fontaine, *Terrorism: The Cuban Connection* (New York: Crane Russak, 1988), p. 97.

3. See U.S. Department of State, "Cuba's Renewed Support for Violence in Latin America," *Special Report* no. 90 (Washington, D.C.: Bureau of Public Affairs, 14 December 1981), p. 10.

4. Douglas W. Payne, "The Drug 'Super-state' in Latin America," *Freedom at Issue,* (March–April 1989): 7.

5. See Michael Isikoff, "Medellin Cartel Leaders Offered U.S. a Deal," *Washington Post,* 20 July 1988.

6. For a book-length account of the Colombian cocaine mafia, see Guy Gugliotta and Jeff Leen, *Kings of Cocaine* (New York: Simon & Schuster, 1989).

7. Richard Gott, *Guerrilla Movements in Latin America* (New York: Doubleday, 1971), pp. 223–29; see also Hubert Herring, *A History of Latin America* (New York: Knopf, 1964), p. 519.

8. Herring, *History of Latin America,* pp. 497–511.

9. For details on Cuba's role in promoting unrest, see U.S. State Department, *Special Report.*

10. Fontaine, *Terrorism,* pp. 95–111. See also, Roger W. Fontaine, *The Colombia Question* (typescript, 1988), p. 25.

11. Fontaine, *Terrorism,* pp. 95–99.

12. U.S. State Department, *Special Report,* pp. 9–10.

13. Testimony of Thomas O. Enders, hearings before the Senate Committee on the Judiciary, Subcommittee on Security and Terrorism on the Role of Cuba in International Terrorism, 97th Cong., 2d sess. (Washington, D.C.: Government Printing Office, 1982).

14. U.S. State Department, *Special Report,* pp. 9–10. See also Fontaine, *Colombia Question,* p. 25.

15. U.S. State Department, *Special Report,* pp. 9–10. See also Fontaine, *Terrorism,* pp. 95–211.

16. Fontaine, *Terrorism,* p. 3.

17. U.S. State Department, *Special Report,* p. 10.

18. GAO, "Drug Control in Colombia and Bolivia," p. 25.

19. Fontaine, *Colombia Question.*

20. Ibid., p. 24. See also U.S. intelligence sources.

21. Ibid.

22. U.S. Department of State, *Libyan Activities in the Western Hemisphere,* August 1986, pp. 3–4.

23. *Colombia: A Country Study* (Washington, D.C.: Foreign Areas Studies, American University, 1971).

24. Michael Getlan and Jurgen Robinson, "Colombia's War on

Drugs Zeroes in on Just Two Men," *Washington Post,* 29 October 1989.

25. All figures on cocaine and marijuana are U.S. estimates in GAO, "Drug Control in Colombia and Bolivia," p. 23.

26. Ibid., p. 18.

27. *Economist* (London), 2 April 1988, p. 63.

28. Gugliotta and Leen, *Kings of Cocaine,* p. 22.

29. Rensselaer W. Lee III, "Why the U.S. Cannot Stop South American Cocaine," *ORBIS,* 32 (4 [Fall 1988]): 501.

30. GAO, "Drug Control in Colombia and Bolivia," p. 13.

31. James Baker, "Threat to Global Security," Current Policy no. 1251 (Washington, D.C.: U.S. Department of State, Bureau of Public Affairs, 20 February 1990), p. 2. See also, Tina Rosenberg, "The Kingdom of Cocaine," *New Republic,* 27 November 1989, p. 30.

32. James Brooke, "Bush and Colombia to Assess the Drug War," *New York Times,* 5 June 1990, p. A15.

33. *New York Times,* 21 August 1989, p. A3.

34. Alan Riding, "Intimidated Colombia Courts Yield to Drug Barons," *New York Times,* 11 January 1988.

35. Lee, "U.S. Cannot Stop South American Cocaine," p. 503.

36. Gugliotta and Leen, *Kings of Cocaine,* p. 171.

37. *New York Times,* 21 August 1989, p. A3.

38. Michael Hedges, "U.S. Races Deadline to Extradite Drug Financier," *Washington Times,* 24 August 1989.

39. Joan Moody, "Noble Battle, Terrible Toll," *Time,* 19 December 1989, p. 33; and Brooke, "Bush and Colombia," p. A15.

40. George J. Church, "Going too Far," *Time,* 4 September 1989, pp. 12–13.

41. Sarita Kendall, "Colombia Steps Up War on Drugs," *Financial Times* (London) 22 August 1989.

42. James M. Dorsey, "Colombians Not Confident of Triumph Over Cartels," *Washington Times,* 6 September 1989, p. A7. See also, U.S. Department of State, *International Narcotics Control Strategy Report* (Washington, D.C.: Department of International Narcotics Matters, 1 March 1990), p. 126.

43. Foreign Broadcast Information Service (Latin), 90-058, 26 March 1990, p. 51.

44. Special Report from Consuelo Ahunede, ed., *Ciencia Politica* (Bogotá), April 1990.
45. FBIS-LAT-90-062, 30 March 1990, p. 37.
46. Fontaine, *Colombia Question*, p. 31.
47. Rosenberg, "Kingdom of Cocaine," p. 31.
48. Fontaine, *Colombia Question*, p. 52.
49. Isikoff, "Cartel Leaders Offered U.S. a Deal."
50. Juan Guillermo Cano, *El Espectador,* 7 February 1988.
51. Riding, "Colombia Courts Yield to Drug Barons."
52. U.S. Department of State, *Country Reports on Human Rights Practices for 1987* (Washington, D.C.: Government Printing Office, February 1987), p. 427.
53. Ibid., p. 431.
54. Peter A. Lupsha, professor of political science of the University of New Mexico, Albuquerque, quoted in Roger W. Fontaine, "Colombia" (typescript, 1 June 1990), p. 20.
55. Herring, *History of Latin America,* pp. 497–511.
56. GAO, "Drug Control in Colombia and Bolivia," p. 25.
57. Testimony of Thomas O. Enders; also quoted in *Castro and the Narcotics Connection* (Washington, D.C.: Cuban-American National Foundation, 1983), p. 23.
58. From U.S. intelligence sources.
59. U.S. State Department, BINM, *Strategy Report,* p. 129.
60. Elaine Shannon, *Desperados: Latin Drug Lords, U.S. Lawmen, and the War America Can't Win* (New York: Viking Press, 1988), p. 147.
61. U.S. State Department, BINM, *Strategy Report.*
62. Lee, "U.S. Cannot Stop South American Cocaine," p. 502.
63. Ibid., p. 503.
64. Bruce Michel Bagley, "Colombia: The Wrong Strategy," *Foreign Policy* (77 [Winter 1989–90]): 163.
65. Gugliotta and Leen, *Kings of Cocaine*, pp. 91–98. See also Alan Riding, "Colombia Drug Lords Acquire Ranches and Allies," *New York Times,* 21 December 1988; and Mark A. Uhlig, "Colombia's War on Cocaine: Farmers' Fears Help Cause," *New York Times,* 3 July 1989.
66. Gugliotti and Leen, *Kings of Cocaine*, pp. 91–98.
67. Michael Isikoff and Eugene Robinson, "Colombia's Drug

Kings Becoming Entrenched," *Washington Post,* 8 January 1989.

68. Jonathan Hartlyn, "Drug Trafficking and Democracy in Colombia," paper prepared for presentation at the Conference on Drug Trafficking, Human Rights and Democracy in Colombia, Washington, D.C., March, 1989, pp. 20–21.

69. As quoted in Fontaine, *Colombia Question,* p. 27.

70. Ibid., p. 47.

71. See FBIS-Latin, 1 March 1989, p. 12.

72. Bagley, "Colombia," p. 161.

73. See U.S. intelligence sources.

74. Bagley, "Colombia," p. 164.

75. *Washington Post,* April 1988.

76. Fontaine, *Colombia Question,* p. 41.

77. Ibid., p. 40.

78. Moody, "Noble Battle, Terrible Toll," p. 33.

79. James Brooke, "High Cost of Fighting Drugs Strains U.S.-Colombian Ties," *New York Times,* 4 June 1990, p. D1.

Chapter 5. Peru and Bolivia: The Spreading of the Empire

1. U.S. Department of State, *International Narcotics Control Strategy Report* (Washington, D.C.: Bureau of International Narcotics Matters, March, 1990), pp. 157–60.

2. Merrill Collett, "Drugs, Rebels Persist on Andes Frontier," *Washington Post,* 11 August 1987.

3. U.S. State Department, BINM, *Strategy Report,* p. 157.

4. Richard Gott, *Guerrilla Movements in Latin America* (New York: Doubleday, 1971), p. 9.

5. Roger W. Fontaine, *Terrorism: The Cuban Connection* (New York: Crane Russak, 1988), p. 102.

6. Ibid.

7. Ibid., p. 103.

8. James Brooke, "U.S. Pilots in Peru Join Battle Against Forces of Coca Trade," *New York Times,* 12 April 1990, p. A1.

9. José Carlos Maríategui, *Siete Ensayos de Interpretación de la Realidad Peruana* (Lima: Editorial Anauta, 1965).

10. See U.S. intelligence sources.
11. Gabriela Tarazona-Sevillano, "The Personality of Shining Path and Narco-Terrorism" (typescript, 29 February 1988), p. 2.
12. Ibid., p. 13.
13. Ibid., p. 3.
14. Ibid.
15. Ibid.
16. Jonathan Cavanagh, ed., *Peru Report* 1 (2 [February 1987]): 42.
17. Ibid., pp. 39–40.
18. Tarazona-Sevillano, "Shining Path and Narco-Terrorism," p. 10.
19. U.S. State Department, BINM, *Strategy Report,* p. 154; and James M. Skinner, "Narco-Guerrilla Warfare," *Defense and Diplomacy* 8 (5 [May 1990]): 51.
20. Tarazona-Sevillano, "Shining Path and Narco-Terrorism."
21. Lima Television Peruana, 3 May 1989, and found in Foreign Broadcast Information Service (Latin), 4 May 1989. See also Jose Gonzalez, "Shining Path Receives Alarming Aid in Tingo Maria," *Congressional Research Service*, Library of Congress, 12 May 1989.
22. Tarazona-Sevillano, "Shining Path and Narco-Terrorism," p. 13.
23. Ibid., p. 14.
24. See James Brooke, "Peru Builds Base to Combat Coca Production," *New York Times*, 13 June 1989.
25. See Eugene Robinson, "Peruvian Rebels' Influence Extends to Lima's Doorstep," *Washington Post*, March, 1989.
26. Michael Isikoff, "U.S. Suffering Setbacks in Latin Drug Offensive," *Washington Post*, 27 May 1989.
27. Alan Riding, "Rebels Disrupting Coca Eradication in Peru," *New York Times*, 26 January 1989.
28. Isikoff, "U.S. Suffering Setbacks."
29. Michael Isikoff, "U.S. Expands Role in Peru's Drug War," *Washington Post*, 29 January 1989.
30. Isikoff, "U.S. Suffering Setbacks."
31. Brooke, "Peru Builds Base."

32. Ibid. For an equally grim assessment of the problem, see Roger Cohen, "Peru's Guerrillas Draw Support of Peasants in Coca-Rich Regions," *Wall Street Journal,* 17 January 1989.

33. Guy Gugliotta and Jeff Leen, *Kings of Cocaine* (New York: Simon & Schuster, 1989), p. 120.

34. Ibid.

35. Joseph B. Treaster, "In Bolivia, U.S. Pumps Money into the Cocaine War, but Victory Is Elusive," *New York Times,* 11 June 1989.

36. U.S. State Department, BINM, *Strategy Report* (March 1988), pp. 69–78.

37. Merrill Collett, "Leftists Challenge Airfield Project," *Christian Science Monitor,* 31 May 1989.

38. Treaster, "U.S. Pumps Money into the Cocaine War."

39. Ibid.

40. Ibid.

41. Charles Garcia to Ann B. Wrobeleski, "Bolivia Trip Report" (November 5–12, 1988), Department of State memorandum, 17 November 1988, p. 2.

42. Ibid., p. 3.

43. Ibid., p. 4.

44. For an equally pessimistic assessment of Bolivia's efforts, see the U.S. General Accounting Office, "Drug Control, U.S.-Supported Efforts in Colombia and Bolivia," GAO-NSIAD-89-24, November 1988, p. 3.

45. Collett, "Leftists Challenge Airfield Project."

46. Isikoff, "U.S. Suffering Setbacks."

47. Madrid EFE, 1 July 1989, and published in FBIS (Latin), 3 July 1989.

Chapter 6. The Other America: From Grass to Crack

1. *New York Post,* 11 August 1989, p. 1.

2. For the facts about Fort Wayne, Indiana, see Julie Johnson, "Drug Gangs and Drug Wars Move into the Rural States, U.S. Warns," *New York Times,* 4 August 1989.

3. U.S. General Accounting Office, "Drug Control, U.S.-

Supported Efforts in Colombia and Bolivia," GAO-NSIAD-89-24, November 1988, pp. 25–26.

4. Quoted in Michael Isikoff, "Drugs Are Top Problem in U.S., Poll Shows; Tougher Laws Favored," *Washington Post,* 13 August 1989, p. A4.

5. Steve Twomey, "Public Lists Drugs as Number One Problem," *Washington Post,* 18 August 1989.

6. Ibid., for Wirthlin's separate survey.

7. Michael Wines, "Poll Finds Public Favors Tougher Laws Against Drug Sale and Use," *New York Times,* 15 August 1989.

8. Ibid.

9. Ibid.

10. Richard Morin, "Drug Abuse Leads Nation's Worries," *Washington Post,* 23 August 1989, p. A22.

11. Ibid.

12. Twomey, "Drugs as Number One Problem."

13. Ibid.

14. Dan Sperling, "Cocaine Use among College Grads Is Rising," *USA Today,* 7 August 1989.

15. Elaine Shannon, *Desperados: Latin Drug Lords, U.S. Lawmen, and the War America Can't Win* (New York: Viking Press, 1988), p. 33.

16. Ibid.

17. See *The Heroin Trail* (New York: Holt, Rinehart and Winston, 1973), pp. xi–xii, written by the staff and editors of the Long Island newspaper, *Newsday.*

18. U.S. Department of State, *International Narcotics Control Strategy Report,* (Washington, D.C.: Bureau of International Narcotics Matters, submitted to Committee on Foreign Affairs and Committee on Foreign Relations, 1 March 1988), p. 15.

19. *USA Today,* 6 February 1989.

20. Richard L. Berke, "Record 14 Officers Killed in '88 Drug Incidents, a Study Shows," *New York Times,* 3 September 1989.

21. Associated Press Wire Service, "Drug-Related Police Deaths

Hit Record," *Washington Post,* 4 September 1989. See also Berke, "Record 14 Officers Killed."

22. AP, "Violent Crimes Increase by 5.5% for 1988, Establishing a Record," *New York Times,* 13 August 1989.
23. Ibid.
24. Ibid.
25. See Sari Horwitz, "Homicides in District Push Past the 300 Mark," *Washington Post,* 30 August 1989, p. A1.
26. Philip Shenon, "Bush Officials Say War on Drugs in the Nation's Capital Is a Failure," *New York Times,* 5 April 1990, p. A1.
27. Horwitz, "Homicides Past 300 Mark."
28. Shannon, *Desperados,* p. 369.
29. James Q. Wilson and John J. Dilulio, Jr., "Crackdown," *The New Republic,* 10 July 1989, p. 21.
30. Ibid. For the grisly details, see Gina Kolata, "In Cities, Poor Families Are Dying of Crack," *New York Times,* 12 August 1989.
31. Wilson and Dilulio, "Crackdown."
32. Ibid.
33. Ibid.
34. Ibid.
35. "Cocaine's 'Dirty 300'," *Newsweek,* 13 November 1989, pp. 36–41.
36. Tracie Reddick, "Gangland Killings in D.C. Emulate Capone-Era Style," *Washington Times,* 31 August 1989. See also Nancy Lewis and Michael Isikoff, "By Highway and Air, California Connection Supplied D.C.," *Washington Post,* 4 September 1989; and Michael Isikoff and Nancy Lewis, "Making a D.C. Link to the Colombian Source," *Washington Post,* 3 September 1989.
37. Reddick, "Gangland Killings."
38. State of New York, Division of Substance Abuse Services, "Street Drug Alert, Street Research Unit" (pamphlet), Bureau of Research and Evaluation, November 1989.
39. Ibid.

40. Michael Isikoff, "Bennett to Crusade Against Crack," *Washington Post,* 26 July 1989.
41. Michael Marriott, "Heroin Seizure at 3 Queens Sites Is Called Biggest U.S. Raid," *New York Times,* 22 February 1989. See also National Drug Enforcement Policy Board, "National and International Law Enforcement Strategy," executive summary submitted to the Congress, 20 January 1987, p. iii.
42. See U.S. Department of Justice, "The Twenty City Report: The Illicit Drug Situation in Twenty Metropolitan Areas Mid-Year 1984," October 1984, p. 60.
43. See Jay Mallin, "Heroin-Crack Mix Headed for Schools," *Washington Times,* 1 September 1989.
44. Steven Erlanger, "U.S. Debates Aiding Burmese in Drug Fight," *New York Times,* 1 April 1990, p. 6.
45. Michael Isikoff, "New Drug Crisis Feared as Purity of Heroin Rises," *Washington Post,* 2 August 1989.
46. Quoted in Sperling, "Cocaine Use Among College Grads."
47. John Kifner, "As Crack Moves Inland, Ohio City Fights Back," *New York Times,* 29 August 1989.
48. Ibid.
49. Ibid.
50. See Charles Mohr, "Deaths and Arrests Mount, but the Drug Trade Is Flourishing," *New York Times,* 1 February 1989.
51. Johnson, "Drug Gangs and Drug Wars."
52. Richard L. Berke, "New Form of Interstate Commerce: Drugs Are Stealing Through U.S.," *New York Times,* 28 August 1989.
53. Ibid. See also Nancy Lewis and Michael Isikoff, "By Highway and Air."
54. "Cocaine's 'Dirty 300'," pp. 36–41.
55. James Barron, "Medellin Cartel's Top Chemist Lured to New York and Held," *New York Times,* 12 August 1989.
56. Mona Charen, "Tracing Drug Woes to Culture," *Washington Times,* 29 August 1989.
57. Ibid.

58. Gina Kolata, "Experts Finding New Hope on Treating Crack Addicts," *New York Times,* 24 August 1989.
59. Ibid.
60. See Shannon, *Desperados,* pp. 28–29.
61. Ibid.
62. Ibid., pp. 30–31.
63. Lead editorial, "A 'Right' to Drugs?" *Wall Street Journal,* 26 September 1988.
64. The myth of the generation gap is ably explored by Joseph Adelson, "Drugs and Youth," *Commentary* (May 1989): 24–28.
65. For the rare skeptical view of at least the politics of the era, see Peter Collier and David Horowitz, *Destructive Generation: Second Thoughts about the '60's* (New York: Summit Books, 1989); for their thoughts on Newton and Seale, see pp. 12, 22, 39, 61, 96, 161, 242, 266, and 320.
66. Quoted in Adelson, "Drugs and Youth," p. 24.
67. Ibid., p. 27.
68. Ibid.
69. Shannon, *Desperados,* p. 33.
70. Ibid., p. 35.
71. Ibid.
72. Ibid.
73. Ibid.
74. Peter G. Bourne, "The Great Cocaine Myth," *Drugs and Drug Abuse Education Newsletter,* August 1974; and quoted in Shannon, *Desperados,* p. 36.
75. Ibid., *Desperados,* p. 37.
76. Quoted in Rowland Evans and Robert Novak, "The Democrats' Dilemma," *Washington Post,* 30 August 1989.
77. Richard B. Foster, "Strategic Dimensions of the Drug War," paper presented at Freedom House Conference on *The Drug Trafficking Threat to Democracy,* New York City, 30 September 1988.
78. Richard Berke, "Corruption in Drug Agency Called Crippler of Inquiries and Morale," *New York Times,* 17 December 1989, p. A1.

79. Mike McQueen and Sam Meddis, "D.C. Fights Image of 'Dodge City'," *USA Today,* 6 February 1989.

80. "Former Lawmaker Given Year in Jail," *New York Times,* 29 August 1989.

81. Jose de Cordoba, *Wall Street Journal,* 13 December 1988.

82. Michael Isikoff, "Cali Cartel, a Rival to Medellin, Expands Reach in U.S.," *Washington Post,* 3 September 1989.

83. See de Cordoba, *Wall Street Journal.*

84. Howard Kurtz, "Arrested U.S. Drug Agent Admitted Carrying Cocaine, Court Is Told," *Washington Post,* 25 August 1989. See also "Federal Drug Agent Nabbed in Boston with 62 Lbs. of Coke," *New York Post,* 16 August 1989.

85. AP, "U.S. Indicts 3 Ex-Drug Agents," *New York Times,* 4 February 1989.

86. Michael Isikoff, "DEA Investigates Possibility Official Aided Cocaine Ring," *Washington Post,* 17 August 1989.

87. Dana Priest and Nancy Lewis, "Threats of Death, Maiming Muzzle Witnesses in Area Drug Trials," *Washington Post,* 20 August 1989.

88. DeNeen L. Brown, "Some Residents Won Over By the Enemy in D.C. Drug War," *Washington Post,* 13 August 1989.

89. James R. McKinley, Jr., "The Price of Fighting Drug Dealers: a Wife's Death," *New York Times,* 10 August 1989. See also Lisa W. Foderaro, "Hundreds Mourn Brooklyn Drug Fighter," *New York Times,* 13 August 1989; and Michael Marriott, ". . . While Citizens Risk Lives to Combat Dealers in Streets," *New York Times,* 14 August 1989.

90. Brown, "Some Residents Won Over."

91. Priest and Lewis, "Threats of Death."

92. Ibid.

93. Ibid.

94. Stephen Labaton, "Bank to Plead Guilty to Laundering Drug Money," *New York Times,* 12 August 1989; and Stephen Labaton, "Banking's Technology Helps Drug Dealers Export Cash," *New York Times,* 14 August 1989.

95. *Economist,* (London) "Mission Impossible," 2 September 1989, p. 15.

96. Hodding Carter III, "We're Losing the Drug War Because Prohibition Never Works," *Wall Street Journal*, 13 July 1989; and his earlier piece, "U.S., Soviets Learn an Old Lesson About Drugs," *Wall Street Journal*, 27 October 1988; see also William F. Buckley, Jr., "Drug Talk Across the Way," *Universal Press Syndicate*, 23 March 1989, and Milton Friedman, "An Open Letter to Bill Bennett," *Wall Street Journal*, 7 September 1989.

97. Wilson and Dilulio, Jr., "Crackdown."

98. Peter Kerr, "Crack and Resurgence of Syphilis Spreading AIDS Among the Poor," *New York Times*, 20 August 1989.

99. Mark A. R. Kleiman, professor of public policy at Harvard, Kennedy School of Government, as cited by David Corcoran, "Legalizing Drugs: Failures Spur Debate," *New York Times*, 27 November 1989, p. A15.

100. James B. Jacobs, "Are We Really Ready for Legalized Drugs?" *Newsday*, 9 January 1990.

101. Wilson and Dilulio, Jr., "Crackdown," p. 22.

102. "Notable and Quotable," *Wall Street Journal*, 15 December 1989.

103. Ibid.

104. Wilson and Dilulio, Jr., "Crackdown," p. 23.

105. Shenon, "War on Drugs Is a Failure," p. A1.

106. Lead editorial, "Cracking Down," *Wall Street Journal*, 10 August 1989.

107. For the full argument on antidrug legislation, see Tracy Thompson, "Cracking Down, Reluctantly, on Low-Level Drug Offenders," *Washington Post*, 28 August 1989.

108. Marshall Ingwerson, "Rise in Drug Offenses Crams Prisons," *Christian Science Monitor*, 13 December 1988.

109. Ibid.

110. See "News," a press release for Senator Charles B. Rangel, 18 July 1989, p. 1.

111. Letter from William von Raab to President George Bush, 31 July 1989. See also "A Loose Cannon's Parting Shot," *Time*, 7 August 1989, pp. 18–19; and David Johnston, "Customs Chief Asserts U.S. War on Drugs Is Stalled," *New York Times*, 28 July 1989.

112. von Raab, letter to Bush.
113. Ibid.
114. "A Loose Cannon's Parting Shot," p. 19.
115. See Barbara Bradley, "Formidable Tasks Awaits Drug Czar," *Christian Science Monitor,* 4 January 1989.
116. Michael Hedges, "Bennett Pledges Drug Plan in 6 Months," *Washington Times,* 6 February 1989; and Michael Isikoff, "Bennett Says Status Is No Slight," *Washington Post,* 4 February 1989.
117. Shannon, *Desperados,* pp. 37–38, 375–76.
118. Ibid., p. 371.
119. Ibid., pp. 380–81.
120. "Key Sections of the Paris Communique by the Group of Seven," *New York Times,* 17 July 1989.
121. Jerry Lewis, "Drug Bonds: Money Is Not the Only Issue," *Washington Post,* 14 August 1989.
122. Michael Isikoff, "Bennett to Crusade Against Crack," *Washington Post,* 26 July 1989.
123. Michael McQueen and Paul M. Barrett, "Bush Launches Drive Against Drug Abuse Aimed at Punishing Users and Middlemen," *Wall Street Journal,* 6 September 1989.
124. Bradley, "Formidable Tasks"; See also Paul M. Barrett, "Federal War on Drugs Is Scattershot Affair, with Dubious Progress," *Wall Street Journal,* 10 August 1989.
125. Richard L. Berke, "Bush's Drug Plan Aims at Capturing Mid-Level Figures," *New York Times,* 31 August 1989; see also "What the Plan Would Aim to Do," *New York Times,* 3 September 1989, sec. 4.
126. Jefferson Morley, "Contradictions of Cocaine Capitalism," *The Nation,* 2 October 1989, p. 347.
127. Richard L. Berke, "Drug Chief Calls for a Vast Prison Plan," *New York Times,* 3 August 1989.
128. A. M. Rosenthal, "The Drug Czar's Report," *New York Times,* 14 July 1989.
129. Morley, "Contradictions of Cocaine Capitalism," p. 346.
130. Ibid. See also James J. Kilpatrick, "Confiscate the Cars of the Drug Users," *Washington Post,* 20 August 1989.

131. Michael Isikoff, "Bennett Proposing Forced Treatment for Addicts," *Washington Post*, 4 August 1989.

132. Wilson and Dilulio, Jr., "Crackdown," p. 25.

133. Kenneth H. Bacon, "Little Is Known About Tenants," *Wall Street Journal*, 6 September 1989.

134. Ibid.

135. "What the Plan Would Aim to Do," *New York Times*, 3 September 1989.

136. Berke, "Drug Chief Calls for a Vast Prison Plan."

Index

─────────── ▮▮▮▮▮ ───────────

Abbell, Michael, 165–66
Ackroyd, Dan, 159
Adams, Nathan, 5, 8
Addiction, 150; cocaine, 152; heroin, 151, 152
Adelson, Joseph, 155–56, 158
Agca, Mehmet Ali, 15–16
¡Alfaro Vive Carajo! (AVC), 116–17
Allende, Salvador, 24, 25n, 86
Altamont (CA), 154n
Anderson, Jack, 6n
Andropov, Yuri, 6, 16
An-Nahar (Beirut), 60
Anti-Drug Abuse Act (1986), 177–78
Antonov, Sergei Ivanov, 16
Aoun, Michel, 53
April 19 Movement, see Movimiento 19 de Abril
Arafat, Yasir, 69, 72n
Arango, Andres Pastrana, 93
Arsan, Henri, 9
Arsencio, Diego, 80
Assad, Hafez al-, 71n

Assad, Rifaat al-, 67–68
Atta, Paul, 49
AVC, see ¡Alfaro Vive Carajo!

Baldizon, Alvaro, 48, 49–50
Banks, money laundering and, 168
Barco, Virgilio, 82, 88–89, 90, 106, 111, 137
Barrantes, Alfonso, 122
Barriman, Adler (Barry Seal), 46, 47n
Barry, Marion, 143
Bateman, Jaime, 75n
Batista, Fulgencio, 21, 23, 24
Belushi, John, 159
Bennett, William J., 137–38, 142–43, 154, 172–73, 176–77, 178–79, 180, 181
Berke, Richard L., 149–50
Betancourt, Rómulo, 114
Betancur, Belisario, 83, 92, 106, 111
Bias, Len, 177

Big Chill, The (film), 155
Bilotnick, Richard, 36
Black markets, 98n, 104–5
Black tar, 147n
Blanco, Hugo, 122
Blandon Castillo, Jose, 43–45
Bolivia: coca production in, 130; drug trafficking in, 130–31; United States assistance to, 131–35; Zarate Willca Armed Forces of Liberation, 135
Borge, Tomas, 46, 47
Borja, Rodrigo, 117
Bourne, Peter, 162–63
Boyatt, Tom, 35–36
Buckley, William F., Jr., 169
Buitrago, Samuel, 96–97
Bulgaria: communism in, 3–4; Italy and, 15–16; KINTEX, 5–10; money laundering by, 13–14; narco-terrorism by, 1–2, 4, 10–19, 190n31; Turkey and, 2, 4, 14–15; USSR and, 2–3
Bush, George: Cuba and, 41; drugs, views of, 178, 179–80; Federal Drug Task Force, 31

Cano, Juan Guillermo, 93
Carter, Hodding, III, 169
Carter, Jimmy, 162, 163–64
Castrillon, Dario, 97
Castro, Fidel: Colombia and, 77, 82; drug trafficking and, xiv, 24–25, 26, 40–41, 50–51; Palestine Liberation Organization and, 71n; Panama and, 43; political standing, 50; revolutionary goals, 25–26; Soviet Union and, 50–51; United States and, 20–21, 25–26, 28; Venezuela and, 114; *see also* Cuba
Castro, Raul, 21n, 38, 40, 48
CCSB, *see* Simón Bolívar Coordinating Committee
Charen, Mona, 151
Chile: cocaine trafficking, 24n–25n, 86; drug trafficking, 74
China, Palestine Liberation Organization and, 72n
Christian factions, Lebanon, 54n, 56–57, 58, 60, 63, 64–65, 67
CIMEX, *see* Cuban Corporation for Import and Export
CNG, *see* Simón Bolívar Coordinating Committee
Colombia: cartels and drug lords of, 43, 76–78, 86–97, 98–104, 110–12, 145–46, 149–50; Catholic church in, 96–97; Cuba and, 29–30, 32–34, 74, 79–82, 99–100; drug trafficking and, xiv, 35–36, 44–45, 74–78, 85, 86–88, 105–6, 115, 118; drug usage in, 101–2; economy of, 104–5; Ecuador and, 116–17; extradition processes in, 88–89, 90, 92, 94–95, 100, 137; guerrilla groups, 78–79, 82–83, 84–85, 98–101, 102–3, 111; his-

tory of, 76–77, 78–79, 97–98;
legal system in, 75, 87–88, 91,
94–96, 100; Medellín, 76, 77–
78, 84, 88, 90, 100, 102, 109;
military of, 106–10; Panama
and, 92; Patriotic Union, 84;
Peru and, 124, 125; Vene-
zuela and, 115–16; *see also*
Movimiento 19 de Abril
Colombian Communist Party
(PCC), 78
Colombian Revolutionary Armed
Forces (FARC), 78, 79, 82–
84, 98–99, 102–3
Columbus (OH), 148
Comprehensive Drug Abuse Pre-
vention and Control Act
(1970), 160
Comrad Gonzalo, *see* Guzman,
Abimael
Cordero, Leon Febres, 117
Costa Rica, 48–49
Craig, Richard, 104
Crips, 145
Crump, Juan (Johnny), 32
Cuba: Angola and, 27, 29, 39, 41;
censorship in, 40*n;* Colombia
and, 29–30, 32–34, 74, 79–
82, 99–100; Departamento de
América (DA), 29, 30*n*, 31;
drug trafficking and, 21–22,
24–25, 26–27, 29–38, 41–42;
economy of, 22, 27–28; his-
tory of, 22–24; narco-terror-
ism by, 38–39, 42–45, 50;
Nicaragua and, 45–51; Soviet
Union and, 20–21, 26; United
States and, 20–21, 23, 27, 36;
see also Castro, Fidel
Cuban Corporation for Import and
Export (CIMEX), 36
Culture, role of, 151–52, 154–62

DA, *see* Cuba, Departamento de
América
Dabbagh, Sallah, 69
DEA, *see* Drug Enforcement
Administration
Death to kidnappers movement
(Colombia), *see Muerte a Se-
cuestadores*
Detroit (MI), 61
Di Carlo, Francesco, 67–68
DiIulio, John J., Jr., 144, 173–74,
181
Domestic Council Drug Abuse
Task Force, 161
Dornan, Robert, 68
Doyle, Sir Arthur Conan, 152*n*
Dozier, James Lee, 15
Drug Enforcement Administration
(DEA): agents, 166–67; drug
trafficking information, 8
Drug trafficking, international: de-
livery of drugs, 12; goals of,
xvii; in Latin America, 74;
money laundering in, 10, 13–
14, 18–19, 88–89, 168, 182,
185; weapons and, 4–5, 7–8,
9, 31–36; *see also* individual
countries
Drugs: *basuco,* 101–2; coca, 118,

Drugs (*continued*)
119, 123–24, 126–27, 128–29, 130, 133–34, 141; cocaine, 31, 32, 35, 37, 46–47, 48, 50, 61, 85, 101, 102, 105*n*, 115, 123, 130, 140, 144, 161, 162; crack, 140, 141, 143–44, 145, 146–47, 148, 170, 177; hashish, 56, 58–59, 60, 70; heroin, 8, 10, 17, 25, 56, 60–61, 141, 145, 147, 161, 169; ice, 146; marijuana, 32, 35, 59, 60–61, 85, 86, 115, 141, 161, 162; methaqualone, 32, 35; morphine, 8, 9, 17, 60–61; opium, 56, 59*n*, 60–61, 147; PCP (angel dust), 141, 143, 146–47; sales of, 85–86, 140–41; *see also* Addiction

Drugs, legalization of: cocaine, 162, 180*n*; marijuana, 162; recommendations against, 169–73; recommendations for, 169

Druze faction (Lebanon), 53–54, 57–58, 60

DS, *see* Komitet za Durzhavna Signurnost (KDS; Bulgaria)

Dukakis, Michael, 164

Durzhavna Signurnost (DS), *see* Komitet za Durzhavna Signurnost (KDS; Bulgaria)

Economist (London), 53–54, 85–86, 169

Ecuador: *¡Alfaro Vive Carajo!* (AVC), 116–17; Cuba and, 116; drug trafficking in, 116; terrorism in, 116–17

Education, 158

Edwards, Don, 153

El Colombiano (Medellin, Colombia), 92

ELN, *see* National Liberation Army

El Espectador (Colombia), 93

El Salvador: Faribundo Marti National Liberation Front (FMLN), 83, 117; guerrilla war in, 22; military, 108–9

El Siglo (Colombia), 82

El Tiempo (Bogatá, Colombia), 93

Enders, Thomas O., xiv, 99

Escobar, Carlos Ossa, 87

Escobar, Pablo, 59*n*, 88, 90, 103

Estenssoro, Victor Paz, 131, 132

Europe, Eastern, *perestroyka* and, xvi–xvii

Farach, Antonio, 48

FALN, *see* *Fuerzas Armadas de Liberacion Nacional*

FARC, *see* Columbian Revolutionary Armed Forces

Faribundo Marti National Liberation Front (FMLN), 83, 117

Fernandez, Jose Antonio, 37–38

First Conference of Solidarity of the Peoples of Africa, Asia, and Latin America (OS-PAAAL), 27

Flupenthixol, 151*n*

FMLN, *see* Faribundo Marti National Liberation Front

Forbes, 13, 88

Foreign Assistance Act (1987), 66

"Forty-eight Hours on Crack Street," (CBS), 177*n*

Foster, Richard, 164*n*–65*n*

Franjiyeh, Soloiman, 65*n*

Franjiyeh, Tony, 64–65

Freeh, Louis, 16–17

Freud, Sigmund, 152

Fuerzas Armadas de Liberacion Nacional (FALN; Venezuela), 114–15

Fujimori, Alberto, 118, 124*n*, 129

Fulwood, Isaac, 174

Gacha, Jose Gonzalo Rodriquez, 111

Galán, Luis Carlos, 88, 89–90

Gallup, George, Jr., 138

Garcia, Alan, 118, 123, 125, 127

Garcia, Calixto, 23

Gaviria, César, 112

Gemayel, Amin, 53, 55*n*

Gemayel, Bashir, 55*n*, 63, 64–65

Gemayel, Pierre, 63

Gerasimov, Geradny, 19

Germany, East: narco-terrorism by, xx*n*, 71

Glasnost and *perestroyka:* Bulgaria and, 3–4; Cuba and,

26*n*, 42–43; Nicaragua and, 45*n*

Globus, 13–14, 18

Gold, Mark, 148

Gomez, Alvaro, 82

Gomez, Carlos Jimenez, 92

Gómez, Juan Vicente, 114

Gonzáles, Mário Estévez, 32, 35

Gorbachev, Mikhail: Marxism-Leninism and, xvi–xvii

Goren, Roberta, 63–64, 73

Granma (Cuba), 40

Guerrilla groups, *see* individual countries

Guevara, Che, 27–28, 120, 134

Gugliotta, Guy, 130

Guillot-Lara, Jaime, 32–35, 80, 99

Guns-for-drugs trade, *see* Weapons and drug trafficking

Gutierrez Marquez, Alfredo, 87–88

Guzman, Abimael, 120

Habash, George, 63–64

Hall, John Wesley, Jr., 166*n*

Harrison, Tubby, 164

Hawkins, Paula: hearings, Miami 1983, 35

Hearts and Lives of Men, The (Weldon), 155–56

Hendrix, Jimmy, 154

Henze, Paul, 12, 15

Hernandez, Martha, 167

Herring, James, 47

Higgins, William, 54
Hisballah (Party of God; Lebanon), 53, 54, 68
Hobbes, Thomas, 54–55
Honecker, Erich: drug trafficking by, xvii, xxn
Hostages: Lebanese, 54; M-19 and, 80
Howard, Roscoe, 167–68
Hoyos, Carlos Mauro, 74–75, 87
Hrawi, Elias, 53

INAIR, 36
International Narcotics Control Strategy Report, 17, 101, 141
Israel: drug trafficking in, 55; Israeli Defense Force, 66; Lebanon and, 65–66; Palestine Liberation Organization and, 71
Israeli, Raphael, 72–73
Italy, Bulgaria and, 15–16

Jamaican posses, 145, 146
John Paul II, 15–16
Joplin, Janis, 154

Kaufman, Irving R., 46–47
KDS, *see* Komitet za Durzhavna Signurnost
KGB, 7
KINTEX, 5–10, 12–14, 18

Kissinger, Henry, 28n
Kleiman, Mark, 170
Komitet za Durzhavna Signurnost (KDS; Bulgaria), 6, 7
Kooistra, Jitze, 47

La Republica (Italy), 15
Lawn, John C., 11
Leary, Timothy, 158
Lebanon: army in, 52n, 53–54, 63; Baalbek, 68; Beirut, 52–53, 63; drug trafficking in, 55, 56–67; economy of, 59–60, 62; hostages in, 54; Israel and, 65–66; Jūniyah, 63; narco-terrorism in, 52–54, 58, 64, 66–73; political groups in, 53–54, 56–58, 60, 62–63, 64–66; Syria and, 53, 56, 57–58, 60, 65, 66–69; Tripoli, 62–63; Tyre, 63–64
Lee, Rensselaer, 86, 88, 102
Leen, Jeff, 130
Legalization, *see* Drugs, legalization of
Lehder, Carlos, 37, 92
Lehtinen, Dexter, 38
Levitsky, Melvyn, 147
Lewis, Jerry, 179
Llosa, Mario Vargas, 118
Lombard, Florentino Azpillage, 38
Lopez, Alfonso, 97
Losada, Manuel Pineiro, 29, 31, 44
Lupsha, Peter, 97

M-19, *see* Movimiento 19 de Abril

Mafia, 145

Marcuse, Herbert, 155

Mariátegui, José Carlos, 119*n*

Martinez, Tomas Borge, 46

Marxist-Leninist ideology: drug trafficking and, xv–xvii, xxi–xxii; Popular Front for the Liberation of Palestine and, 64

Maryland, witness intimidation in, 168

MAS, *see Muerte a Secuestadores*

Matallana, Jose Joaquin, 109

Medellin, cartel, *see* Colombia, cartels and drug lords of

Media, role of, 159, 177

Mendoza, Plinio Apuleyo, 93

Miami Herald, 37–38, 130

Michel, James H., 36

Michelsen, Alfonso Lopez, 92

Mikoyan, Anastas, 21

Military, Colombia, 106–10

Mitchell, John, 160

Mladenov, Petar, 1, 4

Moawad, René, 53

Money laundering: Bulgaria, 13–14, 18–19; Colombia, 88–89; Switzerland, 10, 13; United States, 168, 182, 185

Morganthau, Henry, Jr., 152–53

Movimiento 19 de Abril (M-19), 32, 33, 35–36, 43, 74–75, 79–82, 98, 99–100, 116; *see also* Colombia

Muerte a Secuestadores (MAS; Colombia), 103

Mullen, Francis, 30, 34, 190*n*31

Mulvihill, Thomas, 38

Murta, Enrique Low, 95

Muslim factions, Lebanon, 56–57, 60, 65–66

Narcotics, terrorism as: democracies and, 43–45, 96; denial of, xiv–xv; evidence of, xviii, xix–xx, xxi–xxii, 42–43, 75, 100; narco-terrorism, definition, xiii; reasons for, xviii–xix, 27, 98–99, 104; spread of, 137, 150, 184–86; *see also* individual countries; Palestine Liberation Organization

Nasser, Gamal Abdel, 57

National Guerrilla Coordinator, *see* Simón Bolívar Coordinating Committee

National Liberation Army (ELN; Colombia), 78–79, 82–85, 115

Newman, Barbara, 55*n*

New Republic, The, 144

New York: cocaine market, 103–4; law enforcement in, 174–75

New York City Tribune, 18

New York Post, 136

New York Times, 37, 41, 93, 103, 128–29, 149, 153, 180

Nicaragua: drug trafficking by, 46–50; Heroes and Martyrs, 49; *perestroyka* and, 45; Sandinista regime, 45–47, 48–49, 79; USSR and, 45–46

Nixon, Richard, 159–60

Noriega, Manuel Antonio, 43, 81, 164, 165n

O'Brien, Edward K., 166
O'Brien, Patrick, 42
Ochoa, Jorge Luis, 88, 95
Ochoa Sanchez, Arnaldo, 39–40
Orejuela, Gilberto Rodriguez, 103, 165–66
Ortega, Daniel, 45n
Ortega, Humberto, 48
Ortodoxos (Cuba), 21
OSPAAAL, *see* First Conference of Solidarity of the Peoples of Africa, Asia, and Latin America
Ossa, Bernardo Jaramillo, 90

Pabon, Rosenberg, 82
Palestine Liberation Organization (PLO): communist representation in, 72–73; drug trafficking by, 68–73; in Lebanon, 54n, 57, 64; USSR and, 70–72; weapons purchases by, 5
Panama: Colombia and, 92; Cuba and, 43, narco-terrorism and, 44–45, 75n, 81
Panic in Needle Park (film), 159
Partido Socialista Popular (PSP; Cuba), 21
Party of God (Lebanon), *see* Hisballah

Payne, Douglas, 75
PCC, *see* Colombian Communist Party
Pell, Claiborne, 41
Perestroyka, see Glasnost and *perestroyka*
Pérez, David Lorenzo, 32, 35
Peru: Columbia and, 124, 125; drug trafficking in, 118–19, 123–24, 125; economy of, 120–21, 123; government in, 118, 126–27; military of, 127; narco-terrorism in, 119; *Sendero Luminoso* (Shining Path), 118, 119–23, 124–26; society in, 120–21; United Left coalition, 122–23
PFLP, *see* Popular Front for the Liberation of Palestine
Piffani, Daniele, 73
Pinochet, General, 86
"Pizza Connection," 16–18
Platt Amendment (1901), 23
PLO, *see* Palestine Liberation Organization
Police, Colombian, 109–10
Pope, Sam, 71n
Popular Front for the Liberation of Palestine (PFLP), 63–64
Prohibition, 169, 170–71
PSP, *see* Partido Socialista Popular

Rangel, Charles B., 175n
Ravelo-Renedo, F., 29, 32, 33, 44–45

Razvedochni Otdel (RO; Bulgaria), 6n
Reagan, Ronald, 66, 177
RO, *see* Razvedochni Otdel
Rockefeller, Nelson, 161
Rojas Pinilla, Gustavo, 75, 79–80
Rolling Stone, 155, 159
Romero, Eduardo Martinez, 88–89
Rosenthal, A. M., 180
Ross, Brian, 31
Ruiz, Jaime, 100
Ruiz, Reinaldo and Rueben, 38
Rumania, Soviet Union and, 2–3

Sakaharov, Vladimir, 15n
Sanchez, Celia, 20
Sandinista regime, *see* Nicaragua
Santander, Francisco de Paula, 75n, 111
Saturday Night Live, 159
Say, Jean-Baptiste, 141
Schalck-Golodkowski, Alexander, xxn
Seal, Barry, *see* Barriman, Adler
Sendero Luminoso (Shining Path; Peru), 118, 119–23
Sessions, William, 142
Shannon, Elaine, 143–44, 152, 160–61, 163, 177–78
Sherman, Lawrence, 141
Shihaby, Hikmat al-, 68
Shils, Edward, 156
Shining Path, *see* Sendero Luminoso

Shultz, George P.,: Bolivia, trip to, 134; drug dealing, international, xi–xxii
Simón Bolívar Coordinating Committee (CCSB), 84
Somoza, Anastasio, 79
Soviet Union, *see* USSR
Soviet Union and Terrorism, The (Goren), 63–64
SUMUD, 64, 69
Svirdlev, Stefan, 6
Swindell, Patrick, 165
Switzerland: money laundering in, 10, 13
Sydney Morning Herald (Australia), 65n
Syria: drug trafficking in, 61, 66–69; Lebanon and, 53, 56, 57–58, 65–69
Szulc, Tad, 41

Tarazona-Sevillano, Gabriela, 120, 121, 124, 125
Terrorism: Cuba, use of, 28; existence of, xx–xxi; in Peru, 119–23; *see also* Narcotics, terrorism as
Terry, Fernando Belaunde, 118
TIR, *see* Transport International Routier
Tlass, Mustafa, 68
Transport International Routier (TIR), 12–13
Treatment, 181–82
Tupac Amaru Revolutionary Movement (Peru), 120n

Turkey: Bulgaria and, 2, 4, 14–15; USSR and, 15
Tutwiler, Margaret, 39

Ucede, Luis de la Puente, 122
UL, *see* Peru, United Left coalition
United Kingdom: drug legalization in, 169–70
United States: drug culture in, 151 –65; drug-related crime, 141–45, 148, 164–65, 173–75; drug-related expenditures, 179–80, 182; drugs and opinion polls, 137–39; drugs, distribution of, 145–46, 148–50; drugs, politics and, 182; drug usage in, 140–41, 146–48, 151–53; National Institute on Drug Abuse, 140; prevention efforts of, 169–83, 184–86
United States, international drug trafficking and: Bolivia and, 131–34; Bulgaria and, 10–13, 16–19; Colombia and, 88–89, 93–94, 105, 106, 110, 111–12, 145–46, 149–50, 166–68; Cuba and, 23–25; Drug Enforcement Administration, 127–28; Peru and, 127–29; reasons for, xiv; recognition of, 16–19; Syria and, 66, 68
UP, *see* Colombia, Patriotic Union
Uruguay: Colombia and, 117; *Tupamaros,* 117
USSR: Cuba and, 26; drug traf-

ficking and, xv–xvi, xvii; Palestine Liberation Organization (PLO) and, 70–72; Peru and, 127; Turkey and, 15; Western society, undermining of, xv–xvi, 70–73

Vasquez, Fabio, 78
Vaughn, Frederico, 46–47
Venezuela: Colombia and, 115; democracy in, 114; drug trafficking in, 113–16
Ventanilla siniestra ("side window," Colombia), 104–5
Vesco, Robert, 37, 47
Vietnam War, 154
Village Voice, 155
Vizzini, Sal, 25
von Raab, William, 18, 176

Wall Street Journal, 36, 153, 166*n,* 174
Washington, D.C.: crack distribution in, 149*n;* law enforcement in, 173–74; mayor of, 143; murder rate in, 142–43; witness intimidation in, 167
Washington Post, 38, 41–42, 109, 139, 162, 167, 168
Washington Times, 146
Weapons, Colombian army, 107–9
Weapons and drug trafficking, 4–5, 7–8, 9, 35–36, 44; Bul-

garia, 4–6; Cuba, 32–35; gun running, 11; Lebanon, 58; Palestine Liberation Organization, 69, 70, 72, 73; Panama, 43
Weldon, Fay, 155–56
Wenner, Christopher, 59n
Westrate, David, 167
Wilson, James Q., 144, 173–74, 181
Wirthlin, Richard, 138n

Withdrawal, 151
Witnesses, intimidation of, 167–68
Woodstock, 154
Workman, Robert, 24

Zarate Willca Armed Forces of Liberation (Bolivia), 135
Zemin, Jiang, 72n
Zhivkov, Todor, 1, 3–4, 4n